THE REAL ARSENAL

THE REAL ARSENAL

From Chapman to Wenger – The Unofficial Story

Brian Glanville

BOOKS

First published in Great Britain in 2009 by
JR Books, 10 Greenland Street, London NW1 0ND
www.jrbooks.com

1 3 5 7 9 10 8 6 4 2

Printed by MPG Books, Bodmin, Cornwall

Dedication

For Samuel and Joshua

Contents

FOREWORD

THIS BOOK, FOR ME, IS A KIND OF COMPANION VOLUME TO MY official *The Arsenal Stadium History*, filling in gaps. Not, I hope, in any sensational way. Indeed, much of the added material appeared in one form or another in my columns for the *Sunday Times* during my 33 years as Football Correspondent, *The People* where I had four years as Sports Columnist and in my autobiography *Football Memories*.

But this does give me the chance to thank, most warmly, the many former Arsenal players who so kindly and generously gave me their help in writing the official history. That was by far the most enjoyable aspect of the project.

Chapter 1

NORRIS, KNIGHTON AND OTHERS

IN THE PANTHEON OF ARSENAL'S HEROES, NONE SURELY STANDS higher than the supreme Herbert Chapman, rivalled as an exceptional manager only by Arsene Wenger. But in my opinion, the most influential figure in Arsenal's long and remarkable history is Sir Henry Norris. A name surely long since forgotten in the annals of English football, yet equally surely, to my mind, the man who by hook, crook, persistence and wealth made everything possible for the club which he took across the Thames in 1913.

Took across the Thames, wangled and connived into the First Division, from which it had been displaced, in 1919, and brought Chapman himself to Highbury. What Chapman thought of him – though by contrast with most of Norris' employees, he could plainly handle him – is unknown. Apart from one rather banal book, a treatise rather than an autobiography, Chapman wasn't given to committing his thoughts to paper. Remembering, perhaps, the nightmarish nature of his end at Leeds. He had been managing Leeds City when, in 1919, the Football Association accused the club of making illicit payments to players and demanded the books, which they failed to produce. The word was that Chapman, protecting his players, told the investigation that he had burned them, though this may be apocryphal. In any event, he was thrown out of the game, obliged to work in a factory, but soon amnestied, becoming first assistant manager then manager of Huddersfield Town; Chapman turned them into the best team in England.

Henry Norris was, in the Fulham area and in Wimbledon, an entrepreneur by profession, an estate agent, who built more than two thousand homes in the two boroughs. The face, when you see contemporary photographs, is formidable, all but ugly, the eyes uncompromising and challenging, the nose long and prominent, below it a bushy grey moustache. An implacable, inscrutable mandarin. A man who wanted and insisted on his own way though his career in football, and perhaps beyond it, would end in bleak anticlimax. However, he would be knighted, be the first Mayor of Fulham, become a Member of Parliament; and he would bring the ailing Woolwich Arsenal club to Highbury.

It was not his original intention. His ambition had been to amalgamate Woolwich Arsenal with Fulham Football Club, which he controlled, but the Football Association defused his plan. So Woolwich Arsenal, instead of disappearing, would make the move North across the Thames to Highbury, and the grounds of the St. John's College of Divinity. It was an inspired decision, though not one easily implemented. It cost Norris £125,000, then a massive sum, and cost him too the bitter enmity of Arsenal fans who followed the team in South East London's Plumstead. He was said even to have received death threats.

But the club, founded – and taking its original name from – the Dial Square workshop in the massive Woolwich Arsenal, had been steadily losing support. Yet there was plainly no truth in the rumours among Woolwich fans that he was deliberately starving the team of money so as to diminish the crowds and strengthen the case for a move. One which would take the club from the rough and ready purlieus of Plumstead, with its aggressive supporters, to more genteel surroundings in North London. Whose own residents were not at all content at the advent of a football club in their enclave. There were protest meetings, but Norris used the tentacles of his widespread influence to see that they were not mentioned in the local press.

There was also the angry opposition of nearby Tottenham Hotspur.

This would soon rise to crescendo when Norris finessed Arsenal's eventual post-Great War promotion to the First Division at the expense of a Spurs team which had finished 20th and bottom of the First Division in season 1914–15, when 'official' football was suspended for the duration of the Great War.

But since the First Division was to be extended by two clubs, Spurs fully expected to remain there. Woolwich Arsenal, meanwhile, had finished a mere fifth in the Second Division in 1915 and therefore seemed to have neither legal nor moral right to promotion. This, however, was to reckon without the machinations of Norris, who had been knighted in 1917.

Football, in that last 1914–15 season, had hardly been immune from scandal. Manchester United, in severe danger of relegation from the Championship, had won a dubious victory in their very last match against Liverpool. The matter came to court but nothing was proved and United survived.

Woolwich Arsenal had slid into the Second Division in 1913 after an abysmal season which included a 23-match run without a win. C. E. Randall, the top scorer, got a pitiful four goals. Yet the first season at Highbury had brought a colossal improvement, the Gunners finishing third and so missing promotion by a single place. The 1914–15 season saw them drop two places. Yet they still found themselves by hook or by crook in the top division after who knows what chicanery and wheeler dealing in 1919.

'Honest John' McKenna was then President of the Football League, chairman of Liverpool and a friend of Henry Norris. McKenna it was, after much conniving, who shamelessly proposed that Arsenal rather than Spurs be installed in the senior division, since Arsenal had been members of the League for 15 years longer than Spurs! For that matter Wolves, who had finished fourth in the Second Division in 1915, had been League members longer than Arsenal, but this did not prevent Arsenal with 18 votes gaining 10 more than Tottenham and thus being promoted. Who could blame Spurs for their outrage?

Arsenal needed a new manager, and Norris' choice fell on Leslie Knighton, then assistant manager of Manchester City, having previously pre-war held a similar position at Huddersfield Town. Knighton had never been more than a schoolboy footballer, his career quickly ended by an ankle injury. Yet fast forward to our own era and we find the phenomenon of Arrigo Sacchi, so poor a young player that his local club told him to stop playing and to coach the juniors. In due course he would become manager not only of Milan but also of the 1994 Italian World Cup team. Remarking at times that you did not need to have been a horse to become a jockey.

Knighton in fact, from the most obscure managerial beginnings, forged a career which began with the tiny Yorkshire non-League club of Castleford, where as a very young man he performed a multiplicity of tasks. He moved on to Huddersfield, Manchester City, Arsenal, Bournemouth (then of the Third Division South, where he had three productive seasons), Birmingham (whom he took to the 1931 FA Cup Final at Wembley), then in 1933 to his second major London club, Chelsea.

Knighton may not have been a great tactician, but he had an astonishing flair for finding and securing young talent. An ability made all the more vital at Arsenal, since Norris kept the purse strings so tight; and would ideally have liked to keep them even tighter. Fascinated and dominated by the overpowering Norris, Knighton left a memorably vivid portrait of him in his autobiography.

Their first meeting was at the House of Commons in 1919, and Knighton said that he would never forget it. 'Sir Henry Norris had the most formidable assurance of anyone I had ever met. He gave the impression that he had always got his own way, and could not fail; and it was very nearly true. He walked me up and down, talking and staring at me with his fierce, masterful eyes, giving me a very fair and candid statement of the condition of things at the club.' The Great War, with football officially suspended, had torn great holes in the Gunners' finances, and they were in huge £60,000 debt. 'In fact,' Knighton reflected, 'I had to make bricks without straw!'

This he was metaphorically able to do, thanks to his extraordinary flair for singling out young talent and bringing it to Highbury some-times under the most onerous circumstances. 'Nothing over £1,200!' decreed Sir Henry, who would even cavil at a £1,000 fee.

Alf Baker was lured away from Huddersfield Town, where his brother Jim was playing, a hugely versatile player whose best position, in which England capped him, was right-half. Baker had played for the Naval Brigade and, as a guest, for various major clubs during the war. When Knighton, encouraged by Jim, travelled to Ilkeston to try to persuade Alf to come to Highbury, it was to find, on the doorstep where he had been for the last couple of days, a scout from Aston Villa. Knighton simply walked past him, put a form on the table and persuaded Alf to sign. He played 311 League games for Arsenal and was at right-half when they won their first FA Cup at Wembley in 1930; ironically enough against Huddersfield Town.

Jimmy Brain, from Ton Pentre, was another persuaded amid great competition to join the Gunners though on this occasion Knighton sent down a scout, who succeeded even though the Spurs manager and former Newcastle United star, Peter McWilliam, was to be seen loitering nearby with intent, wearing a cloth cap and a false moustache! Brain, actually a Bristolian, had seven productive years with Arsenal, scored 34 League goals in season 1925–26 by which time Herbert Chapman was in charge, and ended his Arsenal career with a total of 123 goals in 204 League games.

With supreme subterfuge, Knighton acquired the resilient Bob John, destined for a splendid career in Wales and Arsenal colours at left-half, scorer as a makeshift outside-left of the Gunners' only, opening, goal against Newcastle United in the ill-starred Cup Final of 1932. It was one of many instances in which Knighton's vast network of contacts served him well. In this instance, his informant was Bob Chatt, Manchester City's trainer when Knighton was there, by then trainer to the little Welsh club, Caerphilly. But, warned Chatt, John was said to be signing for Cardiff City.

Cardiff's Chairman at the time was Sid Nicholls and with typical bravura, Knighton took Caerphilly's other officials to lunch in the local hotel which Nicholls owned, unbeknown to the Chairman. Indeed, it transpired that while Knighton was signing John in one room, Nicholls and another Cardiff director had been discussing the acquisition of John in the next room! Walking out of the hotel with the Caerphilly officials, for a celebratory drink, Knighton ran into an astonished Nicholls. 'Well, of all the nerve!' said Nicholls. 'You not only come down here to pinch my stars, you actually sign them on in my own hotel!'

Nerve of a stronger nature was needed when Knighton travelled to Belfast in pursuit of the 17-year-old full-back, Alec Mackie, then with a junior club. Another old friend, the former Derby County winger Toby Mercer, would tell Knighton when local talent emerged. Belfast then was a violent and threatening city. Knighton soon saw a dead man slumped against a wall. Through dangerous streets, the Protestant Mercer escorted Knighton, but when it came to the Catholic quarter, he turned him over to the Catholic Irish international, Micky Hamill. Thus, the deal was done. Mackie, a talented eccentric who'd have great success with Arsenal then Portsmouth, used his first wages at Highbury to buy a pet monkey.

Such coups were the delight of Henry Norris who imposed not only financial but physical stipulations on the club's recruiting policy. 'Nobody under five feet eight or eleven stone! Nobody, mind!' was Sir Henry's forbidding dictum. Arsenal must, he insisted, have big men. By a great irony, Knighton, the very next day after this ukase, received a letter from an old friend in Huddersfield, telling him of a remarkable but tiny outside-right, 'Midget' Moffatt. Norris had left for his villa on the French Riviera, so Knighton took matters into his own hands. By bizarre coincidence Knighton had received a letter from Moffatt himself, in answer to an advertisement eliciting players – strange to relate – in the old, influential *Athletic News*.

Meanwhile, Knighton had travelled overnight to Workington, wandering the town for eight hours, half awake, till he was brought briskly to life by seeing Moffatt play. Back at Highbury, he sent the boy a telegram, telling him to come to London at once.

But when, next day, he met the 11.30pm train at Euston, no Moffatt could be seen. It was not till the following morning that, arriving at Highbury, Knighton was greeted by an amused groundsman who told him, 'Something's come for you. A little tiny chap. Says he's come to play for Arsenal! He's asleep in the dressing room.' So he was, curled up in a corner, 'his shock of hair sticking out like a squirrel's tail.' The poor fellow had taken an earlier train and made his way not to Highbury but to Woolwich! A kindly road sweeper bought him a cup of coffee and took him on board his van. Through the night Moffatt rode, eventually finding his way to Highbury.

Knighton signed him, and took him immediately on Arsenal's European tour, where he delighted the crowds, as he did on the return to London. When Sir Henry heard the news he smiled and was silent. But before long, Moffatt was off to Luton, thence to Everton.

Board meetings, for Knighton, were an ordeal. He had, he said, never met Sir Henry's equal 'for logic, invective, ruthlessness against all those who opposed him. I knew more about footballers than he ever could have known, but I am a poor hand with words, and can only say a thing bluntly and straight out. When I disagreed with him at Board meetings, as I soon had to do to justify my own position and stand up for what I *knew* as best for the club and boys, he used to flay me with words until I was reduced to fuming, helpless silence. Then, as I sat there not knowing what to say next and trying to bottle up what I was tempted to say, he would whip round with outstretched finger and shout: "Well, Knighton, we pay you a great deal of money to advise us – and all you can do is sit there as if you were dumb. Can't you talk?"'

Having thus reduced poor Knighton to impotent fury, he would call him back 'ask my advice, smile, wheedle . . . and I was falling over myself to help him again.' Pavlovian tactics *par excellence*.

How ironic that Knighton's downfall at Highbury, in 1925, should be occasioned by his abortive pursuit of Charlie Buchan, the inside-right whom Arsenal long before had foolishly discarded. The player who, that very year, would return to the club he had left in disgust in 1909, soon to invent the Third Back Game, which would revolutionise Arsenal's tactics, and those of the English game at large. Buchan was beyond doubt one of the salient figures in the history of the English game.

Tall and powerfully built, Buchan would win only a handful of England caps; one of those players, as my father, an Irishman who had fervently supported Arsenal, assured me was simply 'too clever' for the international selectors. A story which would repeat itself frequently across the years: Len Shackleton, Stanley Matthews, Glenn Hoddle, Paul Gascoigne. In 1909, then an amateur on the books of Woolwich Arsenal, son of a Scottish policeman who had come South to London, Buchan was refused 11 shillings' expenses in 1909 by a mean Arsenal manager, George Morell. How dear in every way it would cost the club! Buchan joined the East End amateurs of Leyton. From there he went all the way North East to Sunderland, and by the time the Great War – in which he served bravely in the trenches – broke out, he was established as a major star in a famous Sunderland attack.

Badly wanting a major force for his forward line, Knighton was encouraged by hearing that Buchan had fallen out with Sunderland and had not played for two weeks. Just as in the Moffatt episode, he knew that Sir Henry, with his deep disapproval of large transfer fees, was back on the Riviera. When the cat's away . . . Knighton called a Board meeting and harangued the members for hours, till at last they gave him permission to go to Sunderland and negotiate for Buchan. This he duly did, having even been given permission to spend £6,000, a record transfer fee at the time.

For another three hours, Knighton tried in vain to persuade the Sunderland manager, Bob Kyle, to sell, even daring to up the ante to £7,000. Still no deal, and now he had to return to London to face Sir Henry Norris who, he was sure, never forgave him. He was doomed to dismissal; partly, he believed, for daring to bid for Buchan, partly because Norris had promised him a large bonus. Taxed with this, Norris responded with evasive *longueurs*.

In fairness to Norris, there was another cogent reason. Arsenal in 1924–25 were enduring a wretched season in the League, once losing half a dozen matches in a row, and ending in 20th position; out of 22. An extraordinary series of three third-round FA Cup ties against West Ham United ended in defeat, even though Knighton had made use of a box of pills given him by a specialist who supported the club. Pills which induced both raging thirst and frantic energy in his players when fog caused the game at West Ham twice to be postponed. So Knighton left and never got his full bonus.

Norris himself, however, was destined not to last long, even though in 1925 he brought off the colossal coup of persuading Herbert Chapman, then manager of a Huddersfield Town team which had won the last two Championships, to come to London, where he would promptly sign Buchan and revolutionise club and team.

First, Buchan had to be persuaded and – however illicitly – compensated for leaving his sports shop in Sunderland. Arsenal had then to agree to the extraordinary arrangement of paying £100, no mean sum then, for his every goal, on top of the transfer fee. Buchan proceeded to score no fewer than 21 goals. Knighton's belief that Chapman exerted 'a sort of hypnotic spell' over Norris may well have had some basis in reality, for he would not be the first one, nor the last.

Norris' departure, indeed ejection, from the game was the stuff of sad anticlimax. In 1927, a Football Association commission of inquiry found him and his long-time partner, William Hall, guilty of a number of offences, such as Norris' use of club funds to pay for his motor car and chauffeur. There was, about this, an aura of somewhat petty revenge, evoked by Norris' famous intransigence. So Norris was obliged to leave the club for which, in his autocratic way, he had done so much for so long.

Two years later, hubris unquenched, he sued the FA for libel in the High Court, and lost the case disastrously. Had he been, in his latter years at Highbury, in financial trouble after all those years of grandiose wealth? What else could explain the fact that the case uncovered the almost comical episode of the club's motor coach, an episode more easily connected to a minor confidence trickster than to a renowned plutocrat. Though the story of the Arsenal motor coach rang down the years, one had to read the court reports of the time, in 1929, to appreciate the full fiasco of it all.

What emerged at the hearing, under pressure from defence counsel, was that Norris had sold the club's motor coach for £300, then quite a substantial sum. Worse, when he received the consequent cheque, he signed it on the back with Herbert Chapman's name – and put the money in his wife's account! There seemed scope, here, for a criminal prosecution, though none took place. Norris, however, had no option but to concede defeat.

A few years later, perhaps significantly, he was in court again, this time successfully suing, of all people, a racing tout, who, he claimed, had swindled him. What, you might ask, was a man of Norris' previous substance doing in dealing with such a man at all? One can only surmise.

Yet Knighton, with supreme generosity, bore no grudge against the man who sacked him. Instead of paying him the promised thousands, Norris fobbed him off with £500. In his autobiography, Knighton gives a confused and inaccurate account of Norris' vicissitudes, alleging that it was the episode of the motor coach which had him thrown out of football, rather than something which emerged only in his abortive libel action, which Knighton ignored, further alleging that Norris did not bother to defend himself. He quotes Norris as saying generously, 'I only made one mistake in my career, and that was sacking Knighton.' And indeed, he would leave money to Knighton in his will. Knighton's assertion was, 'It is not vanity that makes me say that if he had kept me, he could have stayed in big football all his days.'

A claim which goes unexplained. Knighton pursued, with a generosity to surpass Sir Henry's own, 'Despite it all, I still say he was the best Chairman I have ever had. He did miles more for football and for footballers than the public will ever know. If he had not been so consti-tutionally a rebel against petty authority he would have risen to the greatest position in the game. A financial genius, football was his hobby and delight, even though only a bagatelle compared with some of his business deals. He spent thousands of pounds and thousands of hours for its benefit. The game was immensely the poorer for his passing out of it, and it was a tragedy indeed that such a man should have gone under a cloud.'

Chapter 2

—

THE CHAPMAN
LEGACY

For almost three quarters of a century, Jacob Epstein's famous bust of Herbert Chapman stood in the entrance hall of the Arsenal Stadium's East Stand, inspiring or perhaps intimidating. For George Graham, long after Chapman's death in March 1934, it would certainly have been inspiring. As a student of Arsenal's history, he aspired to follow in Chapman's footsteps in terms of the club's success, even though where Chapman's regime had been paternal, if not paternalist, Graham's in a very different era was autocratic, if not abrasive. And, in sharp contrast with Chapman's, it ended in anticlimax and disgrace.

The main elements of Chapman's career are well enough known. A Yorkshireman, he played at inside-left for Spurs in the old Southern League, later to become the Third Division (South) before the Great War. He was an unexceptional player, not always in the first team, notable for the colour of his yellow boots. One day, in the dressing room, he heard the Tottenham centre-half, Walter Bull, remark that he had been offered the player-managership of another non-League club of lesser standing in Northampton Town. Chapman took it instead.

There, his managerial flair soon grew apparent. His original plan to become a mining engineer was abandoned; he had originally studied for it at Kiveton Park, in the colliery zone of South Yorkshire. It wasn't long before he showed his flair for discovering new talent. Though his reputation at Highbury would be that of a high spender, he complemented this with his ability to find and develop talent.

In this case, the talent was that of the tiny right-winger, Fanny Walden, who stood little over 5 feet 2 inches (1.57m), and weighed 8 stone 9 lb (55kg). Chapman saw him play at Wellingborough and left the game deciding Walden was simply too small to succeed. Then, according to Ivan Sharpe, once a flourishing amateur left-winger who played for Derby County and the United Kingdom Olympic winners of 1912, Chapman wondered, were Walden to succeed, just how great an attraction he might be. So he retraced his steps, Walden was signed, and Walden excelled. It was almost literally impossible for defenders to touch him. In time, appropriately perhaps, he went to Spurs, and was capped by England. Moreover, he became an accomplished cover point fielder in the county championship for Northamptonshire; and later, an umpire.

From Northampton, Chapman moved back to his native county to manage Leeds City in the Second Division, where Sharpe himself played for him. In 1919, however, things went badly awry. Accused by the Football Association of making illegal payments to players, he typically safeguarded them by refusing to produce the club's books, and was suspended. For a time, after the club itself had been consigned to oblivion, he worked unhappily in a factory.

Amnestied, he became manager of another Yorkshire club in Huddersfield Town. With them, he won the Championship in successive seasons. They would win it in yet a third successive season, but by then Chapman had come to London and to Arsenal. Why, you might ask, did Chapman appear to gamble by leaving Huddersfield Town on the crest of a wave, and join – in Arsenal – a club which had seriously shipped water in the previous season, finishing in 20th position in the Championship and thus so narrowly escaping relegation?

The answer is given in the beguiling autobiography of Ivan Sharpe who wrote, 'Outside his family circle, no man in the country knew him better than I did.' Chapman had once exclaimed to Sharpe, 'What a chance there is in London! I would like to build a Newcastle United there.' And so he did, *par excellence*. The Newcastle United to which he referred being the team of 1905 to 1911. He also told Sharpe, 'There's a change of management coming at Highbury. You have a friend there, Sir Samuel Hill-Wood (then the Chairman). Can you drop a hint?' So Chapman, audaciously, left a club just about to attain its third successive title, for one which was struggling in the shadows, because he believed that London was where the true challenge lay.

In one major respect, he was extremely fortunate. He was able to acquire Charlie Buchan. Leslie Knighton had tried hard to do so before him, and who knows how different Arsenal's and his own history, might have been had he succeeded. But Chapman persuaded Norris to disgorge his funds, and Buchan, properly compensated for the loss of his sports shop, to come South to the club which had once so foolishly let him go. There was also the famous contractual clause, whereby Sunderland pocketed £100 for Buchan's every goal; which would prove expensive, however ultimately beneficial.

Chapman arrived at Highbury at a highly significant time; the offside law had just been radically changed – and changed in the most indifferent way. Perhaps in retrospect it was appropriate that the solitary trial of the new law should be staged by the FA at Highbury itself, where the Third Back Game would be born. That the change in the law, which would affect the game worldwide, should be uniquely entrusted to the FA – the British countries then were not members of FIFA – was extraordinary. And the trial consisted merely of playing the old offside law, whereby three opponents were needed to put an attacker onside, for one half of the game, the proposed new one, whereby the number would be restricted to two, for the other. After which it was decided that the revised law would prevail, with all its massive implications.

Perhaps this had been made inevitable by the machinations of that wily Ulsterman, Bill McCracken, and his fellow full-back F. Hudspeth, at Newcastle United. They had refined the tactic of putting opponents offside to a fine art, moving forward time and again to entrap them. So much so that the apocryphal tale was told that when a visiting team arrived at Newcastle station for a game and a guard's whistle was heard, one of the players remarked, 'Blimey, offside already!'

How ironic it now seems that Arsenal were spurred into changing their style by the 7–0 defeat they suffered earlier in the season . . . at

Newcastle. Charlie Spencer, the Magpies' centre-half of that era, told me years later that he that day had been playing as a stopper; *avant la lettre*, one might say.

The conception of the Third Back Game has been variously attributed to Chapman and Buchan, though Buchan always insisted to me that the idea was his. He had, he once told me, been urging from the start of the season that given the change in the law, the centre-half, traditionally something of a rover, should be withdrawn wholly into defence, his absence from what we now call midfield being compensated by playing one of the inside forwards in a deeper role. He expected this player to be himself but for the League game the following Monday at West Ham, Chapman decided, almost whimsically, that it should be the third team inside forward, a Scotsman bought from Brighton, Andy Neil. Chapman described Neil as 'slow as a funeral', but praised his ball control and his ability 'to stand with his foot on the ball.'

At all events, the new tactics worked wonderfully, Arsenal winning the game 4–0. They were up, up and away. With Chapman, counter attack would be the name of the game, a policy with which he would imbue his players. Though his Arsenal teams would in due course score a multitude of goals, he'd tell his teams that when they went out on the field, they went out with one point. If they didn't give away a goal, they'd come off with at least that point.

Even if his team won, he would insist on a tight defence. Eddie Hapgood recalled an occasion when, after the team had won handsomely, Chapman subsequently harangued them in his office for an hour, declaring that the one goal they gave away should not have been conceded.

His first season in charge, with the new tactics, saw an astonishing transformation; the team soared from 20th position to second. Andy Neil who had played 16 times the season before would now play 27, though by the following season, he would be gone. Charlie Buchan scored 19 League goals plus a couple more in the FA Cup in which Arsenal, having eliminated Aston Villa 2–0 in a fifth-round replay, succumbed 2–1 at Swansea Town in the sixth round. But even Buchan's scoring feats were quite eclipsed by the 34 goals, a club record, scored by the centre-forward, Jimmy Brain, who surely deserved to be well remembered in the Gunners' history.

Brain was one of the many transfer coups brought off by Leslie Knighton who had conjured him away from little Ton Pentre. It should be emphasised that even when it came to the 1927 Cup Final, no fewer than eight of that Arsenal team were Knighton's men.

Buchan wasn't, of course, and neither was Joe Hulme, the dashing right-winger bought from Blackburn. He would go on playing for Arsenal till the season of 1937–38, joining Huddersfield Town with whom he would play in his fifth FA Cup Final. An interesting aspect of his long career with Arsenal is that in his first four seasons, he never got out of single figures as a scorer, yet his tally in the next three was 14, 14 and 20.

The following season, 1926–27, Arsenal slipped down the League to 11th, scoring 77 goals but letting in 86, despite the Third Back tactic. Six games were lost in succession, but by way of compensation, in the next seven games, only a couple of points were dropped.

The Cup was the consolation; or would have been, were it not for one of the most bizarre goals seen in a Wembley Final. Sheffield United, Port Vale, after a replay, Liverpool, Wolves and Southampton, in the semi-final at Chelsea, were defeated en route. Southampton were then a Second Division club – which indeed they would be so many years later when they eventually won the final – but they pressed the Gunners hard. Hulme and Buchan scored the goals in Arsenal's 2–1 win. During the Cup run, Buchan would score four times, Brain twice. How ironic that when Arsenal, against Cardiff in the Wembley showpiece, had an easy chance to equalise, Brain and Buchan would leave it to each other, and chance and ball had gone.

It was only thanks to the devoted ministrations of Tom Whittaker that Alf Baker, the diligent right-half whom Knighton had contrived to bring to Highbury, was fit to play. Whittaker had been made the first team trainer only that season when Chapman, perhaps somewhat impetuously, dismissed George Hardy, a highly regarded, pre-war survivor, who had taken on himself to give instructions during a game. This was the more poignant since Hardy and Whittaker, his assistant, were close friends. But Chapman had previously assured Whittaker, whom he had so generously looked after when he returned, crippled by a knee injury, from the 1925 FA Australian tour, that he would make him the greatest trainer in the world. Perhaps he was impatient to promote him.

Whittaker, a solid, competent rather than exceptional wing-half from the North East and a qualified engineer, who at a pinch could have embraced that career, had been badly injured in a match at Wollongong. His initial good fortune was that on the boat home, he met a woman who told him there was one person who could help him, a brilliantly eccentric Liverpool surgeon called Sir Robert Jones.

Chapman, sympathetic from the first, did what he could to increase the FA's meagre offer of compensation, and paid for Whittaker to see Jones. The surgeon told Whittaker that though he would never play football again, he'd be able otherwise to use his right leg in the future. Thanks to the innovative operation Jones performed on Whittaker's cartilage, this duly came to pass.

What inspired Chapman to make Whittaker a promise which would be so abundantly fulfilled? Was it merely wish fulfilment, or was it a case of clairvoyance? For Whittaker proved to be a remarkable, natural healer, so accomplished that in time, sportsmen of many kinds, including the celebrated tennis champion, Fred Perry, consulted him. His success in treating a knee injury to Alf Baker so severe it seemed he had no hope of playing was an early example of his unusual powers. Many Arsenal players would have cause to be grateful to him.

The farcical goal whereby Arsenal lost the game, and Cardiff took the Cup out of England for the first and so far only time, has been described *ad infinitum*. In an undistinguished game, played on a slippery pitch, Fred Keenor, a famous Cardiff figure, right-half rather than centre-half that day, threw the ball to his Scottish centre-forward, Hugh Ferguson, some 25 yards out. It seemed an easy ball for Dan Lewis, Arsenal's goalkeeper, to gather. But as Ferguson advanced on him, Lewis let the ball slip out of his grasp. It slid under his left arm. Turning, he could do no better than knock the ball with his elbow, propelling it inexorably over the line.

After the match, Lewis was so distraught that he dropped his loser's medal on the pitch. At this his teammates rushed back on to the field, where his compatriot Bob John recovered it for him. To follow one anticlimax with another, Arsenal's defeated players got on their team coach, which had been blocked in traffic on the way to the stadium, and got off it at Marylebone Station. There, Charlie Buchan bought them a drink in a nearby pub, and they made their way home.

Arsenal's right-back and future captain was the sturdy Tom Parker. Signed from Southampton the previous season, he had made only seven League appearances, yet managed to score three goals in those games.

He would be a regular choice till, in 1932, Chapman decided it was time to replace him, and George Male was promoted at his expense.

Cliff Bastin thought Male a better full-back, while 'temperamentally, Tom was the last person to skipper a team. Far from being the cool, firm, steady type, he was one of the most nervous footballers I have ever met. He would go through agonies before a game began, and nobody would be more happy when it eventually started. Once the ball had been kicked off, Tom's nervousness would disappear, and for the rest of the afternoon, he would be imperturbability itself. Tom, who took very seriously his duties as captain, would make brave efforts to maintain an unruffled demeanour in the dressing room; but one could always sense the undercurrents of uncertainty which lurked beneath.'

Praising Parker's loyalty to his club and gentlemanly behaviour, Bastin felt Parker's greatest strength 'lay in his uncanny positional sense. His bald head was like a magnet for passes by the opposite side.'

Knowing how Arsenal under Chapman have in retrospect been seen as a resiliently defensive team, it's revealing to see how the statistics of his early seasons at Highbury tell a very different tale, suggesting that the Third Back Game was anything but impregnable. Thus, in season 1926–27, en route to the Cup Final, Arsenal conceded no fewer than 86 goals, in the League. The following season, another 86 were given away. 1928–29 was somewhat better, with 72 goals conceded, while 77 were scored. While in the Cup-winning season, 1929–30, things continued to improve, with 66 against.

1927–28 would be Charlie Buchan's last season, in which he was still good enough to score 16 goals in 30 League appearances. He was disappointed, however, in his hopes to go out a winner in his final match, the last of the League season, when he was overshadowed by Dixie Dean's hat trick for Everton, one of them a penalty, which gave him the astonishing, impregnable total of 60 for the season.

1927–28 was also notable for the debut, plus another couple of appearances, of a left-back destined to become one of the club's greatest exponents, Eddie Hapgood. And seeing how he came to join them goes to emphasise the abyss between what happens now, when it seems that unless a boy doesn't join a major club by the time he is nine, he has no future, and then, when Hapgood was ignored for years.

Born in Bristol, a city which had produced so many famous players, he played just two games as a schoolboy. He was already 18 when in

1927, playing for a local club called St Phillip's Adult School Juniors, he was at last spotted by Bristol Rovers, who gave him a trial and offered him a contract which would entail driving a coal cart in the summer. Hapgood, who was already driving a milk cart for his brother-in-law, felt this *infra dig*, and refused.

A month later, he was approached not by any other League club, but by non-League Kettering Town, who offered him only half what he'd have earned at Bristol Rovers in the season – £4 rather than £8 a week – but allowed him to go on driving his milk cart in the summer. After a dozen games for Kettering, Herbert Chapman 'a chubby man in tweeds whose spectacles failed to hide the shrewd, appraising look from his blue eyes' turned up in the manager's office with George Allison, and demanded: 'Well, young man, do you smoke or drink?' Hapgood said no, and he was signed.

He'd come to worship Chapman. Years later, long retired, he said to me, 'He told you how to do your hair. He told you how to dress.' In his early months at Arsenal, Hapgood tended to faint when heading the heavy ball. Tom Whittaker built him up on beefsteaks and the following season saw him play 17 League games. He went on to become club captain and legend.

His partner was Tom Parker, who would play his 100th consecutive game, though Bastin insisted 'he was not well versed in the finer points of the game.' Hapgood, by contrast, was 'far different, the finest full-back I have ever seen. Even when I first came to Highbury, when Eddie was but twenty years old, he bore the stamp of greatness. Eddie had football developed into a meticulously exact science. His method of tackling was all his own. Never would you see him rush at an opponent, hoping blindly for the best. . . . Allied to his tackling skill was a positional sense every bit as good as Tom Parker's, and the ability to kick with equal power and accuracy either with the right or the left foot . . . Eddie besides all this was terrifically enthusiastic, and possessed a wonderful fighting spirit. He was, indeed, an ideal captain, and fully deserved the honour of captaining England.'

To succeed Charlie Buchan, Chapman, in the summer of 1928, paid the then record fee of £10,890 to Bolton Wanderers for David Jack, a renowned English international, scorer of the first goal in a Wembley Cup Final in 1923. Jack was an immediate success, becoming top scorer in the League for the Gunners with 23 goals. Close behind him came the ever reliable Jimmy Brain, with 21. Third on the list was Joe Hulme, with a mere half dozen.

Jack, who had begun with Plymouth Argyle when it was managed by his father Rollo and had gone to Bolton in 1921 for just £3,000, was a remarkable ball player who for Chapman represented the best bargain he had ever made. Three years after coming to Highbury, he scored a goal there against Aston Villa which almost beggared belief. Taking a short pass from Alex James, just inside the opposing half, he saw Beresford, the Villa inside-left, approaching him, and swerved towards him. Beresford stopped, Jack ran on. Next he was confronted by a celebrated right-half in Gibson. One more swerve, inducing Gibson, too, to pause, and Jack was away again. And still he hadn't touched the ball! Two more body serves, to elude first Talbot then the full-back Smart, and only the keeper, stood in his way. Biddlestone advanced to narrow the angle. David feinted to go left, Biddlestone plunged at his feet, Jack rolled the ball into the net with the outside of his right foot.

Arsenal in 1928–29 came only ninth in the First Division but had another good run in the Cup, going down eventually at Aston Villa in the sixth round 1–0, Tom Parker putting through his own goal.

The 1929 close season saw two hugely important arrivals, who would form a left wing partnership of historic fame: Alex James from Preston North End, Cliff Bastin from Exeter City. They could scarcely have been more sharply differentiated in character. Bastin, the quiet, shy, 17-year-old Devonian. James, the tough little Scot with supreme ball control and a wide repertoire of passes, a salient member of Scotland's Wembley Wizards attack which thrashed England 5–1 in 1928. He cost £9,000 from Preston North End, another huge fee for the times, albeit not as big as David Jack's.

Chapman's intention was to modify James' game to make him the architect of the attack, and he was richly rewarded. Though he could on sporadic occasions pick his way through a defence to score as nimbly as David Jack, his role was essentially constructive. With Bastin, basically an inside-left, somewhat reluctantly turned by Chapman into an incisive, even prolific, left-winger. James would feed him with the pass inside the opposing back, would send his centre-forward racing down the middle after through balls, or find the galloping right-winger Hulme with his long, crossfield pass.

Erroneously, James was supposed to have said to Bastin, 'Stay out on the wing and I'll give you the ball!' In fact, Cliff would stand some 10 or 15 yards away from the touchline. In his endless quest for the right centre-forward, Chapman kept picking, dropping and recalling the big Yorkshireman, Jack Lambert, who had come in 1926 from Doncaster Rovers. After 32 games in two seasons, he was picked only half a dozen times in season 1928–29 with Brain still the acknowledged first choice. But by 1929–30 Brain was marginalised and Lambert, brave, strong and fast – a far better footballer, in Bastin's view, than he had credit for being – edged his way into favour and eventually into the Cup Final.

The 1929–30 season had, for Chapman, an almost poignant climax when, in the Cup Final at Wembley, Arsenal, the team he was making great, confronted Huddersfield Town, the team he had made great. In the League, it had not been a distinguished season for Arsenal. They could do no better than 14th place, losing three more games than they won. It took time for James and Bastin to blend into the side. James didn't find it easy at first to refine his style. Bastin first played at inside-right, and it was only when it came to Christmas and he was short of an outside-left that Chapman, to Bastin's surprise, played him there. He hadn't occupied the position since he was nine years old, but once again, Chapman was vindicated. Bastin settled down quickly, though he would score only seven League goals, an amount he would quadruple the following season.

In the Cup, however, he scored four of Arsenal's goals on the way to the Final, beginning with the second against Chelsea in a derby victory at Highbury in the third round. Jack Lambert got the first; he would finish top scorer in the Championship with 18 goals, and would stave off the challenge of another of Chapman's centre-forward purchases, Dave Halliday, for the Final.

The Monday before the Final, in a somewhat chaotic game at Leicester City, Halliday scored no fewer than four times and Bastin twice in a 6–6 draw, Arsenal having been 3–1 down at half time. In 1971, Arsenal of course would also be contentiously forced to play on the Monday before the Final, though in that case, the very League title rested on the match at Tottenham.

On the way to Wembley Arsenal first defeated Chelsea, then a Second Division team, 2–0 at Highbury. Bastin's goal was his first for the club and there had been some surprise when he was picked on the left wing in preference to the Welsh international, the experienced

Charlie Jones. Next, Bastin scored again at Highbury against Birmingham – 'putting all I knew into a shot which whizzed past Harry Hibbs [then England's goalkeeper] struck the underside of the bar, and hit the back of the net.' But Birmingham forced a 2–2 draw and Arsenal were obliged to win 1–0 at St Andrews. It was the turning point for Alex James, who rose from a sick bed to excel.

A 2–0 win at Middlesbrough, an even better 3–0 derby win at West Ham, and Arsenal were in the semi-final, where their unexpected opponents would be Hull City, shortly fated to be relegated from the Second Division. Hull, you could say, were not a team which stood on ceremony, bruising, indeed, might be the word. At Leeds, they rose above themselves. Thanks to another of Danny Lewis' bizarre blunders, they even took a 15th-minute lead. Lewis, destined poor soul to miss the Cup Final and the chance of redemption, picked up a loose ball and essayed to kick it clear. The ball, however, travelled barely 30 yards. Howieson, Hull's inside-left, lobbed it back, side footed. Lewis assumed it would sail out of play and stood still, but he was wrong; the ball finished in the net! An own goal by of all people Eddie Hapgood made it 2–0 to Hull, and who knows what might have happened had Hull in the opening minutes of the second half not been obliged to put Walsh, their injured right-half, out on the wing.

So David Jack scored from Hulme's centre, and Bastin, served by James, went past his man to shoot into the far top corner. Characteristically, Bastin would later reflect, 'The relief of my Arsenal colleagues was remarkable to see. I was naturally very happy myself, but even in this moment, my latent coolness did not desert me, with the result that I, who should have been the most excited of the whole team, was probably the least affected.'

The return, at Villa Park, suffered, in Bastin's view, from 'memories of how we had shocked one another in turn'. In Hapgood's somewhat euphemistic view, 'some of the Hull players tried to play without the ball'. Childs, their centre-half, was eventually sent off. Six minutes after that, Arsenal scored the only goal, and it was set up by the reserve right-winger, Joey Williams, who'd make but a dozen League appearances all season, standing in for Joe Hulme. With exceptional speed, he kept a pass from Alex James in play, tore down the wing, and crossed for David Jack to volley the winner.

So the final would be against Huddersfield Town, with Alec Jackson, the Wembley Wizard who had scored three times against England at Wembley two years earlier, on the right wing. Arsenal would have to replace two first-choice players, Lewis in goal and the quietly effective red-haired centre-half, Herbie Roberts, both unfit. Bill Seddon proved a solid replacement for Roberts, an inexorable marker, who once in a Cup tie would head the decisive goal against Huddersfield themselves. Lewis's place went to a goalkeeper substantially more erratic, indeed eccentric, than himself: Charlie Preedy. Jack Crayston, later to become Arsenal's immaculate right-half, once recalled to me a match in which he was playing for Barrow against Wigan Borough, when he himself was a mere 16 years old, 'and very new to the game. My conception of what a goalie had to do was to stand between the posts. Charlie certainly made one or two very fine saves in goal – but the best of his work that day was at right-back; or even left-back!'

Even the official match programme adumbrated what would indeed happen. 'Preedy', it said, 'never hesitates to leave his goal if he thinks the occasion demands such a measure. After all, it's odds on the goalkeeper who advances at the right time. Better than "stopping at home" and having to pick the ball out of the net, says Charlie.'

That afternoon, wrote Bastin, 'Charlie's far too daring antics nearly caused heart failure among his colleagues.' But in the event, he got away with his antics, and his goal remained intact.

In the coach on the way to Wembley, Alex James caused some amusement when he turned to Bastin and said, 'If we get a free kick, I'll slip the ball out to you right away. Hold it, then let me have it back, and I'll put it into the net!' This was greeted by general amusement since, by that time, James – even if on a later occasion he'd score a memorable hat trick at Highbury, joking that the goalkeeper flung two of them in the net for safety – was known for the rarity of the goals he got.

And yet it would come to pass. When Goodall, the England right-back, fouled James, in a match exceptional for its few free kicks, James raised his eyebrows to Tom Crew, the referee, received an assenting wave of the hand, and duly found Bastin outside him. Cliff drew Roy Goodall, returned the ball to James who, while the Huddersfield defence seemed preoccupied with Jack and Lambert, advanced and scored.

This calmed and reassured the Arsenal team, and though in the second half Town largely forced the pace, a typical through ball from James sent Jack Lambert galloping through to make it 2–0.

The following season saw Arsenal win the Championship in imperious style, with Lambert scoring no fewer than 38 of their 127 goals. David Jack chipped in with 31, Bastin with another 28. Fifty-six were conceded, 28 games won, four lost. Chelsea were beaten 5–1 at Stamford Bridge in the League, all five goals, after going 1–0 down, coming in the last half hour, three of them for Jack. Yet when it came to the Cup, Chelsea, eternally unpredictable, would knock out the Gunners 2–1 on the same ground. When Blackpool were beaten 7–1 at Highbury, Jimmy Brain scored three of the goals, but he only scored one more all season, though he did play 16 League games.

A 5–1 thrashing at Villa Park put a temporary spoke in the wheel. The defence, and especially Charlie Preedy, in goal that day, could never master Villa's robust centre-forward, Pongo Waring, who always made a point not only of unsettling Preedy with mock threats but also in teasing Chapman, 'You'd like to buy me, wouldn't you Herbert?' reducing even Chapman to silence.

Eventually, Arsenal established a new record number of points for a Championship victory, half a dozen more than the previous best. Cliff Bastin called Arsenal's 'the finest eleven I ever played in.'

1931–32 was the season which saw the Gunners second in both major competitions, runners-up by just two points to Everton in the League, and beaten in the FA Cup Final by Newcastle, a game notorious for the Over The Line goal the Magpies scored and notable for Arsenal for the catastrophic absence of Alex James.

Arsenal had squeezed through the semi-final against Manchester City at Villa Park in the 89th minute. Herbert Chapman, in the stand, was already discussing where the replay should take place, City had been the better team, when Jack Lambert, faithful to lost causes, chased a long pass from Bastin, which seemed certain to run out of play for a goal kick on the right. But Lambert caught up with the ball and pulled it back, for Bastin to score the winner. Hapgood would admit that the team was so weary it was 'dreading the game going into extra time.'

Alas, in the weeks before the Final, James was seriously injured playing at West Ham. Hopes rose when the team was in pre-Final training at Brighton, and Alex seemed fit at last in a test on the Brighton and Hove Albion Goldstone ground. Chapman, however, wasn't satisfied and told Tom Whittaker to subject James to a hard tackle. Whittaker did, and Alex, hobbling in pain, was out of the Final.

Bastin was happy enough to take his place at inside-left, which was always his favourite position. But Bastin was surprised when he learned that Bob John, the team's resourceful Welsh left-half, would play on the wing, while the young and inexperienced George Male would replace John as the left-half. Chapman, Bastin would later say, had made 'one of his very few mistakes.'

Bob John had in fact lately been operating on the left wing but Bastin felt he'd never looked happy there. He himself, though inside-left was his ideal role, had seldom figured there since joining Arsenal. His view that George Male, certainly a right-footed player – as he would so impressively show when switched by Chapman to right-back – should have been picked at right rather than left-half was in retrospect somewhat less germane, given the fact that after the war, and during it, Male's usual position for the Gunners would indeed be left-half.

Bastin would have put John in his usual place, kept himself on the left wing, and had another Welsh international, in the highly competent Charlie Jones at inside-left. As it transpired, John actually put the Gunners ahead. Bastin to Hulme, a right-wing centre, a collision between Newcastle's keeper and right-back, enabling John to head in the bouncing ball.

But then came the notorious Over The Line equaliser. Davison, the Newcastle centre-half, was first to a long clearance by Hapgood which he promptly banged up the right wing. Jimmy Richardson chased the ball, but seemed to have scant chance of catching it. But just as it seemed he wouldn't, and with Arsenal's defenders fatally relaxing, Richardson reached the ball, crossed and Allen headed into the goal. The referee, W. P. Harper, indicated a goal. Arsenal's players moved towards him in angry protest, but Tom Parker called them back. Later, newsreel and photographs showed clearly that the ball had crossed the line.

In the second half Allen scored again. David Jack, by then at centre-forward with Bastin and Lambert flanking him, missed a point blank open goal, and the Cup went to Newcastle, just as it would 20 years later.

For Bastin, if not entirely for Arsenal, the following season, 1932–33, provided abundant consolation. Arsenal would win the League again and he, from the left wing, would score the astonishing number of 33 goals, out of the Gunners' 118. The record included an 8–2 home win against Leicester, a 9–2 win at home to Sheffield United, and an astonishing 7–1 victory away to Wolves. But the season also included the historic debacle of defeat in the FA Cup third round at Third Division Walsall.

It was arguably another of those rare occasions when Chapman erred. Indeed, for all the fact that several Arsenal first choices were absent through illness or injury, hubris seemed to be involved in at least two of the choices he made to replace them. Joe Hulme, however, even if he had lately been out of form, was perfectly fit to play. Play indeed he did, most impressively that Saturday afternoon . . . for the reserves. Billy Warnes, the amateur who took his place, was manifestly out of his depth.

Absent through influenza were Eddie Hapgood, Jack Lambert and Bob John. To deputise for Lambert, Chapman made a truly disastrous selection: Charlie Walsh, a centre-forward who had never played a League game, and never would. He had for some time, however, been begging Chapman for a chance. In the dressing room, before kick off, he assured Chapman, 'I'm ready to play the game of my life.'

'Good lad,' said Chapman, 'you'll do,' then added, 'Oh, by the way, you'd better put your stockings on, or the crowd will laugh at you.' A bundle of nerves, poor Walsh had put his football boots on over his day socks and suspenders. Nor did he show more confidence during the game. Once in the first half, a cross by Bastin was coming straight to his head, unmarked. He misjudged it so badly that it bounced off his shoulder. In the second half, he was switched with David Jack, but when another cross from Bastin was coming to Jack's head, Walsh suddenly leaped in, to divert the ball away from him. The look Jack gave him was apparently memorable.

In Bastin's view, five Walsall players could have been sent off in the first quarter of an hour, Arsenal being given 10 free kicks in the first 10 minutes. On the hour, Gilbert Alsop, destined to become a Walsall hero, headed in a corner from Lee to thunderous applause. When Tommy Black, a young Scottish left-back standing in for Hapgood, fouled his man after rancorous exchanges, Sheppard scored Walsall's second from the penalty. Black soon afterwards was sold to Plymouth, Walsall won 2–0, turning form on its head.

Chapman had little more than a year to live, and the manner of his death was in a sense the concomitant of his extraordinary sense of duty.

But at least he had the delight, in December 1933, of seeing his Arsenal side beat the illustrious Austrians, the pride and joy of his great friend, the Viennese innovator Hugo Meisl, at Highbury. The so-called *Wunderteam*, which had just drawn with Scotland in Glasgow, had come to Chelsea a year earlier and given England a tremendous and sometimes baffling run for their money, though ultimately losing 4–3. Since under FA rules English club teams couldn't play against foreign international teams, the Austrians had to call themselves A Vienna XI. It was sure to be a contrast in styles. The Gunners, with their swift, functional, breakaway tactics, the Austrians with their Vienna School intricacies, their supreme ball control and rapid passing.

Arsenal just then were going through a somewhat indifferent period, but they raised their game for the occasion, especially the attack. James and Bastin had lost form, David Jack his place, though he regained it for that Monday. 'We may lose,' said an Austrian official, 'we know that, but after seeing Arsenal play (against Liverpool) we know we shall be the better footballers.'

There could have been a fascinating contrast in centre-halves, but neither Herbie Roberts, a stopper *par excellence*, nor Smistik, the elegant, ubiquitous Austrian, was fit to play. Arsenal set about the Viennese at speed. Jones and John were swift to react to the Austrians' short passing, but Arsenal couldn't score till five minutes before half time. Bastin was tripped and scored himself from the penalty. Three minutes more, and Hulme raced in from the right to crash home a pass from Alex James.

Only in the final minutes, by which time they were 3–1 behind, did the Austrians come to dazzling life. Immaculate ball control, effortless, elusive switching of positions. A goal by the hard shooting inside-left Schall, a header against the bar at a corner by the full-back Szesta. But football being football and Arsenal being Arsenal, they typically broke away, and Bastin made it 4–2.

'It looks fine, it is fine', wrote the perceptive Roland Allen in the *Evening Standard*. 'When the Austrians have learned how to turn all their cleverness into something that counts; when in a few words they have organised the winning of football matches as highly as they have organised the taming of a football, they will make (everyone) sit up and take notice.'

'We learned three vital lessons from Arsenal', said Hugo Meisl. 'One was that we must play a much more open game. Our inside forwards were prone to keep the ball much too close. Another thing demonstrated to us was that our play is not fast enough. We must develop our speed. I also realised that our covering was defective. Arsenal's victory has made us feel that club strength in Britain is greater than international strength.'

Chapman was only 55 years old when he died on 6 January 1934; arguably the consequence of his extraordinary, even excessive, devotion to duty. How many managers then, or even now, you wonder, would have driven himself as Chapman did, in the days before his death? On the previous Saturday, he had taken his team to play Birmingham; a goalless draw. The subsequent Monday he was at Bury, presumably in quest of talent, watching their game against Notts County. The following day saw him at Hillsborough to see Sheffield Wednesday, due soon to play Arsenal, meet Birmingham. Next day, he had incurred a heavy cold.

Returning to Highbury he entered the dressing room, looking unwell to Tom Whittaker, and complaining of backache. 'Relax a while,' Whittaker advised, 'and then I'll run you back to Brent.'

Chapman responded, typically, perhaps, that he couldn't relax; there was a player he had to look at in an Arsenal third-team match, to be played at Guildford. In retrospect and in such circumstances, it seems an almost obsessional decision, especially for so illustrious a figure. Chapman assured a concerned Whittaker that he would 'get back early and go straight to bed.'

He did so, with a high temperature. Pneumonia set in, and on the Saturday, he died. 'Chapman', wrote Whittaker in his autobiography, 'had worked himself to a standstill. His resistance had gone and he had nothing left.' On the Thursday, he had found Chapman 'tired and weak, but brightened considerably when I told him that I had learned that morning that, for the first time since he had taken over at Highbury, Arsenal were out of debt.' At this, Chapman smiled, saying, 'That's good news, Tom. Now we can really go places.' As if they hadn't.

His death came as a horrific shock to Whittaker and his devoted players. Clearly he was much more than a manager, he'd been a father figure. 'The news', wrote Bastin, 'came as a terrible shock. I could not have felt it more had it been the death of my own father. . . . In the Arsenal dressing room, nobody had anything to say, yet each of us knew what his companions were thinking. Herbert Chapman had been loved by us all. His fairness, his kind heartedness, his consideration, above all else, for the players under his charge, were qualities which, besides his transcendent genius, ensured a cherished place for him in the memories of all who had come under his magic spell at Highbury.'

How cruel an ordeal it was for the players, who on that very day should have to go through the motions of a home match against Sheffield Wednesday. Played out in almost total silence from a dejected crowd, the game was drawn, 1–1. It seemed, said Bastin, to last not 90 minutes but 90 years.

After the funeral, recalled Bastin, Tom Whittaker, more affected than anyone else, 'was wandering about in the road outside the church, dazed by grief.'

Chapman had been an extraordinary innovator. As early as November 1932, he successfully staged a floodlit match at Highbury, but the obscurantist Football Association would then have none of it. Not till 1951 would Arsenal at last with official blessing put on a floodlit game. It was Chapman who persuaded the old London Electric Company to change the name of the Gillespie Road tube station, right opposite the stadium, to Arsenal; though you can still see here and there the name Gillespie Road painted on the white tiled walls.

It was Chapman who first put numbers on the back of players' jerseys. He once suggested that to take the competitive heat out of football, half the top division would be relegated, half the second division promoted, each season. He introduced white sleeves on the Gunners' red jerseys, given originally to the Dial Square club of Woolwich Arsenal by Nottingham Forest. He changed the club title of The Arsenal, adopted when the word 'Woolwich' was dropped, to 'Arsenal', simply to put the club ahead in alphabetical order. Austria's Grand Panjandrum Hugo Meisl and Italy's *commissario tecnico* Vittorio Pozzo, were his close friends, the three great figures of European Football.

Bastin felt that the obvious successor to Chapman should be Joe Shaw, then manager of the reserve team, but in his playing day a significant figure, joining Woolwich Arsenal from Accrington Stanley in 1907. He went on playing for the Gunners till 1921 at right-back. Initially he and Whittaker took over the team, but Shaw, a shy and modest man, had no desire to be the manager. He was said to embody the whole Arsenal tradition, but how disappointing it was, when I wrote my first book about the club in 1952, to meet him at Highbury and find it was like getting blood out of a stone. During the war, he moved for a few years across town to Chelsea, allegedly because there was no reserve team to run at Arsenal, only to return after the war. Yet one wondered whether his departure and return had something to do with the appointment in 1934 and departure in 1947 of George Allison. Shaw was a much-respected captain of the Gunners – he played 308 League games for them, which would have been many more had it not been for the Great War.

So it was George Allison who became the new Arsenal manager. Never beloved by the players, often condemned for an alleged lack of knowledge of the game. And yet, did things really go so wrong?

Chapter 3

THE ALLISON
YEARS

GEORGE ALLISON, IN THE VERNACULAR, WAS HARDLY 'a football man', though there could be no doubt about his commitment to an Arsenal – originally a Woolwich Arsenal – club with which he had been connected since before the Great War. That connection began when he was a young journalist who had come to London from Teesside, though any trace of a North Eastern accent would be submerged by the orotund, patrician tones which would become so familiar in later years, not least as a radio broadcaster.

As a publicist, he was exceptional, constantly promoting the club in the press. As a journalist, he became the London representative of the then mighty Hearst Newspapers of America, whose owner was purportedly the model for Orson Welles' *Citizen Kane*.

Allison even became the first BBC radio commentator on football, with 'Uncle Mac', famous on *Children's Hour*, intervening to explain which square on an imaginary chart the action was taking place. Allison himself recalled in his memoirs a match in which action came to a standstill, enabling him to fill in time by describing imaginary developments.

One could, I suppose, evoke in Allison's case a clever American political cartoon strip called *I Go Pogo*, its characters a group of animals in the Florida Everglades. In one such strip, the animals are deeply dejected as they trudge their way through the pouring rain. Eventually they decide to make the alligator their new leader, whereupon the rain stops. 'There you are!' he boasts. 'Look what's happened!'

'Ain't got nothing to do with you!' they retort, to which he memorably replies, 'Happened during my administration, didn't it?'

In Allison's 13-year administration, all sorts of positive things happened. After Chapman's death, Arsenal proceeded to win the Championship again, won it a third successive time for good measure, and again in season 1937–38. They regained the FA Cup in 1936, and in the war years, at least until season 1943–44, they won a clutch of titles.

Chapman, the inspirational paternalist, was an almost impossible act to follow, not least for a man cut from such different cloth as Allison. But what, or rather whom, Allison did have was Tom Whittaker. Chapman had had him too, of course, but in very different circumstances, essentially as supporting cast, as a remarkable healer. He would indeed continue to be immensely valuable in this role, but over and above that he would largely inherit Chapman's own role as father figure. The invaluable corrective to Allison's uneasy relationship with the players.

Yet as we shall see later on, a manager, such as Bertie Mee, even if not beloved by the players and no great tactician, can keep the rain off his assistant. To vary the metaphor, it's the manager who is in the firing line. Just as Don Howe, as coach, was protected from pressure. When eventually he found himself out on his own, success eluded him. Whittaker was not a coach, but effectively, he was Allison's deputy. Becoming manager himself, he was able for some years to live productively on the capital he had built up as the revered trainer. But when things began to go wrong, which they never did for Chapman, he grew increasingly puzzled and dejected.

'We must rebuild', Chapman had told Allison, and, surely to his credit – for the decisions on transfers must ultimately have been his – Arsenal did, quickly and rewardingly. Just two months after Chapman's death, Ted Drake, the Southampton centre-forward, was signed for £6,000; and at last, however ironically, Arsenal had acquired the very kind of centre-forward which Chapman had pursued for so long, so expensively but unavailingly.

A Hampshire man who played cricket for his county, Drake was fast, powerfully built and utterly fearless, victim, alas, to a seemingly endless series of bad injuries. The sight of his being carried off the field on the back of Tom Whittaker would become all too sadly familiar. In the weeks that remained of his initial season at Highbury, he made just 19 appearances, scoring seven goals. But the following season found him in irresistible form, scoring no fewer than 42 League goals in 41 games. Bastin, the second top scorer, had 20. Drake's most extraordinary achievement came at Villa Park in December 1935, when he scored all seven of Arsenal's goals, hit the bar, and had another shot splendidly saved by the much put-upon Villa goalkeeper, Morton.

Constantly in the wars, constantly coming back, he was severely injured in what a teammate described as 'the heaviest tackle I have ever seen' by the Wales centre-half, Hanford, in February 1936. Yet by April his knee festooned in bandages, he was able to play and score the only goal of the Cup Final at Wembley against Sheffield United.

He could be at times a droll fellow. At half time in a match against strong opposition in Europe, played in intense heat, the general view in the Arsenal dressing room was, 'Brilliant players, aren't they? Pretty clean, too.' To which Drake rejoined, 'Yes, I tripped over my tongue four times.'

When Arsenal met Huddersfield Town, he had famous duels with an equally robust centre-half in Alf Young; endless clashes and collisions but never a harsh word spoken. After one such battle, Young left the field holding his left arm, one eye discoloured, a slight trickle of blood from above the other. In the dressing room, the Arsenal players though weary agreed that it had been a good game. 'Yes,' observed Drake, in all seriousness, 'but Alf Young isn't half using his elbows!' In the summer of 1934, Arsenal, and let us give due credit, Allison, signed two outstanding if sharply contrasted wing-halves, 'Gentleman Jack' Crayston, and pugnacious, indomitable Wilf Copping.

Where Crayston, a right-half, as elegant off the field as on it, still had a reputation to be made when he arrived from his second club, Bradford, Copping, who came from Leeds United, never shaved before a match and would insist, 'First man into a tackle never gets hurt', was already six times an England international. A member of a famous

Leeds half-back line: Edwards, Hart and Copping. Goodness knows why Barnsley originally turned him down.

Crayston, with his cool control, his long throw in, his famously equable temperament, was the ideal contrast and would himself become eight times an England international. Later, of course, he would become the Gunners' assistant manager and manager. Crayston always asserted that Peter Doherty, the red-haired Irish international inside-left, surely one of the original practitioners of Total Football long before it was invented, and later the manager of a remarkable Northern Ireland team, was one of the best inside forwards he had ever had to mark. He wryly remembered a game against Manchester City, and Doherty, when 'I felt as if I'd covered hundreds of miles.' At last he turned to Doherty to ask, 'Blimey, Peter, aren't you tired?' to which Doherty replied, 'Not so bad.'

'Well, I am,' said Crayston, 'but I can't leave you, so you'd better come and sit with me on the touchline!'

Crayston was not one of the seven Arsenal men who played for their country in the notorious Battle of Highbury in November 1934 against Italy, but with typical generosity he walked into George Allison's office the following day to say, 'If we play Italy again tomorrow, there's only one half-back line there can be: Copping, Copping and Copping!'

No fewer than seven may have played but just five were originally chosen: Frank Moss, who would have an outstanding second half in goal, preserving an England victory which nearly slipped away from them, Eddie Hapgood, Copping, Ray Bowden and, at inside-left this time, Cliff Bastin. Subsequent withdrawals through injury enabled George Male and Ted Drake to win their first caps.

The Italians arrived as holders of the World Cup, won in Rome, a competition in which, as a non-member of FIFA, England did not compete. Their *commissario tecnico*, or senior manager, was Vittorio Pozzo, who had learned his football tactics in England as a student before the First World War, and eschewed the Third Back Game.

Only 90 seconds had gone when Drake clashed with the Italian centre-half, Luisito Monti, a notorious Argentinian thug, breaking a bone in his foot and sending him hobbling off the field in intense pain, telling Pozzo, 'He kicked me deliberately.' It has always seemed very doubtful to me. However violent and provocative a player Monti was, and there is much chapter and verse, it was surely far too early in the game for Drake, who always told me of his total innocence, to want to injure him. So far as Pozzo was concerned, his 10 surviving men were 'retaliating'.

Already, the Italians were jumping on the England players, pushing them and, in Drake's case, punching them on the jaw and seizing them round the neck. 'We were playing for England,' said Drake, 'and we had to take it.'

England swept into sustained attack for some 20 minutes, during which they scored three goals. 'We were playing the best football it was possible to play,' Drake himself once told me. 'You could not play any better.' This, despite Eric Brook, the stocky England outside-left, having a penalty kick splendidly saved by the resilient Italy keeper, Ceresoli.

England went ahead when Brook headed in from Cliff Britton's free kick, then doubled the lead when Ceresoli arrogantly waved away his wall, and Brook promptly beat him from another free kick, struck with extraordinary force. Drake himself scored the third goal, after 12 minutes. That goal was scored when Hapgood, captaining England, was off the field for treatment by Tom Whittaker, his nose smashed by an Italian elbow. At the post-match banquet, the perpetrator laughed in his face but Hapgood, who had returned to the field for the rest of the game, restrained himself.

Abruptly, in the second half, the Italians ceased 'retaliating' and began to play elegant football. 'Players who had formerly run wild', wrote *The Times*, 'began to run into position.' Peppino Meazza, a prolific and elusive centre-forward, scored twice. 3–2 was the final score.

England's outside-right was the 19-year-old Stanley Matthews, no doubt alarmed by the flying boots and arms. Of him, the deluded *Daily Mail* sports columnist, Geoffrey Simpson, wrote, 'I saw Matthews play just as moderately in the recent inter-League match, exhibiting the same slowness and hesitation. Perhaps he lacks the big match temperament.' The next 30 years would prove him wrong.

Tom Webster, the popular sports cartoonist on the same paper, wrote on his cartoon, 'With England three up, the good old Latin temperament exerted itself and soon there were so many English bodies lying all over the field that our selectors might have wondered if they had picked more than eleven players. In conclusion, we were very glad when the whistle blew because you never know when this Latin temperament is going to leave the field and set about the spectators.' The caption was illustrated by the drawing of a tiny spectator, cowering away from a gigantic pair of footballer's legs, pleading, 'Can I go now? You've kicked me twice.'

Curiously, neither Bowden nor Bastin, the English inside forwards, thought that the match had been especially violent. Bowden, who joined Arsenal in 1933, was an unusual figure, not least because he was one of those rare Cornishmen to succeed in major football. A man of conscience, he was upset when he joined his previous club, Plymouth Argyle, to be taking the place of a married man, and he twice turned Chapman down, before eventually coming to Highbury. Usually deployed at inside-right Bastin, who thought him an inconsistent player, felt his best position was at centre-forward. Where indeed he would play effectively in Arsenal's run to the FA Cup Final the following 1935–36 season, when Ted Drake returned to lead the line.

It was a season of mixed fortunes, redeemed by the Cup, after disappointments in the League. After those three successive titles, sixth place was a sobering anticlimax, even if Drake did score those extraordinary seven goals at Villa. By contrast, the path to the Final included some notable performances, not least against Liverpool in the fourth round at Anfield, a game won 2–0, which inspired W. K. Johnston, alias 'Recorder', the usually measured editor of the Arsenal programme, to unwonted heights of eulogy:

> The Liverpool Cup tie of 1936 will go down in Arsenal history as one of the most glorious performances. Victories, it is true, have been gained with some regularity on the Anfield ground by visiting Arsenal teams, and it is again true that the actual score on this occasion was not an exceptional one. But nevertheless the triumph was complete and outstanding. Liverpool rose to considerable heights, and their performance was probably one of the best efforts they have made for some time in a Cup match. But in spite of this excellence they were well and truly beaten, and eclipsed in every department. The form of our team, severally and collectively, was superb and would probably have accounted for any team in the land. Each player produced his best form and the combination of the team was magnificent. It was most decidedly our best performance of the season, but we may go further and say that we would have to search a long way before we found so convincing a display.

Bastin himself, who crossed for Drake to head down and Bowden to score the first goal, said that it was a game which 'did not stick very hard in my memory.' Bowden, he recalled, 'made a great run down the left wing, finally crossing the ball for Joey Hulme to volley into the net.'

Sunderland would win the League, losing to Arsenal 3–1 at Highbury but beating them 4–1 at Roker. In the Cup, Newcastle came next, Drake with his badly injured knee, dropping out, to be replaced at centre-forward by Bowden. So Bastin played at inside-right and Pat Beasley, doomed and destined to be dropped at the stage of the Final, became the outside-left. He would, however, play in the Wembley Final of 1938 for Huddersfield Town, he on the left, Joe Hulme on the right; would score for England against Scotland in Glasgow the following year, and against Arsenal as a guest player for Spurs in the war. After which he would still be left-half and captain of Fulham!

On Tyneside, Arsenal drew with The Magpies, then a Second Division side, 3–3, then beat them at Highbury 3–0; two goals by Bastin, one by Beasley. Grimsby Town were the opposition in the semi-finals at Huddersfield. The Gunners had beaten them 6–0 in the League at Highbury but lost 1–0, away. Now a single goal by Bastin was enough to take them into the Final. Bowden, still at centre-forward, played him the pass.

Sheffield United, another Second Division team, would be the opposition in the Final. A few days before it happened, Allison summoned Bastin to his office and told him, 'I'm playing Ted Drake at centre-forward. What do you think about it? I know I'm taking a chance.'

'You certainly are,' responded Bastin. 'I should keep the same team, if I were you. Ray Bowden is doing very well at centre-forward and I think playing Ted is too great a risk.'

The risk, however, was taken, and narrowly paid off. This though it was not a convincing performance, United's clever inside forwards, Pickering and Barclay, largely orchestrating the play flanking the burly Scottish centre-forward Jock Dodds, who during the war would score prolifically for Blackpool and as we shall see help them beat Arsenal in the 1943 North-South Cup winners' play-off. Frank Moss, his shoulder so vulnerable to dislocation, was a major absentee, his place taken by the Scottish keeper, Alex Wilson. He dropped the ball in the opening minutes, then redeemed himself with a spectacular save.

The only goal came after 74 minutes, Bastin beating his man on the left wing and crossing for Drake to score. Hardly a famous victory for an Arsenal team for whom Alex James was nearing the end of his career, Drake was playing his first game for weeks and Hapgood was worrying about his sick mother. Lucky in 1936, unlucky in 1932. Half a dozen of the winning Arsenal team had played against Newcastle.

Nothing was won the following season, though it was significant in various ways, and an honourable third place was taken in the League. It saw the debut at outside-left of the young Denis Compton, a remarkable ball player with a fierce left foot and plenty of pace, besides being a wonderfully exciting batsman, who would make so many runs for Middlesex and England, but miss so many Arsenal games through being on winter tours abroad with the MCC. Denis played 14 League games and scored four times. His big brother Leslie, at Highbury since 1932, made 15 appearances and even, for a time, kept out Eddie Hapgood.

On the right wing, the fast and powerful, two-footed, Alf Kirchen at last succeeded Joey Hulme. As long ago as 1935, in the popular *Topical Times Sporting Annual*, he had been picked out as a future star under the headline 'From Village Boy to Lion of London'. A Norfolk boy in fact and a crack shot, Kirchen took a couple of years to roar but when he did, he would roar his way into the England team which toured Scandinavia in the summer of 1937.

For Bastin, it was a mixed and frustrating season, though he did manage to play 33 matches, even if they brought only five goals. He had trouble with each ear in turn, presaging the gradual impairment of his hearing, caught influenza and by his own admission, 'very nearly had a nervous breakdown.' But when the team's wheels were not turning, he volunteered to play for the first time at right-half, believing he could improve matters from there. The immediate result was a 5–0 win in the annual friendly against the Racing Club, in Paris, and he made a number of other appearances in that position.

At centre-half, the tall, blond schoolmaster amateur Bernard Joy, who in 1936, as a Casuals player, won a full England cap in Belgium and figured in the British Olympic team in Berlin, made half a dozen appearances. The following season would see him succeed Herbie Roberts, seriously injured in his 297th game for the Gunners against Middlesbrough. He would for a time run Arsenal's nursery club at Margate but would alas die in 1943 from erysipelas, when commissioned as a captain in the Royal Fusiliers.

You might also entitle the following 1937–38 season, when Arsenal regained the Championship by the skin of their teeth, as The Apotheosis of Eddie Carr. A centre-forward who stood only 5ft 6in (1.67m), though he was solidly built, Carr could scarcely have been more of a physical contrast with Ted Drake, for whom he stood in. Yet his opportunism was quite remarkable, his seven goals in just 11 games enabling the Gunners to edge Wolves out of the Championship, on the very last day of the season. Five of those goals came in the last three League games.

At one stage, Arsenal had sunk to 11th place, but they steadily recovered, jousting in the final stages with Wolves and Preston, who had put them out of the Cup and eventually won it. Thanks to a splendid display and two goals from Carr, they won 3–1 at Preston (then top of the League), Carr despite his size actually heading an early goal from George Male's centre.

Next came Liverpool at Highbury, the only goal of the game scored by . . . Eddie Carr. And in the decisive last game at Highbury, Carr scored a couple more in a thrashing of Bolton. Eventually the Gunners ran out winners 5–0, while Wolves lost at Sunderland enabling Arsenal to win the title by a single point. Fifty-two in all, jointly the lowest points total to win the Championship.

They had done it without Alex James, now retired, and with George Swindin, destined to be both a famously important, fearless goalkeeper, dividing duties with Alex Wilson and Frank Boulton. It was the season which also saw the debut at centre-forward of the young Reg Lewis, who'd score such a plenitude of goals for the Gunners, and who had been on Surrey's ground staff at The Oval.

Carr played only once for Arsenal in the following season. His later travels, which lasted into the early 1950s, would take him to Bradford, as a guest, recovering from a motorcycle accident which seemed certain to end his career, Huddersfield Town, in 1946, Newport County and Bradford City.

In some games, Carr played inside-left to Drake, sometimes it was Bastin, the Welsh international Leslie Jones, or latterly the blond George Drury, bought for £9,000 from Sheffield Wednesday. A skilful player, he'd make 23 League appearances the following 1938–39 season, but never quite fulfilled his promise at Highbury.

So to the last pre-war season, in which Bastin also made 23 League appearances but, waning, beset by problems with his ears, with duodenal ulcers, obliged to be for weeks in hospital, scored but three goals. He'd later say that had it not been for his hearing problems, he'd have kept his England place throughout the war. He had, after all, struck a fine first goal, a right-footed volley, for England in May 1938, in a famous victory over Germany in Berlin.

It was the season when Bryn Jones arrived so controversially for £14,000 but, though he did play 30 League games, found it so hard to adapt. Yet when the Gunners went on a coruscatingly successful Scandinavian tour at the end of the season, youth had its fling and Bryn Jones struck form at last. All seven matches were won, 33 goals scored against four. Gordon Bremner, a talented young Scottish inside-right, had made 13 League appearances, but the war years took him away from Highbury, though he played twice successfully for Scotland against England in 1942, joining Motherwell after the war.

How strange to think that George Marks, that excitingly gifted goalkeeper, should have made just two League appearances ever for the Gunners, having joined them from Salisbury Corinthians. Joining the Royal Air Force, like so many other Arsenal players, establishing himself as the unchallenged England goalkeeper, who knows how long he might have lasted at the top, both for club and country, if not injured. As it was, he would play after Blackburn for Reading and Bristol City, while George Swindin would flourish for years at Arsenal, though he'd never play for England.

Bernard Joy, who'd train alone at Highbury after teaching, was successfully integrated into the team on and off the field. He was, however, obliged to modify his game. Total Football was a distant mirage, and Joy's penchant, from his amateur days, to move upfield at times was sternly inhibited, Frank Hill, a Scottish international right-half, told him, when he once dared to cross the halfway line to head away a goal kick, not to do it again. Hill had come from Aberdeen in 1934, to take the place of Charlie Jones, but when he developed tonsillitis, Jack Crayston, who'd been acquired at the same time, stepped into the team and stayed there.

When war began in September 1939, and the Football League was indefinitely suspended, Arsenal had played three First Division games, drawing at Wolverhampton, beating Blackburn and Sunderland. But they had lost Len Shackleton, then a teenager playing in their Enfield

Nursery, destined to become one of the most brilliant if idiosyncratic inside-forwards of his time. Summoning him to his office to give him the bad news, George Allison, in a moment of insensitivity, gestured towards the new television set, a novelty indeed then, which stood in a corner of his office. Far from assuaging Shackleton's dismay, it incensed him at what he took to be a patronising gesture to a provincial bumpkin. He never forgave Allison and Arsenal, went down the mines as a Bevin Boy, played for his local club Bradford Park Avenue, and later excelled with Newcastle and Sunderland.

Highbury, alas, would be quickly sequestrated by Civil Defence, and for the next seven years, Arsenal were obliged to seek hospitality down the road at White Hart Lane, with Spurs. George Allison, working hard throughout the war to the point of ultimate exhaustion, had the referees' room converted into a flat as accommodation for air raid wardens to sleep, and a clearing centre in the West Stand for foreign evacuees. A barrage balloon flew above what had been the practice ground.

Alas, in October 1940, a 1000lb bomb fell on the area, killing two RAF men sitting in a hut, though two of their colleagues escaped. In April 1941, five incendiary bombs fell through the roof of the northern end, setting light *inter alia* to the goalposts. Tom Whittaker before he joined the RAF was initially the post warden, besides being the prolific centre-forward of an improvised team which called itself the Arsenal ARPS: after Air Raid Precautions. Cliff Bastin, exempt from military service thanks to his hearing, became a warden at the stadium.

Football resumed on a regional basis. In the first wartime season, Arsenal won the first of two somewhat idiosyncratic sections of the South League 'A' but came third in the South League 'C'. The Football League Cup, however, was a national though also region-alised affair, standing in for the FA Cup. In 1940, the Gunners, beating Notts County 9–1 in the first round, went down 2–1 to Birmingham in the third.

In 1941, however, they went all the way to the Final in a competition now played on a two-legged basis till the semi-finals. There was a notable success against their hosts, Spurs, Arsenal winning the first leg 2–1 and holding Tottenham to a 1–1 draw in the return, despite Eddie Hapgood being forced to play in goal, since George Marks – an endless wartime hazard – failed to turn up.

Leicester were defeated in the semi-finals, then it was Preston at Wembley, in front of 60,000 (22,000 was the limit at White Hart Lane) in the Final. Leslie Compton, now operating at centre-forward, where he would even have a game for England, hit the post from a penalty and Preston, with the then unknown Tom Finney scintillating on their right wing and Fairbrother resilient in goal, held the Gunners to a 1–1 draw.

In the replay at Blackburn, Leslie Compton was replaced by Ted Drake, injured and forced off the field yet again, suffering intense pain from a misguided morphia injection. With Bastin exhausted from his ARP duties, Preston won 2–1.

Arsenal's right-back in those two finals was Laurie Scott. He'd had to wait since 1937, when he came from Bradford City, for his chance, but now he had it, he was irreplaceable; even by George Male. Short and compact, speed of recovery was the essence of his game. He won a dozen appearances for England when caps were not awarded, 17 full caps when they were. A sequence halted after he badly hurt his knee playing at Villa Park against Wales in November 1948. It took him over a year fully to recover.

With most professional footballers going, at the behest of the Government, into the Army or Air Force physical education corps, Arsenal by and large, were able to deploy most of their leading players till well into 1943. Then guest players became more frequent.

In 1942 my father, an Irish dentist and an ardent Arsenal fan, who had regaled me with tales of the team, took me, aged 10, to my first Arsenal match at White Hart Lane. They beat Brighton 6–2. I was also taken to Stamford Bridge where, in the semi-final of the London Cup, the Gunners were held to a draw by Brentford, by then recognised as their 'bogey team'. Time after time the Bees would frustrate them. It was a game I remembered chiefly for an astonishing save by George Marks. Eddie Perry, Brentford's Welsh centre-forward, on loan from Fulham, was clean through the defence and let fly a shot of great power and accuracy. But somehow, Marks hurled himself through the air and turned it one-handed over the bar.

Arsenal themselves, however, couldn't beat Johnny Jackson, the Brentford goalkeeper, a Scottish international actually playing on his own ground since he was still a Chelsea player, kept out of the team by the immaculate Vic Woodley, who was so good that when I saw him,

I could hardly imagine him being beaten. And Brentford, after I'd gone back to school, won the replay, Cliff Bastin, of all people, missing a penalty. Alf Kirchen was in that Arsenal side on the right wing, though, ever versatile, it was at outside-left that he had played a few weeks earlier at Hampden Park, against Scotland. Arriving at the England team's hotel in Glasgow, in his RAF uniform, he greeted one of the selectors, who responded by asking him who he was.

'You ought to know, sir,' answered Kirchen, 'you picked me to play for England.'

'Oh, yes,' said the selector. 'How are you, Matthews?'

It was at Chelsea the following Christmas that I saw Arsenal beaten for the first time, and burst into tears. There were extenuating circumstances. Half a dozen of the regular Arsenal team were condemned to look on powerless from the stand; all of them embargoed because, on Boxing Day, they were due to play either for the Army or the RAF in a representative match at Cardiff.

It was a strange Arsenal team that took the field that morning. The goalkeeper was one Noel Watson-Smith, of Yorkshire Amateurs, and like an amateur he played. The outside-right was somebody called Colley whom my father, sitting beside me, called The Invisible Man. I had been smugly pleased that Joe 'Ten Goal' Payne – he had scored them one day for Luton – had to drop out, injured. In his place played a large centre-forward called Bernard Bryant, borrowed for the occasion from the amateurs, Walthamstow Avenue. It must have been the apogee of his playing career, since he scored four goals. Years later Harry Homer, then Arsenal's programme editor, met him working in the House of Commons as a barman.

Though his name meant nothing to me then, the Chelsea right-back, a late selection, was Walter Winterbottom, later to become for 16 years the manager of the England team; then a Manchester United player. Outside-left was a better known guest, the Liverpool and Scotland left-winger Billy Liddell, a formidable raider, due to be maltreated by Arsenal in the 1950 FA Cup Final at Wembley. Another guest was the forceful Scottish inside-right, Peter McKenna.

Arsenal were overwhelmed, thrashed 5–2, to my tearful despair and to the joy of my honorary Uncle Willy, who'd generously take his honorary nephews to Stamford Bridge and Lord's. Next day, my father and I couldn't face attending the return game at Tottenham, but Uncle

Willy turned up at our house for tea telling us beaming that this time Chelsea had won 5–1!

Christmas, however, proved no more than a transient setback. The team went on to win both the League South and the League South Cup. Reg Lewis, recommended to the club by none other than the revered coach of Austria, Hungary and so many other teams besides, Jimmy Hogan, was in prolific form, scoring 100 goals in three seasons. Strong in the air, a powerful shot, quick off the mark and a skilful ball player, he was unlucky never to win a full England cap, but Wembley would be his playground. Four goals against Charlton Athletic in the League South Cup Final of 1943, both goals, fully seven years later, against Liverpool in the 1950 FA Cup Final.

It could be said that Arsenal's annihilation of Charlton at Wembley was their last wartime hurrah. Without their irreplaceable red-headed goalkeeper, Sam Bartram, Charlton were overwhelmed. Ted Drake, wrote one newspaper, 'worked harmoniously with Lewis, gained reward with two splendid goals.' I still remember Drake, having failed to beat the hapless Charlton keeper Sid Hobbins to the ball, ended with a flamboyant flourish, his arm round Hobbins' shoulders, the other hand raised high in the air. There were reports that Bryn Jones might be brought to London to play at inside-left, but in the event, Cliff Bastin kept his place.

Alf Kirchen, alas, had little left of his career. Later that year, playing against West Ham United at Upton Park, he suffered so severe a knee injury after a collision that only a highly skilled surgical operation, whereby muscle from his thigh was grafted to his knee, enabled him to walk again. It was a loss to Arsenal and a loss to football, but he would flourish as a Norfolk farmer.

Jack Crayston retired about the same time, though the ankle injury which prompted his decision was by no means as severe. One remembers him, some years later, sitting on a table in the boardroom at Stamford Bridge, drily remarking that he'd decided to give up before we journalists 'started using that most worn out of clichés, "a mere shadow of his former self".'

But at least Kirchen had the consolation of playing a major part, shortly before his accident, in the laying of the Brentford bogey. In a match at Griffin Park, he drove a free kick into the Brentford penalty box where the left-half, Bill Sneddon, raised his hands to protect his face. The ball struck them and it was a penalty. Before the game, George Allison had insisted that Compton should take any penalty which arose. This he did, calling out to the Brentford keeper, John Jackson, 'Pick this one out, John!' and suiting the action to the word.

It should be added that the previous season had finished on a note of anticlimax when, at Stamford Bridge, Arsenal as South Cup holders met Blackpool, winners of the Northern equivalent, and lost 4–2. Denis Compton did his best to help Leslie at left-back contain an irresistible Stanley Matthews, one of three gifted guests in the Blackpool forward line; but failed. Matthews, it was alleged, was piqued when Leslie fouled him early in the game and duly sought satisfaction.

Denis, in due course, was shipped out to India to put fellow soldiers through their paces.

'WHAT'S WRONG WITH THE ARSENAL?' was a headline that year in the sports diary of the *Evening News*. The answer was surely and simply one of personnel; or the increasing absence of it. Guest players increasingly appeared, notably the electric Stan Mortensen, the Blackpool and England inside-right, scorer of numerous goals for the Gunners, and destined to score many for England.

Going to White Hart Lane, you could never be sure almost till kick off whom you would see in Arsenal colours. It was the task there of a little old man to put up the names of replacement players along the low wall of the stand with large yellow letters on black squares of metal. One Saturday afternoon, we saw the poor fellow struggle with the name of Liverpool's South African outside-right, Nieuwenhuys.

If, by Arsenal's standards, 1943–44 was a disappointing season, two major stars lost, no title won, at least there was the substantial consolation of the emergence of Walley Barnes. Of whom even the perfectionist Cliff Bastin reflected, 'This boy has everything.'

Recommended to the Gunners by their old right-back, Tom Parker, Barnes at the time was playing outside-left as an amateur for Parker's former club, Southampton, but he gladly turned professional with Arsenal. Son of an Army NCO from Islington, the luck of Wales had it that Walley was born in Brecon, so becoming a Welsh international full-back. But he was utterly versatile and, in his first season for Arsenal, played in a plenitude of positions; even, once, in goal. Acrobatic, quick, positionally astute, technically adroit, he seemed almost too good to be true. But in 1944, he hurt his knee so badly in an Army physical training exhibition that it was feared he would never play again. Sheer willpower had much to do with his recovery, for his knee collapsed again when he tried to return at the beginning of the 'transitional' season of 1945–46. At last he was able to come back to football and the First Division, at Preston, in November 1946.

It was almost six years and many international caps later that in the 1952 FA Cup Final against Newcastle United, his studs caught in the thick Wembley turf, his right knee was wrenched and he had to leave the field.

Season 1943–44 saw the Gunners dropping to fourth place in the League South and making scant progress in the Cup, losing three out of their six games in the qualifying group. The following season, they sank in the League to eighth, but fared better in the Cup. They beat Reading, Clapton Orient and Portsmouth (losing at home, winning away by the same 4–2 score, but somewhat bizarrely qualifying) and went down to Millwall at Stamford Bridge in the semi-final. A game of guests, you might say.

Millwall had Charlton's Sam Bartram in goal and his teammate, the England international playmaker Bert 'Sailor' Brown in attack, probing Arsenal's defence, plus Tottenham's elusive left-winger, Leslie Medley, and their right-half, George Ludford. Arsenal had the burly Fred Hall of Blackburn at centre-half, and Maurice Edelston, the Reading amateur who'd played for England and for Britain in the 1936 Olympics, at inside-right, standing in for the unavailable Freddie Steele, a pre-war star of Stoke City, not to mention Stanley Mortensen.

Millwall won 1–0; Arsenal, in the last 10 minutes, missed two penalties. Why, it was asked, did Cliff Bastin, captaining the Gunners from right-half, not take them? The answer lay in what transpired to be a less happy decision taken by George Allison, since Cliff had recently missed a couple of penalties. In his place, Stanley Mortensen was deputed, but Bartram saved his kick. When a second spot kick was awarded, Edelston begged Bastin to take it, but he, having seen Hall send in a couple of fierce free kicks, gave it to the big centre-half. Who promptly shot over the bar.

Both Drake and Mortensen scored 24 goals that season, but it was doomed to be Ted's last, a particularly heavy fall on the Reading ground finally proving an injury he could not overcome. His spine was beyond adequate repair. By an irony, he would become the manager of Reading, then a Third Division (South) club, moving up and on to Chelsea with whom, 10 years later, he'd win their first ever Championship.

Season 1945–46 saw a reorganisation of the League tournaments, the League South being enlarged to a full 42-match competition, now including clubs from the Midlands. Arsenal finished a mere 11th and crashed out of the FA Cup in January 1946, a two-legged affair, to West Ham, beaten 6–0 at Upton Park, finding scant consolation in a meaningless 1–0 win at White Hart Lane in the return. Little Horace Cumner, a lively Welsh international outside-left, scored that goal.

But much the most remarkable match of that season was that in November, at Tottenham, against the touring Moscow Dynamos. One of the provisions Dynamo had made before their tour was that they should play a match against Arsenal. Another was that they should bring their own referee, who would officiate at one of the games. Arsenal's.

Training at White City, Dynamo were crassly written off by the sports columnist of the then-popular *Sunday Express*, Paul Irwin, who dismissed them as 'a bunch of earnest amateurs, so slow you could almost hear them think,' no match for 'our professional teams.'

At Stamford Bridge, where Dynamo opened their tour before a massive crowd which broke down gates, swarmed over fences and sat along the touchlines, Dynamo would ridicule such idiocies. They moved with great speed and bewildering fluency, eventually drawing the game 3–3, though their equalising goal, however well deserved, was palpably offside.

George Allison, meanwhile, had been subjected to a protracted grilling at the offices of the FA by the Dynamo's Manager Yakushin, a large man with a sandstone cliff face, seemingly skilled at ice hockey, the referee, Nicolai Latychev and a female interpreter. Where did Allison live? Where did he work? And an infinity of other questions.

For their second game, Dynamo played Cardiff City, then a Third Division team, and thrashed them 10–1, to the wonder of the Cardiff manager Cyril Spiers, himself once a Welsh international goalkeeper. How could Allison in no time at all raise a team capable of giving Dynamo a game?

In the event, he called on six guest players, at outside-right no one less than the illustrious Stanley Matthews, partnered by Stan Mortensen. Bernard Joy on RAF service was flown in from the Continent. Fulham provided two players, Joe Bacuzzi, an England full-back, who'd played against Dynamo for Chelsea, and Ronnie Rooke, who within a year would sign for Arsenal. Cliff Bastin captained the team from right-half. Dynamo promptly decided they were playing England, though Wyn Griffiths, a Cardiff City goalkeeper, and Cumner were both Welsh.

What a game it might have been had it not been for the fog. Thick, implacable fog which closed in over White Hart Lane, reducing visibility to a few yards at best and making play palpably impossible. But not for Latychev, who insisted the game should go ahead, and compounded his decision by whimsically placing both his linesmen on the opposite touchline to himself, making communication impossible.

What went on in the fog frequently had little or nothing to do with football. A situation compounded by the fact that Latychev had told his linesmen that he alone would pronounce on incidents in the penalty area.

Dynamo went ahead early on when Constantin Beskov, an incisive centre-forward, later to manage the national team, headed in an obscurely awarded free kick. Wyn Griffiths, the Arsenal keeper, was hurt in the process, and replaced by Queens Park Rangers' Harry Brown. At half time, Ronnie Rooke, though once thwarted in the box when Semichastny, the Russian centre-half and skipper, jumped on his back (to be awarded a free kick when Rooke shook him off!) had scored once and Mortensen twice for Arsenal, who were leading 3–2.

At half time in the Dynamo dressing room, an English interpreter heard Manager Yakushin instructing Latychev to stop the game if the Dynamo continued to lose but to let it run, should they regain the lead. This they duly did, though with the help of having 12 men reportedly on the field, both outside-rights, for 20 minutes.

George Allison did what he could to put an end to the fiasco, but with Dynamo going ahead at 4–3, and the left-back Stankevich constantly pulling Stanley Matthews back by the shirt, on the many occasions when he beat him, there was no chance. In vain did Allison appeal to a Soviet Embassy secretary.

Vadim Sinyavsky, the commentator who had come with the Dynamo team would publish on his return home a shamelessly scurrilous account of the tour in a magazine read supposedly by children. Though his account of how on arrival they were initially billeted in a military barracks with mildew on the walls – they quickly left – rang embarrassingly true. Sinyavsky wrote:

Because of the fog, Dynamo suggested to Allison that the game should be postponed since we knew that fog, occurring so frequently in London, would be a help to Arsenal. But Allison refused, because people had paid for their seats and bets had been placed. After the first Dynamo goal, Arsenal became furious. They always play rather roughly and here in the fog they gave us a full demonstration of their 'style'. They used their studs on our players again and again. Rooke, their centre-forward, was particularly bad; so much so that the British themselves beat him after the game. Allison was also most gallant. When the English had scored three goals he suggested to Yakushin, with an oily smile, that the game should be postponed. But Yakushin stopped understanding English – even through an interpreter – and the match went on. When the Arsenal goalkeeper took the fourth ball out of the net Allison fainted. He had bet a large sum on the match and had lost.

The Russians even made a presumably comic opera about the tour, entitled '19–9', Dynamos' goals total, for and against. George Allison protested through the Foreign Office, who were informed that Sinyavsky had been deprived of his commentating job. But when Dynamo toured again, 10 years later, there he was, once more!

Arsenal's leading scorer that season, albeit with the somewhat exiguous number of 10 goals, was a romantic new figure: Dr K. P. O'Flanagan who had come to London from Dublin to work as a general practitioner. An outside-right with a potent right-footed shot, he was a remarkable all round athlete, once playing soccer and rugby for Ireland on two successive weekend days. An amateur, as he would always remain, he was also an accomplished athlete, adept at hurling and Gaelic football. His brother Mike, who played with him for Ireland teams, was equally versatile.

In the first post-war, fully official, season, his second and last for the Gunners, he made 14 appearances in which he scored but three goals; two of which, however, were memorable.

The first enabled the Gunners, floundering at the time, to win a vital home League game against Stoke City. A fine solo run was crowned with a tremendous right-footed shot. The second goal, also at Highbury, came against Bolton. When Arsenal were given a free kick 30 yards out, O'Flanagan took the heavy ball – no lightweight plastic in those demanding days – studiously cleaned the mud off it with the sleeve of his jersey, put it down, and let fly with formidable power. His shot flew into the net, though on this occasion, the result would be a 2–2 draw.

Many years later, at the Tokyo Olympics, I had the unexpected pleasure of meeting him by chance in the Olympic Village, sturdy in a dark green tracksuit, when he was acting as medical officer for the Irish team.

Chapter 4

Of Bastin, Allison
and Bryn Jones

'THE TEAM'S PLAYED OUT, MR ALLISON, WE MUST REBUILD!' IS what Herbert Chapman is supposed to have said to his designated successor, George Allison, shortly before he died in March 1934. Perhaps he was exaggerating. Arsenal, at the time of his death were, after all, on the way to winning a second successive Championship. And Ted Drake was about to arrive.

Yet you wonder why, in previous years, Chapman should put so little faith in Jack Lambert; himself scorer of a cornucopia of 38 League goals when Arsenal, for the first time, in season 1930–31, scored an astonishing 127 goals in the process. He also scored Arsenal's second goal in the 1930 Final against Huddersfield.

Of him, Cliff Bastin, never effusive about his teammates, wrote:

> Jack Lambert, our crashing centre-forward, was one of the finest
> whole hearted players I have ever seen. Many people label Jack as
> a mere crasher, asserting that any centre-forward placed between a

couple of inside men like David Jack and Alex James just could not help getting goals. I disagree with this point of view entirely.

No one can deny that Jack was blessed with a ball service which had probably never been afforded to any other centre-forward, before or since. Nevertheless, he didn't always get the ball placed right on to his toe or head, practically asking to be put into the net. More often he would have to go racing hell-for-leather down the field, with an assorted collection of enemy half-backs and full-backs tearing, wolf-like, at his heels. And even when he had outstripped them, there was still the goalkeeper to come. True, a forward bearing down on goal with only the goalie to beat is presented with a big advantage. But how often does one see that advantage abused? Few forwards have used it more often and more efficiently than Jack.

Bastin went on to emphasise that Lambert 'had skill, too', describing a goal he had scored in a Cup tie at West Ham, running half the length of the field before 'walking the ball into the net.' Bastin thought Lambert most unlucky in that 1930–31 season not to be picked for England. Bastin said he would always remember Lambert's feat on Christmas Eve 1932, of scoring five out of nine Arsenal goals against Sheffield United.

Yet, as Bastin recorded, Chapman was forever buying in expensive centre-forwards to take Lambert's place, listing no fewer than five of them, all scorers of renown, of whom only Tim Coleman, bought for what was then the huge fee of £8,000 from Grimsby Town in 1931, had some success at Highbury. In season 1932–33, when the Gunners regained the Championship and Bastin scored a phenomenal 33 goals from the left wing, Coleman scored 24 in only 27 games, while Lambert played only a dozen. But the next season was Coleman's last at Highbury with just one goal in a dozen games of his own. Jimmy Dunne, the big, blond Irishman, played half the League matches but was past his best. Thereafter, enter Drake.

Chapman, the innovator, the internationalist, the man who prolif- erated new ideas, has sometimes come under criticism for making his hugely talented Arsenal teams play such functional football, renowned for the breakaway. Bastin himself once told me that when Arsenal had a lot of the play, they began to worry. It is true that Chapman put large emphasis on defence, emphasising to his teams, however platitudi- nously, that when they went out onto the field with the score at 0–0, they had one point. If they did not concede a goal, they would come off with at least one point. But does any defensive team, Chapman might have argued, score 127 League goals in a season?

The choice of George Allison to follow Chapman seemed and still seems a strange one. Chapman after all was steeped in football even though he had been, with Spurs and other clubs, no more than a moderate inside forward. Leslie Knighton was much less than even that, yet he himself was steeped in the game. Allison, however, though unquestionably committed to the club, was essentially a journalist and a publicist.

He had been involved with the club before the Great War, initially as a match reporter for his newspaper, chiefly because no colleague was keen to make what was then the dismal journey across the river to cover Woolwich Arsenal at Plumstead. After the war, with the team at Highbury, he would write polemically and sometimes incandescently for the match programme as Gunner's Mate. Rotund, orotund, his Teesside accent a thing of the past, he would successfully work in London for the American chain of Hearst Newspapers. He doughtily played himself in that gloriously silly film, *The Arsenal Stadium Mystery*, which was shown in 1939, and after the Second World War would make sporadic weekday television appearances. How I longed to see it as a wartime schoolboy fan, and what a disappointment when I finally did!

In stark contrast with Chapman, Allison was never *persona grata* with the players, with whom he never established easy relations. It was perhaps inevitable that in such circumstances, the players should turn to Tom Whittaker as much as did Hapgood. Indeed in his autobiography, he devoted a chapter to the greatness of Tom Whittaker.

'During the course of my football career,' he wrote, 'I met hundreds of different personalities, from all walks of life. . . . For none of them did I have greater respect and admiration than for Tom Whittaker. . . . Tom was always a great friend to me, personally. I can never thank him enough for the care and expert treatment he lavished on me whilst I was at Highbury. . . . There was about him a touch of genius. To him, as much as any man, was due the amazing success enjoyed by Arsenal between the two World Wars. Men who, under any other pair of hands, would have remained on the injured list for three or four weeks, Tom would have fit again in three or four days.'

Bastin gave several cogent instances of how Whittaker came to his rescue, not least when he tore a muscle in his formidable left leg. 'He bound that foot with yards and yards of plaster, twisting deviously sly this way and that. And that Saturday, I played! Tom, in effect, had manufactured me an artificial muscle!'

For Bastin, and indeed for other players, notably Eddie Hapgood, 'the Chapman tradition had been broken under George Allison.' For Bastin, Allison, whom he disliked and told me so unequivocally, 'was not a successor shaped in the Chapman mould. Indeed, relations between him and Mr Chapman had not always been of the happiest. With consummate ease, he had the name of Arsenal splashed across the front pages of the English press, but he lacked Herbert Chapman's gift of getting the best out of his players.' But then, how many managers had it?

Bastin, when I was working with him on his autobiography, told me with some amusement of a time when Allison saw a player he was impressed by, in a rival team, and sent a scout to look at him. But the player had been dropped on the basis of his last performance. Whittaker apart, and he had a number of good years when made Arsenal manager in 1947, what manager could have carried on in Chapman's footsteps? Nevertheless, the choice of so radically different a figure as Allison, no 'football man', in the vernacular, was a strange one by his fellow directors.

For all that, the five pre-war years or so in which Allison was in charge were hardly failures, and success continued well into the war, till so many leading Arsenal players were posted abroad. Taking over from Chapman, Allison retained the momentum, winning the Championship in 1934, and winning again, the third consecutive success, in season 1934–35. The following season, Arsenal won the FA Cup, beating Sheffield United 1–0 in the Final. In 1937–38, the League was regained, if only narrowly. There is little doubt that, were it not for the war, success would have continued for several years. Under Allison's aegis, the formidable left-half Wilf Copping came from Leeds United, while Bernard Joy, a tall, blond schoolmaster amateur, took over from the ultra third back, Herbie Roberts; George Swindin arrived to keep goal, the resilient Frank Moss, a hero of the Battle of Highbury against Italy, had succumbed to his ever dislocated shoulder. But then, there was Bryn Jones.

When Alex James, the supremely inventive Scottish inside-left and fulcrum of the team retired from the game in 1937, Arsenal made do without him to win the League the following season, but the role still plainly needed filling. So it was that in the summer of 1938, Allison splashed out a record £14,000 on Wolves' Welsh international, Bryn Jones. A transfer strongly criticised by both Bastin and Hapgood.

A dozen years after the transfer, Bastin, in his autobiography, gave Jones and Allison no quarter, scathingly dismissing any analogy with how Chapman persuaded Alex James to modify his style to become the team's midfield orchestrator. 'Bryn', wrote Bastin, 'just did not have it in him to become the general and prime mover of the Arsenal attack.' Bastin compared the record fee with the previous record, the £10,890 paid by Chapman to Bolton for Alex James, who in Bastin's opinion 'would have been cheap at twice the price.'

Allison, insisted Bastin, if he wished to metamorphose Bryn Jones' style of play as Chapman had modulated James', should have reflected on their disparate characters. 'Would Bryn stand up to adversity as Alex had done? Either Mr Allison decided that he would, or he did not give the matter any thought. As it was, Bryn didn't. Quiet, modest and self effacing, he possessed none of Alex's almost aggressive self-esteem.'

For Bastin, Jones, by contrast with James, played too far upfield. 'He never pretended to be anything but an extremely efficient attacking player.' Jones, Bastin concluded, 'would have been infinitely happier if he had never left Wolverhampton.' Jones himself, I discovered years later from Ken Jones, his nephew, the sports journalist, had been badly hurt by these strictures. This, as the 'ghost' of Bastin's book saddened me: not least as I myself, as a schoolboy Arsenal fan, had much admired him.

As a 10-year-old, I was taken in August 1942 by my father to Charlton where Bryn was making what was announced as 'a comeback', having been stationed, in the Army, far away from London. The war produced many a strange scenario and when, on this occasion, George Swindin, designated as Arsenal's goalkeeper, himself serving in the Army, failed to appear, Leslie Compton, chosen at left-back, but with the safe hands of a Middlesex wicket keeper, went competently in goal. As for Bryn Jones, he excelled, scoring a hat trick in Arsenal's 6–2 win.

Jones had had just one pre-war season with Arsenal 1938–39, in which he played 30 games, scoring a mere four goals; scarcely emphasising his reputation as an attacking inside-forward. But those three goals at Charlton suggested that given time – and the outbreak of war saw to it that he wouldn't get it – he might well have settled down to make a proper contribution. As it was, he, in common with so many other footballers, lost half a dozen years of his career.

In the first 'official' post-war season, 1946–47, Jones successfully resumed his place in the Welsh international team, though in his 26 League games for the Gunners he would score just once. Later, he would drop back to left-half with some success. But the following two seasons saw him play just 15 times.

Eddie Hapgood was no more enthusiastic about Bryn Jones than Bastin. 'I've nothing personal against Bryn, but I'll always have it that Arsenal should never have paid £14,000 to Wolves for his transfer. It was unfair to Jones, and to the rest of the team. The little Welshman . . . came to us like a man with a millstone round his neck. He was a grand footballer, but I am convinced the responsibility of being the most expensive player of all time was too much for Bryn and he never played like a £14,000 player for Arsenal. . . . We had to change our whole style of play when Bryn stepped in to fill the gap left by Alex retiring.' Which, however, takes no account of the fact that prior to Jones' arrival, Arsenal had already played a full season without Alex James.

Here, I must declare an interest: in both senses of the word. When I left school at 17, in 1949, to become a very reluctant articled solicitors' clerk, I began immediately and concurrently to work as a freelance football journalist. Driving with my family along the North Circular Road, I saw a sign: The Cliff Bastin Café. Far, far away from the multi millionaire footballers of today, even the greatest stars of those remote years were so often obliged to make modest livings. Bryn Jones, returning to London from a spell with Norwich City, opened a news-agents' shop not far from Highbury. And here was Cliff Bastin, second only to Eddie Hapgood, in my admiration, as a legendary figure.

But Hapgood, I reflected, had had an autobiography; Bastin none. In all rationality, I might have considered that he had retired from the game four years earlier, and by contrast with a country such as Italy, footballers were quickly forgotten, rather than venerated, whatever their attainments. And Willy Meisl recalled what his brother Hugo, father figure of the pre-war Austrian Wunderteam, had told him on the eve of the 1934 World Cup finals in Italy. 'We cannot win, my team is too tired. But if I could have just one other player, we could win it: Bastin.'

So, in hope rather than great optimism, I wrote to Bastin suggesting that I help him write a book. To my delight, I had a promising reply: 'Thank you for your letter and glowing tribute to my career.' He had, in fact, he wrote, received an offer for a book from Findons, who published what were not much more than extended pamphlets. But the publication would have sold at only a shilling, which he regarded as 'something of an insult'. So I went to see him in the rooms above his café and we agreed to collaborate. For me, it would turn out to be a turning point in my journalistic future. When the book eventually appeared in December 1950, I hardly awoke to find myself famous, like Lord Byron, but, given the controversy it aroused – much to my surprise – at least I was on the journalistic map.

Surprise, because I had never intended the book as anything but a labour of love, an act of piety. My hope, doomed to be sadly frustrated, was that the autobiography would be published by Sporting Handbooks, well known for publishing the ghosted memoirs of Eddie Hapgood, Tommy Lawton and Frank Swift, books which I and my schoolboy friends had swooped on eagerly, as soon as they appeared. Hopes which seemed justified since, during my office lunch hours, I escaped from the white tiled miseries of my city building and raced down to Bloomsbury, and the basement office of Sporting Handbooks' Robin Owen, who gave me a genial audience.

Yet when I'd finished the book, after many a Sunday evening visit to Cliff's café, and as many to the British Museum Newspaper Library, Owen, to my despair, rejected it. I still, after so many years, cannot understand why. Robin suggested I look at their latest autobiography, that of the famed England inside forward Raich Carter, to see how it should be done. I never have, but I imagine it must have resembled the pleasantly anecdotal first three, rather than *Spotlight on Football*, the bitter autobiography of Peter Doherty, Carter's inside-forward partner when Derby County won the 1946 FA Cup.

Doherty's book was in sharp contrast with the easy blandness of the others. At one point he even said that were the game to rely on the sons of professional footballers, it would die. Published by a small, hitherto obscure, firm called Art and Educational, it sold a handsome 30,000 copies.

It was to Art and Educational, or more exactly its Scottish publisher, Peter Finlayson, that my father was recommended by one of his patients. The world of publishing then, let alone that of literary agents, was unknown to my father and myself. The book went to the Ettrick Press, in Bloomsbury Street, successors to Art and Educational, though, in essence, indistinguishable, their current best-seller a little book called *Tea Time Tips*, though its sequel, *With Ring and Grill*, was less successful.

I made infinite visits to Bloomsbury Street, where the amiable little Mr Finlayson was wont to sit on a convenient perch, gently swinging his feet. Assisted by the long haired opera buff, Harry Bryett, whose chief interest, and many phone calls, involved his Verdi Society. A poster of a corpulent soprano hung on a wall, a decision on the book was endlessly postponed: until my father himself generously agreed to invest in the book.

Today, so many years later, it sells, second hand, at a reported £170. If autographed by Cliff himself, then £200. Hardly a book to win the Nobel Prize for literature yet 'Boy' Bastin had a strong story to tell, and his own strong opinions ensured publicity. Was Cliff conceited, as one magazine editor and at least one Sunday columnist – adducing copious chapter and verse – insisted? Willy Meisl, transmuted into a didactic London football journalist, wrote 'it is obvious Bastin likes Bastin a lot and considered him to be an outstanding footballer.' Yet this was to oversimplify a complex and unusual character.

Bastin, you might say, lived in a kind of psychological cocoon, exacerbated by his increasing deafness. Yet even as a 17-year-old in Exeter, where he was playing for the local club, he was remarkably detached and self-sufficient. As even the formidably persuasive Herbert Chapman found when he came down to Exeter to pursue and ideally sign him for Arsenal. As he sat in his home, where Chapman had followed him from a local solicitors' office, hoping to convince him, Cliff, by his own account, was more interested in getting out while the light still lasted to finish a tennis match. Eventually, Cliff succumbed, but only when his mother said he should. 'The fact is,' wrote Cliff about this episode, 'that I am, and always have been, essentially phlegmatic in temperament. I am not easily elated; and I am not easily depressed.'

Season 1946–47 would be George Allison's last. He was wearied by the war years, in which a powerful Arsenal team as we have seen inevitably disintegrated after the 1943–44 campaign. By way of consolation, there was a major discovery in the shape of the supremely versatile young Walley Barnes. Though born in Brecon, where his father was serving in the Army, and thus destined to play many games for Wales, Barnes' family actually came from Islington, on Arsenal's doorstep. But his bright promise was to be threatened by a shocking knee injury in an Army PT display in 1945, which seemed likely to end his playing career.

The war years also saw the belated emergence, at full-back, of Leslie Compton, who had been waiting for an extended chance since he joined the club in 1932 from amateurs Hampstead. He was hoping to succeed the sturdy right-back and captain, Tom Parker, but Chapman decided he was too slow, preferring to switch the young left-half, George Male. Leslie was largely overshadowed by his protean younger brother Denis Compton, a superb batsman as well as a highly talented outside-left. The great irony being that while Denis, playing a dozen 'unofficial' internationals in the wartime and immediate post-war years, never won a full England cap, Leslie, converted to centre-half by Tom Whittaker on a European tour just after the war, was twice picked for England at centre-half in 1950 at the age of 38. To the displeasure of the England manager, Walter Winterbottom, who didn't pick the team.

The Gunners made a shocking start to the first post-war season, crashing 6–1 at Molineux against Wolves in their opening League game. Relegation loomed, for the first time since they were finagled by Henry Norris into the First Division in 1919. George Allison must surely take some credit for the two signings, which would transform the team.

Joe Mercer arrived from Everton in November 1946, Ronnie Rooke from Fulham the following month. Two inspired transfers, two players resuscitated and rejuvenated. Mercer, of Everton, had been left-half in a celebrated England wartime half-back line: Britton–Cullis–Mercer. But Everton treated Joe callously, allowing him to limp all the way home after one match on a badly injured knee. When he came to Arsenal, it was the phenomenal healer Tom Whittaker who put it right. As left-half and an outstanding captain, Mercer by his own admission had to moderate his old attacking game but he was a huge influence on the team.

As for Rooke, no one was more surprised than he when one morning at the Fulham ground at Craven Cottage, he was informed that Allison and Tom Whittaker were there to see him. And, it transpired, to buy him. He was 33, a rugged centre-forward with a ferocious left foot who couldn't cut it at Crystal Palace – though as fate would have it, he ultimately became their player manager. Fulham acquired him in 1936 and goals began to flow. He'd actually already played for Arsenal: in the notorious fog bound match against the Moscow Dynamo at Tottenham in November 1945. A match so bizarrely and ineptly refereed by the Russian Nicolai Latychev, who will figure again in this story.

Rooke's impact at Highbury would be immediate and Arsenal clearly had a bargain. Fulham surely felt, and Rooke himself most probably agreed that he was in the last throes of his career. So Fulham let him go for £1,000 and a couple of moderate Arsenal reserves, in Dave Nelson and Cyril Grant. Whereupon Rooke on that December Saturday at Highbury proceeded to rise typically high to a corner and head the only goal of the game against Charlton Athletic. He would go on to score another 20 in the League in just 24 appearances. Arsenal heaved themselves clear of the relegation area and finished a safe, if modest, 13th.

In the immediate post-war years Arsenal, just as they did after World War One, had severe financial problems. They were in hock to the Prudential insurance company, to the extent of £150,000: huge money then. The situation would ease when the debt was transferred to Barclays Bank. Rooke, operating as an advanced inside-left with the fluent and incisive Reg Lewis at centre-forward – he had scored 100 goals in three wartime seasons – scored an astonishing 33 goals. Arsenal under the new applauded managership of Tom Whittaker, were Champions.

During the close season, Whittaker, to his credit, had made two important acquisitions: Archie Macaulay and Don Roper. Macaulay had begun as an inside-right with Rangers, come South to play for West Ham, and from there moved across London to Brentford. He had blossomed as a right-half during the war, so much so that he was chosen for Great Britain against the Rest of Europe at Hampden Park in May 1947, by then a classical wing-half with fine technique and a strong tackle. That same summer found Brentford relegated from the First Division, to which they have yet to return, and Whittaker pounced to buy him for Arsenal.

As for Southampton's Don Roper, he was a strong, quick, straightforward winger whose two good feet enabled him to play successfully on either flank. He began on the right, later switched to the left where he once gave Alf Ramsey, at right-back, a chasing at Tottenham. On occasion, he could even operate effectively at left-back as he once, in an emergency at Highbury, did, even against as elusive an opponent as Stanley Matthews.

These early years of management were highly positive for Whittaker, whose reputation grew to international dimensions. The Italians would have liked him to run their international teams and he was greatly admired when the team twice toured Brazil.

The FA Cup, after 14 years, was regained when Liverpool were beaten in the 1950 Final, with two goals by Lewis, though the victory was somewhat blemished by a painful challenge by Alex Forbes, a red-headed successor to his fellow red-haired Scot Macaulay, on a third Scot; Liverpool's forceful left-winger, Billy Liddell, which greatly reduced Liddell's effectiveness. 'Lucky Arsenal?' wrote the accomplished columnist and politician J. P. W. Mallalieu in *The Spectator*. 'No, just a little dirty.'

Whittaker promised legal action, but it came to nothing. Years later, in a press box, Liddell, an impeccable sportsman, a wartime bomber navigator, smiled and told me that the following day he had trouble putting on his jacket

In due course, Whittaker would replace Macaulay with Forbes. 'We are always interested in good players', he tactfully said, when it was rumoured in the press that he would be buying Forbes from Sheffield United. His transfer dealings in this early managerial period were sound, though later he would lose his way. As for Macaulay, he would later manage Norwich City and Brighton, yet would end up working as a traffic warden. Such could be the fate of former stars in those iniquitous days of the maximum wage.

In his halcyon period, Whittaker clearly had the complete confidence and affection of his players. He was not, in the new Matt Busby mode, a 'tracksuit manager'. Indeed, in those days when training grounds were unknown, when the Arsenal players trained in the area behind the Clock End of the stadium and played endless games of head tennis, there was scant tactical innovation. The Third Back Game with its W-formation, initiated in the Chapman–Buchan era, prevailed and would do until Brazil revolutionised the game with their 4–2–4 in the 1958 World Cup finals.

Where Whittaker was undoubtedly fortunate was to inherit Jimmy

Logie, who between 1946 and 1955 was the vibrant inspiration of the Arsenal attack. Well might Jack Kelsey, Arsenal's accomplished Welsh international goalkeeper, write of him, 'As far as I was concerned, Jimmy for me just was the Arsenal, the indispensable link between attack and defence.' When the Second World War began, Jimmy had just signed for Arsenal from the Scottish junior club, Lochore Welfare. Alas, too late to play for them until the war, in which he served on a Royal Navy trawler, was done.

In the transitional 1945–46 season, he figured at left-half, but his natural, influential position was at inside forward, and as such he made his League debut, though at inside-left rather than in his future position of inside-right, in the Gunners' disastrous beginning at Wolverhampton, where they crashed, 6–1. Certainly Logie was the most essential Arsenal playmaker since his fellow Scot, Alex James, though they were very different kinds of player. James, physically the stronger, excelled in his long, searching passes through the middle, or crossfield from inside-left to the left wing.

Logie, by contrast, was essentially a 'one wing player', chiefly serving his outside-right or his centre-forward, while his speed and exceptional close control enabled him to take out opposing defenders. Without him, after he left in controversial circumstances in 1955, the Arsenal attack was like a car without an engine. How bizarrely ironic it was that his nemesis should be that very Nikolai Latychev, the Russian who had refereed that farcical game in the Tottenham fog against the touring Moscow Dynamo.

The other major Moscow club, Spartak, came to Highbury for a friendly game, and whom should they bring to referee it than . . . Latychev. At one point, the Arsenal outside-right, blond Arthur Milton, another of the club's footballer-cricketers, capped for England in both codes, raced into the Spartak penalty to be badly brought down. Latychev, to Arsenal's and Logie's dismay, gave no penalty. Logie, incensed, refused as Arsenal skipper to shake hands with Latychev at the end, thereby incurring the displeasure of the reigning Chairman, Sir Bracewell Smith. Something Big in the City, Sir Bracewell reportedly did skilful things to help Arsenal with their finances, but the impression he gave, albeit telephonically, was one of pompous self-importance: 'Well, come on, *boy!*'

Be that as it may, he, in turn, at the club's Christmas party, pointedly refused to shake hands with Logie; and an era ended. Jack Kelsey, in his goalkeeping days, once told me, of Bracewell Smith, 'He comes down to the dressing rooms now and gives us advice, silly little things like, "Pass to a man!"' But Logie would pass no more for the Gunners.

He moved, surprisingly, even mysteriously, not to any other major club, not even to one in the Football League, but to Southern League Gravesend and Northfleet where his former Arsenal colleague, ex-England left-back, Lionel Smith was in charge. Hard to discover why, even when speaking to those who had been close to him at the club. It was suggested to me that the maximum wage may have played a part; he'd have been no better off had he joined a League team.

Alas, thenceforward it would be downhill all the way. Before long one would meet the bizarre and troubling sight of seeing him sitting at the corner of Piccadilly Circus, outside the Swan and Edgar store, presiding over a stall of magazines and newspapers. Then one would encounter him in a commissionaire's uniform, seated behind the reception desk of the Thames Television company in the Euston Road. A gambler and a heavy drinker, he would die young.

His close friend at Highbury was the wing-half Arthur Shaw, another addicted to dogs and horses but one who would survive well into his 80s: and a compulsive, inveterate practical joker. So many friends had he and Logie among the jockeys that a section of the stand which harboured a line of them at matches was christened 'The Paddock'.

Shaw spent seven years at Highbury and though he never kept a regular first-team place, making just 41 League appearances, the 27 games he got in season 1952–53 were enough to gain him a Championship medal. He played football for a string of West London amateur clubs and Queens Park Rangers, before turning professional with Brentford, joining the Gunners in April 1948.

The most celebrated of his practical jokes took place in Scotland, during Arsenal's pre-season participation in a competition called The Coronation Cup, in Glasgow. Its victim was the director, Commander Bone, representative on the board of Barclays Bank, a figure not known for his lavish ways. It happened in May 1953, as the team coach drove away from the golf course, at Skelmorlie.

Arthur Shaw came up to Bone carrying a Scottish pound note. 'Look at this, Commander,' he said. 'Stage money. I found it on the golf course.'

'No, no,' replied the commander, 'it's a Scottish pound note.'

'It's stage money!' said Arthur. 'There's a whole bundle of it up there. We were kicking it about all over the place.'

'I'll give you ten shillings for it,' said Bone.

'No,' replied Shaw, 'I wouldn't take it off you.' Whereupon, switching the pound note into his other hand, he replaced it with a crumpled envelope, which he proceeded to throw out of the window of the coach.

'Idiot!' expostulated Bone. 'You've thrown a pound note away!'

'It's only stage money', countered Shaw.

Later in the day, Joe Mercer, Arsenal's skipper, drove some of the players along the same road. 'Wouldn't it be funny,' a player reflected, 'if we saw Commander Bone looking for the one pound note.'

And they did. There was the Commander, head down, diligently examining the road. Mercer, convulsed with laughter, blew a long blast on his horn and slowed down. The Commander confronted them. 'I've never seen so many cigarette and toffee papers in my life', he said.

Another of Shaw's practical jokes was played on 'Gentleman' Jack Crayston, when acting as reserve team manager. When the team travelled for a match in Bournemouth, their coach was parked on the promenade. Descending from it, Shaw quickly took in a phone box and on the opposite side of the road, a newsagents. Strolling as inconspicuously as possible along the road, having noted the number of the phone box, he reached another one. There, he dialled the number of the first box.

When it duly rang, Joe Wade, the full-back who made a fine beginning in the 1945–46 season, and ultimately won a First Division place, told Crayston, 'Quick, Jack, answer the telephone!' This Crayston did, to be greeted by a voice asking, 'Would you mind doing me a great favour? Pop across to the newsagents' opposite and tell Pegleg that Nobby won't be able to come tonight.'

Agreeing, Crayston crossed the road to the shop, where, peering over the counter, he saw no sign of a wooden leg, but gave the message. 'There's no Pegleg here,' he was told, 'you'd better try the shop up the road.' So up the road went Crayston to the other shop, again to no effect. Walking back to the team coach, he told his assembled players, 'I'm Pegleg.'

Shaw was wont to have fun with telephones, not least in the office that lay between the Highbury treatment room and the dressing room, which had three telephones. Ringing one of them from another, he persuaded Ernie Collett, once a moderate left-half, by then a coach, that he was the Chairman's Secretary and that Collett should come up to give the Chairman a massage. This Collett, confused, would have done, had Shaw not relented.

But the biter, you might say, was bit when, on the occasion of Jack Kelsey's unhappy debut in goal at home to Charlton, the ball came over from a cross. 'Leave it!' shouted a Charlton player, standing behind Shaw. He duly did, and the Charlton player scored; one of his team's five goals.

As for Tom Whittaker, his star, perhaps inevitably, began to wane after the Championship season of 1952–53. Salt, you might say, was rubbed into Arsenal's wounds when, the following season, Sunderland thrashed them 7–1 at Roker Park with Len Shackleton, at inside-left, tearing the Gunners' defence to pieces. That same Len Shackleton who shortly before the Second World War was called into George Allison's office to be told that the club did not intend to keep him.

Shackleton would never forget or forgive. One remembers, during the war, Allison writing in his notes on the back of the flimsy one page ersatz match programme, of 'This once frail boy, who was playing in our Enfield nursery.' Unregarded.

In season 1953–54, the team sunk to 12th place in the League and, after overwhelming Aston Villa 5–1 at Highbury in the third round of the Cup, Don Roper scoring twice, went down 2–1 at home to seemingly far less powerful opponents in Norwich City. None of the first eight League games was won. A bad beginning was made again in season 1954–55. 'What you need, Tom,' said Harry Homer, the Oxonian who'd engagingly edited the match programme between 1946 and 1949, 'is a Tom Whittaker.'

Instead, what Whittaker got, in early 1956, was Alec Stock. Stock was the young, successful manager of Leyton Orient, favoured protégé of the club's ebullient chairman, the East End shoe manufacturer, Harry Zussman. Briefly a pre-war Charlton player, an inside forward, Stock served as a tank captain in the war and was wounded in action. Afterwards, he became the player-manager of the little Somerset club, Yeovil Town, who in January 1949 astonished the football game by knocking out mighty Sunderland, Shackleton and all, on their notoriously sloping pitch. Stock was one of the goalscorers. Orient recruited him.

In 1956, the Arsenal board clearly believed that Whittaker, after all those years in command, and a playing career which ended in 1925, needed somebody who would reinforce and stimulate Tom's paternal, if not paternalist, regime. So Stock arrived, and got off disastrously on the wrong foot. On his first Saturday at Arsenal, Stock accompanied the team to a match at Villa Park. In the dressing room beforehand, Jack Kelsey asked Joe Shaw, whose playing career had begun with Woolwich Arsenal, with whom he crossed the Thames, 'Aren't you going to introduce me to Alec Stock?' Shaw, who had reluctantly left Arsenal for Chelsea under George Allison's regime, but returned under Whittaker, replied, to Kelsey's surprise, 'It'll take place on Monday, when he's officially introduced.'

On Monday, at Highbury, Stock told the players, 'Right, we'll go up in the gym and have a natter.' There, no father figure, he told them, 'There'll be twenty of you away at the end of the season', leaving the players stunned. Kelsey and the left-back, Dennis Evans, were both smoking. Stock handed an ashtray to Danny Clapton, a future England international but then a young reserve, outside-right, telling him to cross the room to Kelsey and Evans, and tell them to put out their cigarettes. When Clapton proffered the ashtray, Kelsey and Evans tapped their ash into it, and continued smoking.

It was an ill-augured beginning and though Stan Charlton, a robust right-back who had played for Stock at Orient, welcomed his arrival, he was the exception who proved the rule. 'Nobody', recalled Kelsey, a World Cup hero of 1958 with Wales, 'seemed to me to enjoy the new methods.' Taking charge of the training, Stock initiated group practice, where before it had been on an individual basis. Kelsey felt that though the method had its advantages, it failed to differentiate between the needs of players with contrasting physical builds. Players now had to sprint between posts, in pursuit of footballs, turn sharply and return the other way.

No one, wrote Kelsey, 'had the nerve' to challenge Stock's methods, probably because they believed he had been recruited to be the new manager. In the event, Stock didn't last very long and returned to Orient. 'But it would be unfair not to admit,' wrote Kelsey, 'that he did some good, as well. Our training had remained more strict, ever since his spell.'

Tom Whittaker, to the deep grief of his players, died in hospital after a serious illness in October 1956. 'To us players,' wrote Kelsey, 'he had been a friend and even a father.' Jack Crayston, then the assistant manager, was, to the relief of the players, fearful that Stock would return, made the new manager. A demoralised team promptly lost 4–0 at Everton, but Crayston took it to fifth place in the League.

As for Stock, he would leave Orient again, and again briefly, in the summer of 1957, this time for far away Roma. It was an episode in which I found myself strangely involved. One day that summer, as I lay reading in my small Chelsea flat, the telephone rang and a high voice emerged from it. That of Sid Hobbins, then Orient's chief scout, well remembered by me as the Charlton Athletic goalkeeper when Arsenal annihilated them 7–1 at Wembley in the 1943 League South Cup Final.

Round and round the mulberry bush Hobbins went, as time went by. If a certain manager, he said – as if I couldn't guess – wanted to work in Italy, would I be able to help? At long last, the high pitched voice – unusual in a red-faced man so large, addicted to big boots – told me, 'That manager is A. W. A. Stock.' I answered that the best I could do was to enlist Gigi Peronace, the ebullient little player-agent, a Calabrese, who, that very summer, had taken John Charles of Leeds and Wales to Juventus, of Turin.

And lo and behold, Peronace went to Roma, convinced their grandiose President Sacerdoti and eventually, after a sustained tug of war with Harry Zussman, never prepared to let Stock go, the deal was done. Stock went, but didn't last long. Roma and Lazio, the Roman clubs, have always been snake pits, and Roma's hierarchy then included schemers who had never wanted him.

They seized their chance when he and his interpreter missed the train from Rome to Naples where the team were due, picking it in his absence. Arriving in Naples, confronted with a *fait accompli*, Stock refused to sit on the bench and was sacked. So Orient and Harry Zussman got him back again.

Chapter 5

THE WHITTAKER ENIGMA

In 1969, Bob Wall published an autobiography called *Arsenal From the Heart*. Wall at that time was Chief Executive at Highbury, an imposing figure in bowler hat and formal overcoat. Hard to imagine that he had risen steadily all the way up from being Herbert Chapman's office boy. The anecdotes of that period were the best things in the book. But there was something else which baffled me. And, had I thought about it more comprehensively at the time – indeed, if Wall had only done so himself – would have seemed impossible rather than merely improbable.

What Wall wrote concerned two leading members of Arsenal's triumphant pre-war teams, Eddie Hapgood and Jack Crayston. Hapgood, my own schoolboy hero, had been the left-back and peerless captain; captain of England, too. 'Gentleman Jack' Crayston had been the accomplished right-half, an elegant user of the ball, a master of the long throw-in and an England international, destined to become, for a time, the Arsenal manager which Hapgood surely longed in vain to be.

Crayston was probably the more sophisticated of the two; both served as RAF officers, during the war. Crayston, a Lancastrian, had come to Arsenal from Bradford Park Avenue. Hapgood, a Bristolian, from non

League Kettering Town. He was devoted to Arsenal, to Herbert Chapman and not least to Tom Whittaker, the trainer whom Chapman, so to speak, plucked out of the chorus and both as an exceptional healer and a kind of father figure, had maintained Chapman's traditions after the manager's untimely death in 1934.

In his book, Wall wrote that at the end of the war, when Arsenal, just as they did after World War One, found themselves deeply in debt, both Hapgood and Crayston demanded a benefit. A man of Wall's long experience should surely have realised from the start that this could hardly be true. Benefits in those days, amounting to £750, after five years' service, were awarded wholly at the discretion of the clubs; a thing of grace and favour. No player could demand one.

Wall went on to write that Arsenal, pleading financial rigours, were not at that time capable of paying such benefits, but might do so in the future. Whereupon, wrote Wall, both Hapgood and Crayston appealed to the Football League, only to have their appeals turned down. Subsequently, wrote Wall, when Arsenal, now more prosperous, did offer to pay the benefits, both Hapgood and Crayston refused.

By an extraordinary coincidence, I happened at the time to be making a BBC television documentary in a series called One Pair of Eyes, a kind of personal statement, in so far as one was allowed to make it. One of my choices was to interview my schoolboy idol, Eddie Hapgood. The first professional match I had ever seen took place at Wembley Stadium in January 1942, England v Scotland. I was 10 years old and my father took me. After all those decades, my memories of it are still surprisingly sharp.

I recall, for instance, that when the Scottish players – including none other than Bill Shankly and Matt Busby as the wing halves; how well I'd come to know them! – were joined by a soldier and a sailor, the soldier wearing a long tartan scarf, no one intervened. The teams were then inspected by Mrs Winston Churchill, who told us that she could not stay long, since she had to go to welcome home her husband, returning from Moscow where he'd seen Stalin.

'Come on, Mannion boy!' a fan sitting behind us shouted, as the blond Boro inside-forward went skipping over the frosty ground. Gloriously talented, doomed to sad penury in his post playing career, Wilf Mannion would become one of the very few leading British players to see active service, most of them being enlisted, by Government preference, in Army or RAF physical training corps, so they could go on entertaining civilian populations at home. England won 3–0 and I, thrilled by it all, soon afterwards returned to board at my prep school in Northamptonshire – its wartime abode, Thenford House, later to pass into the ownership of Michael Heseltine – there to draw crude and untalented pictures of the match. 'Hapgood gets knocked out', was one of them so I suppose he was.

Moreover, I took to writing him fan letters each Sunday, after he had sent me his coveted autograph. One included an adulatory poem: 'When Hapgood takes the field each match, then Arsenal have no fear.'

He did not reply to these tributes and before long, the master in charge of correspondence, the bald, chain-smoking maths teacher, 'Bags' Lawrie, forbade me to send any more. Hapgood, wartime honours included, would go on to play 43 times for England, 34 of the games as captain.

In parenthesis, I should also like to recall George Marks. He kept goal for England on that Wembley occasion and continued to do so till the autumn of 1943; again at Wembley, he hurt an eye playing against Wales and was never the same again, being replaced by the Army and Manchester City keeper, Frank Swift. In due course, Frank would become a revered figure, keeping his place in the international team till 1949. He was in fact no stranger to Wembley, having kept goal there in the 1934 Cup Final for Manchester City, where an early shot slipped through his hands. City revived to win, and the 19-year-old Swift eventually fainted under the nervous pressure of the final minutes.

Yet for all his future fame, it would take him another nine long years before he played for England. When would it have happened at all, had George Marks not been hurt? Marks, solidly built, dark hair creamed carefully back, at once brave and agile, a long kicker, had joined the Gunners from the non-League Salisbury Corinthians, and made his first team debut shortly before the start of the Second World War. Like several other Arsenal men, he played for the RAF.

Alas, he was never to recover his full form, and would lose his place in the Arsenal goal in strange circumstances in January 1946. That was when, for the first and only time in its history, the FA Cup until its semi-finals was played on a home and away, aggregate, basis. The Gunners were drawn in the opening, third round at Upton Park against West Ham United. Both Marks and George Swindin, goalkeeper when

Arsenal, by a whisker, won the 1937–38 League Championship, were then on the Continent, Swindin with the Army, Marks with the RAF. Whoever got back to England first would play in goal, and it turned out to be Swindin.

It was a disastrous day for the Gunners, thrashed 6–0, and it might be thought that Marks would be picked for the meaningless return match at White Hart Lane, where Arsenal, exiled from Highbury, were still playing; and indeed would do till the start of the following season. But Tom Whittaker, by then the assistant manager, serving with distinction in the RAF, where his engineering skills were of significant value, announced that the choice would go to Swindin. His analogy being with an RAF pilot who had crashed, and who would be instantly sent up again, to rebuild his confidence.

In the event, Arsenal kept Swindin, but not Marks. Eddie Hapgood, just made manager at Ewood Park, took him to Blackburn. Irony of ironies, when Hapgood brought Blackburn to Highbury in midweek for the second League programme of the 1946–47 First Division season, Marks was in goal for Blackburn, Swindin for Arsenal, and the Gunners, who had been thrashed 6–1 at Wolves on the opening day of the season, were clearly and comfortably beaten, 3–1.

A 14-year-old Arsenal fan at the time, I remember walking out of the stadium mid-match in a daze of despair, walking back in again through an open gate to the terraces, and seeing things weren't getting any better. To rub salt into the wound, out in Gillespie Road again, I bought a shiny booklet chronicling Arsenal's pre-war success, which made me feel even worse.

George Marks eventually left Blackburn for lower division football with Bristol City and Reading where he was praised as a model trainer: 'You could forget about George Marks.' Long afterwards, when I'd mentioned him in an article, I had a letter from his son, who gave me the sad news that George was in hospital, having had a leg amputated. He would die not much later, undeservedly forgotten; but never by me.

Until I went to Weymouth, where Hapgood was running a hostel for apprentices to the Atomic Agency Authority – he, who in these excessive days, would surely have retired as a millionaire – I had never met Hapgood though we had once spoken, somewhat disappointingly, on the phone. I'd been working on an article about Arsenal for the *Sunday Times* magazine, and found him both resentful and embittered.

Some while before, he had written a published letter to the paper, criticising something I'd written. I told him I couldn't at first believe it was from him. 'Oh,' he instantly and testily replied, 'you didn't think I could write a letter like that?' which had a grain of truth in it. I told him how, as a young Arsenal fan, I'd admired him, but this cut no ice. 'But look at you now,' he answered bitterly, 'you're a successful journalist, and look at me!'

Travelling to Weymouth, to see him and his loyally supportive wife, I told him what Wall had written in his book, and he was horrified. There was no truth in it at all, he said, and went into the next-door room to bring me a file of correspondence. After losing his job at Blackburn, he had had a spell in charge at Watford, then a Third Division South club, finally, outside the League, with Bath City. Losing his job there, as well, and in difficult financial straits, he had written to Arsenal asking for help, pointing out that he had never had a benefit. The cold-hearted reply was to offer him a payment of £30.

Back in London, sad and outraged, I began to investigate. First, I spoke to the Football League, who told me they had no record whatsoever of Hapgood and Crayston making such an appeal. Next, I told Bob Wall as much. Could I, I asked, see Arsenal's minutes for that time? Bob Wall refused: 'I don't think the Chairman would like that.' To which he added, 'You can write whatever you like, Brian, but Arsenal will not reply.' However could they?

So I did indeed write what I liked – or what I fiercely disliked – in the *Sunday Times*, and Arsenal stayed predictably mute; though they made no effort or gesture to atone for their parsimony. Hapgood, it seemed to me, and Crayston too for that matter, had a very good case for libel. But a solicitor who was consulted, himself an Arsenal fan, responded that my article was justice enough. A moot point. A neglected hero.

But for me, the most surprising, even shocking, thing was when I asked Bob Wall who had told him this fictitious, not to say malicious, story? The astonishing answer was: 'Tom Whittaker.' Whittaker, the very embodiment of the Arsenal ethos and of Herbert Chapman's benign tradition. Whittaker, to whom Hapgood had paid such tribute in his 1945 autobiography, *Football Ambassador*. 'Tom Whittaker,' Hapgood wrote, 'was perhaps of all the people who helped me at Highbury, been my closest friend. It was he who, not long after I got into the first team at Highbury and my head was growing fatter than my body, accompanied me when I announced my intention of going upstairs to see Herbert Chapman. And it was Tom, with the Old Boss, who argued long and patiently with me when I said I was fed up with football and wanted to go back to my milk round at Bristol.

'Tom and I often talk about those days. And, looking back, I can see how his calm judgement and guidance played its part in many similar hectic moments.'

It was Whittaker who patiently came to his rescue when Hapgood badly scalded himself, leaping out of bed deep in the night, when his small son, Anthony, cried out, a prey to catarrh. In doing so, he knocked over a bowl of burning oil, all, agonisingly, over his stomach and legs. A doctor told him he might never play football again. Whittaker to the rescue. Day after day, in the Arsenal dressing room, Whittaker not only dressed the burns, but washed and shaved Hapgood into the bargain.

How then, one asked oneself, could Whittaker have betrayed Hapgood in this way; if indeed he did? By the time Wall wrote his book, Whittaker had long been dead, and there was no one to defend him. Besides, why should Wall not be telling the truth? Even if it was unforgivably naive of him to accept Whittaker's story at face value, when it quite clearly could have had scant basis in reality.

One can but speculate, and there does seem some possibility that Whittaker saw Hapgood as a potential rival for the Arsenal managership, which he probably hoped, with good reason, to inherit from George Allison. As it transpired, Whittaker was duly and successfully appointed and with hindsight, made a far more convincing manager than the unfortunate Hapgood, even if things went awry in his latter seasons. For Hapgood failed in all three of his managerial appointments, though he did last three years at Blackburn, between 1944 and 1947. Slipping down the League two divisions to Watford, he endured between 1948 and 1950, after which the best he could do was to move outside the League to Bath City, where he would eventually be sacked. But such was Hapgood's immense prestige as a player, for both club and country, that you could imagine Whittaker being uneasy.

Perhaps there is some significance in my own disappointing experience with Tom Whittaker, over the book *Cliff Bastin Remembers*: of which more later. I had 'ghosted' the autobiography of another famous Arsenal star who had worshipped Whittaker, and for which Tom contributed a eulogistic foreword.

A few months after its publication, as a 19-year-old freelance, I was granted an interview by Tom, in his office at Highbury. When I asked him what he had thought of the book, he answered, to my surprise, that he had never seen it. But hadn't Cliff given it to him, I asked. 'I believe he brought a couple of copies to the ground', was the reply.

Concerned, I went to the offices of the Ettrick Press, who had published it, in Bloomsbury Street; to find a response of anger and incomprehension. They'd given Bastin, they insisted, two very early copies of the book especially to bring to Whittaker, and they wrote Cliff a strong letter of rebuke. To this he replied angrily that I should not go around making such charges: he had given Whittaker the books, himself.

I wrote to Bastin at once, wholly accepting his version of what happened, explaining that this was simply what Whittaker himself had told me. In return, I got a letter saying that he could see I was misled; he had even heard that Whittaker in private conversation had said that he wished he had never written the foreword. Cliff ended with the words, 'But in future, watch your step at Highbury.'

In retrospect, you wonder why Whittaker chose to lie to an obscure young journalist, not least because it was inevitable that I would talk to Bastin, and that Tom's deception would be found out: as indeed it quickly was. In trying so ineptly to conceal his hostility to the book, Whittaker had set off a chain of distressing consequences. The implication was that he feared any kind of confrontation and, in his anxiety to avoid it, simply made matters infinitely worse. An Achilles heel.

Chapter 6

CUPS AND DOWNS

WHEN THE FA CUP WAS REINSTITUTED AFTER THE SECOND World War, it was only at the fourth attempt that the Gunners got out of the third, opening, round. Highbury was at last reopened in August 1946 with a public practice match between the first team and the reserves. In a one-sided cakewalk, Reg Lewis scored no fewer than six goals, but strangely they seemed enough for the England selectors to pick him to lead the attack in a charity match against Scotland, in Manchester. No caps were given for the game and Lewis was never picked again.

January 1946 saw the fiasco, in a competition played for the first and only time on a two-legged basis, of the 6–0 debacle at West Ham, where despite the disaster, George Swindin, arriving from Europe ahead of George Marks, kept his place for years to come.

The following year brought an epic three match London derby saga against Chelsea, each of which I saw. A vast crowd saw a 1–1 draw at Stamford Bridge. Defiant goalkeeping by Swindin kept Chelsea at bay in the return at Highbury, against Chelsea's famed inside-forward trio of Walker, Lawton and Goulden, internationals all. But Ronnie Rooke in the second half scored a breakaway goal and Arsenal, however fortunately, would have gone through, had it not been for an untypical mistake by Walley Barnes, almost miraculously restored to fitness.

I can still see what happened in my mind's eye. The ball reached Walley in the left-back position and instead of clearing, he fatally dallied with the ball, enabling the veteran Chelsea right-winger, Dickie Spence, hardly the quickest of men at that time, to whip the ball away from him, hurry down the right wing and cross. To Tommy Lawton's unforgiving head.

So to a third game at White Hart Lane, where Arsenal committed a kind of hara kiri. They should have had the game well won in the early stages, hitting the bar, missing an open goal and finally, the most unkindest cut of all, missing a penalty given for handling, when Reg Lewis shot wide of the left-hand post. Not the kind of liberties you can take when Tommy Lawton, still in his prime, is leading the opposing attack. He swooped twice in a minute, and Arsenal were out.

There was no shame in being eliminated by Chelsea, least of all after three encounters, but 1948, if it wasn't a Walsall, would at least be an embarrassment.

Just before the surrender to Bradford Park Avenue, then of Division Two, destined alas to disappear in all but ghostly form, my father and I had the great enjoyment – marred only by the game's result – of being invited to a match by Harry Homer, the programme editor. And, in the early days of the war, before he joined the RAF, an enthusiastic member of the so-called Arsenal Arps, running the wing with such speed and enthusiasm that Bastin and Co. feared he might finish somewhere up Highbury Hill!

I'd been writing to him for some time from boarding school, until eventually he invited my father and myself as his guests in the West Stand Enclosure Club, to watch the post-Christmas return match against Liverpool. It turned out, alas, to be a disappointing game. With Walley Barnes injured, Tom Whittaker decided to use Joe Wade, then a reserve team player, in his place at left-back. Liverpool cannily switched Billy Liddell, their locomotive of a Scottish outside-left, to the right flank. He was altogether too fast and powerful for Wade. Twice he went past him, twice he crossed for Albert Stubbins, his red-haired centre-forward, to score. Liverpool won 2–1.

But there was consolation, for Harry took me down to the *sanctum sanctorum* of the Arsenal dressing room. There, I remember seeing the bruises and grazes on the shins of Reg Lewis. Had he been kicked, I asked? 'Just a few little taps,' he said. He also derided the idea that a team in pursuit of the Championship would ever throw away its chance in the Cup. What distant days!

But when Bradford came to Highbury, Arsenal lost. To a goal scored by a future England left-winger in Billy Elliott, while in the West Stand, huge Yorkshiremen bellowed out choruses of 'Ilkley Moor Baht Aht'. There was some consolation when, the following Saturday, Arsenal went to Maine Road and before a crowd of over 80,000, held their Championship rivals Manchester United to a 1–1 draw.

At least in 1949 Arsenal lasted the third round, with the special satisfaction of their victims being Spurs, at Highbury, in the North London derby: by the ample margin of 3–0. One remembers the game well. Tottenham had rashly dropped their most creative player, the England international inside-left Eddie Baily, replacing him with a reserve footballer in Harry Gilberg. If he was anonymous, then the Spurs skipper, the Welsh international left-half, Ronnie Burgess, was recklessly self-indulgent, constantly dashing upfield into attack, leaving acres of space for Jimmy Logie, whom he should have marked, to run riot. Arsenal won with goals by Ian McPherson, Don Roper and their close season recruit, the powerful inside-left, Doug Lishman. Previously and mysteriously left to blush unseen at while at Walsall. But Derby County beat the Gunners 1–0 at the Baseball Ground in the fourth round.

1950, however, would see Arsenal win the Cup for the first time since 1936; without ever having to travel out of North London. At Highbury, with Lewis scoring invaluable goals, Sheffield Wednesday were beaten 1–0; Swansea Town, with a coruscating group of local born players – Jones, Medwin, Paul, Allchurch – in their Second Division team, 2–1; Burnley 2–0, with a memorable left-footed strike by Denis Compton; Leeds, with the 17-year-old John Charles at centre-half, 1–0, in front of 62,573 spectators.

But it is the first of two semi-final matches with Chelsea at White Hart Lane which is surely most memorable. Above all for the astonishing freak of a goal whereby Freddie Cox, the right-winger, himself previously a Tottenham player, brought the Gunners back to life.

Chelsea had dominated the first half with their ubiquitous centre-forward Roy Bentley tormenting the Arsenal defence and scoring twice. There was barely a minute before half time when Arsenal gained a corner on the right. Cox took it, with the outside of his right foot. Caught by the wind, the ball swerved suddenly and unpredictably into the near top corner of the goal. The whistle for half time blew almost at once.

To their credit, Chelsea were not demoralised, though not surprisingly Arsenal now predominated. It was a quarter of an hour from time when the Gunners forced another decisive corner, this time on the left, to be taken by Denis Compton, who beckoned his brother Leslie upfield.

Leslie trotted forward, ignoring the urgent call of his skipper, Joe Mercer, 'Get back, get back!' Mercer arguably had a point. Time after time Leslie had come up for corners, time and again he had been thwarted, even when on target, by a clearance off the line. The one exception being a goal he had headed in Paris, against Racing Club. But now, defiantly and inexorably, he advanced, and when the kick came over, headed it in, somersaulted, and didn't know that he had scored till his teammates embraced him!

So, on the same ground, to a replay, with Cox playing a still more crucial part. The match was in extra time when Cox, collecting the ball, took it across the penalty line while the Chelsea defenders stood and stopped, expecting him to square it. Instead, he suddenly pivoted and drove it past the keeper, Harry Medhurst, with his left foot. Reg Lewis' two crisply taken goals defeated Liverpool in the Final.

The following season was badly blemished when Lishman, who had already scored 17 goals in 26 games, broke a leg playing at Highbury against Stoke City. Reg Lewis was brought back into the side to take his place, scoring Cup doubles against Carlisle away (after an embarrassing goalless draw at home) and Northampton, but the die was cast. The Gunners went out of the Cup 1–0 at Manchester United and took fifth place in the League.

Lewis had, in fact, been displaced at centre-forward by the big, blond Peter Goring, a player who seemed utterly transformed by his experience of the team's 1949 tour of Brazil. Recommended, most appropriately, to Arsenal by their former incisive centre-forward, Jimmy Brain, when playing non-League football for Cheltenham Town, he frankly, when playing for the reserves, looked hopelessly stiff and static.

So much so that a fan, watching from the stand, cried somewhat erroneously, 'Blimey, they shot the wrong one!' But now he was transformed, full of ubiquitous energy. Later destined to turn into an effective wing-half.

February 1951 saw the somewhat ill-starred debut of a future famous Arsenal goalkeeper: Jack Kelsey. Seven years later a hero of the 1958 Welsh World Cup finals team, Kelsey let through five Charlton goals at Highbury that afternoon. Three of them were scored by the formidable Swedish international centre-forward, Hans Jeppson, a hero of the 1950 World Cup, briefly at Charlton, though *en route* to Italy. The following Monday at the nearby Finsbury Park Empire, Old Mother Riley, the comic act, made fun of Kelsey's ordeal. Arsenal soon put a stop to it.

April 1952 saw the Gunners in the Wembley Final again; once more against Newcastle United, as they had been 20 years earlier. And once more, Arsenal lost in unhappy circumstances. No Over The Line Goal this time, but Arsenal, like so many Cup Final teams of the time at Wembley, were obliged to play much of the game with 10 men. This because Walley Barnes, operating at right-back, twisted his right knee in the thick turf, came back with the knee bandaged, but was forced off definitively after 34 minutes.

Arsenal had again reached Wembley after twice meeting Chelsea in the semi-finals at Tottenham. Two drab matches, with Freddie Cox again the nemesis of the West London club. He put Arsenal ahead in the first game, Chelsea equalising, with George Swindin laid low on the ground. But Arsenal dominated the replay with Cox, first with a bold dash through the defence, then with a header, scoring twice.

When it came to the Cup Final, both Logie, with a substantial hole in his thigh, and the young centre-half, Ray Daniel, who only a few weeks back had broken his wrist at Blackpool, were barely fit to play. Daniel, whose talented older brother, Bobby, had been killed during the war in a bombing raid over Germany, insisted, 'If we win the Cup tomorrow, they can break my arm in four places, for all I care!' He did, indeed, break his wrist again, but continued to play resiliently. Though he was a fervent admirer of Leslie Compton, he was a very different centre-half, swift, mobile and adventurous, even to excess. That Arsenal – shades of the way Bernard Joy had been discouraged by Frank Hill – should let him go to Sunderland in 1953, after he had asked for a transfer, was surely an expensive decision; however headstrong a player this exuberant character may have been.

Twice in the first half Lishman came very close to scoring, and the team held out gallantly until five minutes from the end, when a header by the Chilean international, George Robledo, flew in off a post. Stan Seymour, Newcastle's overlord, who had himself scored for them in the 1924 Cup Final, told Tom Whittaker, 'Yours is the honour and the glory.'

The following season saw Arsenal win their seventh Championship and their last for another 18 years; by the skin of their teeth, on mere goal difference.

Yet they scored no fewer than 97 goals, the most since season 1934–35. Nineteen of them went to the powerful centre-forward Cliff Holton, so profitably converted from full-back, in only 21 games. Doug Lishman headed the League scorers with 22, but it took him 29 games to get them. Even Ray Daniel scored five, a tribute to his enterprise. He'd be replaced the following season by Bill Dodgin junior, from Fulham, a devoted student of the game but with none of the pace, mobility and natural talent of Daniel. He'd become an outstanding coach.

During the Championship, Arsenal found it all but impossible to shake off Preston North End, still a power in those far-off days, before the harsh realities of money marginalised the teams from smaller towns. But Preston then was still the Preston of Tom Finney.

It went right to the wire. When Preston beat the Gunners 2–0 at Deepdale, it meant that with just one match to play, the teams, joint top, had 52 points each. A surprisingly low total, it is true. In their final game played four days later, Preston beat Sheffield Wednesday from the penalty spot; then went to Europe on tour. This meant, in the somewhat strange circumstances, that the Gunners, knowing exactly where they stood, had to beat Burnley in an evening match at Highbury.

This they duly did, though the 3–1 lead they established in the first half through goals by Alex Forbes, Doug Lishman and Jimmy Logie looked increasingly fragile in the second half, when Burnley made it 3–2. But the Gunners held out, the title was theirs, only for long, disappointing years to lie ahead.

In parenthesis, it was in this season that the ebullient, inspirational Logie won his single, sparse cap for Scotland; at home to Northern

Ireland. And this, it seems, only because the Scottish selectors, such as they were, happened to watch a televised friendly from Highbury in which Arsenal, with Logie irresistible, thrashed Hibernian 7–1. Parochialism still ruled in Scotland; just as it had in the case of Alex James.

Chapter 7

CRAYSTON, SWINDIN, GREENWOOD

LOOKING FAR BACK OVER THE YEARS, IT'S DIFFICULT TO understand why Arsenal did not keep Ron Greenwood. Destined, at West Ham's so-called academy of arts and sciences, to emerge as the outstanding managerial innovator of his time, Greenwood joined Arsenal as their first ever coach. He quickly revolutionised the training. It seems incomprehensible that as late as December 1957, when Greenwood was appointed, the Gunners still did their training on the hard surface at the back of the south stand, prey to many a bump and graze. Greenwood it was who had them training on the actual pitch. But how remote even that seems from the supremely lavish training grounds of the Wenger era, at London Colney. Another world.

Four years after the Hungarians came to Wembley, thrashing England 6–3, breaking their unbeaten record against foreign teams, and prompting an agonising reappraisal of tactics and preparation, Arsenal's players had still been lapping the pitch. Now to the particular delight of Jack Kelsey, praising Greenwood's fertile ideas, training, though 'harder than it ever was', was always varied and interesting. Greenwood, enthused Kelsey, was 'one of the best coaches I have ever met'. His appointment was beyond doubt inspirational, but should Arsenal not have kept him?

Following the death of Whittaker, it seemed something of a matter of Buggins' Turn. First Jack Crayston, then the former brave, long-serving goalkeeper, George Swindin. Neither could take the club back to its erstwhile heights: not even with Greenwood beside them in his four years at Highbury. Bill Dodgin junior, an Arsenal centre-half and a dedicated student of the game, watching an infinity of matches when he wasn't playing, said that Swindin and Greenwood were 'like night and day'. As for Crayston, urbane, humorous and genial, even if he once did keep the young Jack Kelsey waiting five hours for an interview, he arguably lacked the dynamism and originality which the job, post Whittaker, demanded.

His goose was cooked when the Gunners, dismally lethargic, were knocked out of the 1958 FA Cup immediately at Third Division Northampton Town, to lurid uproar in the press: perhaps inevitably, the humiliation was compared with the historic defeat by little Walsall in the third round of 1933, though then Arsenal were the dominant team in England. Two–nil had been the margin of defeat at Walsall, it was 3–1 at Northampton who, by contrast with Walsall, whose methods had been robust to a degree, were thought to have played the better football. One of their best players, the attacker, Tebutt, who scored one of his team's three goals, was actually making his debut. He would seldom be heard of again.

To add insult to injury, the Arsenal players – when they played their next home match, and lost to Blackpool – were lambasted in the club's own match programme, to their bitter resentment. 'The vital difference between the two teams', wrote the programme, so far from the editorial days of Harry Homer, 'was effort'. Here, too, a comparison was drawn with the debacle at Walsall. Northampton, the programme asserted, somewhat enigmatically, was 'a different kettle of fish'. It implacably pursued, 'The present position is the culmination of an insidious trend dating back to 1952. The team then being carried forward to reasonable success by determination and the superb captaincy of Joe Mercer.'

To give Crayston his due, he rallied the team when he took over in 1957, finding it in a parlous condition, but eventually taking it to an honourable fifth place. And in February, effort was hardly lacking in a splendid recovery at Highbury, a match I was lucky enough to report, against Manchester United, eventually going down 5–4. It would, alas, be the final game in England played by the exhilarating young United team, five days away from the horrific disaster of Munich airport.

Kelsey thought the programme article a wounding and implicit slur on Tom Whittaker. True, Whittaker seemed to be losing judgement when, in his last full season, he signed two obscure wingers from Cardiff City in Mike Tiddy and Gordon Nutt. Yet he also bought an impressive patrimony of players. The big, incisive inside-left, Doug Lishman, was plucked from modest Walsall. He was the top Arsenal scorer for five seasons and ended with 125 goals in 226 League games. Two gifted young attackers, from either side of London, Jimmy Bloomfield from the West, Vic Groves from the East, in 1954 and 1955 respectively, each contributed substantially. Bloomfield at inside forward had elegant close control and distributed shrewdly, in the Arsenal tradition of playmaking inside forward. The versatile, vigorous Groves could play on the wing, at centre-forward, and latterly at wing-half. David Herd, signed from Stockport where he played with father Alex, would score freely.

Then there was the Welsh attacker, effective alike on the right wing or inside-right, Derek Tapscott, picked up from little Barry Town. Small, very fast, a notable opportunist, he made an explosive debut in April 1954, scoring twice in a 3–0 home win over Liverpool, a feat overshadowed by it being the last match played by Joe Mercer, waving bravely to the crowd as they carried him off on a stretcher with a broken leg.

The following three seasons saw Tapscott gain a regular place with prolific results, scoring respectively 13, 17 and a remarkable 25 goals, putting him 13 ahead of the second scorer, the successfully converted defender Cliff Holton, by then a centre-forward. But there would be a sadly abrupt end to his Arsenal career, injury restricting him the following season to an anticlimactic eight games, after which he moved on. So far as Greenwood was concerned, he was the exception who proved the rule. 'I'd like to hit him!' he once told me, miming a punch.

So Crayston, always liked by his players, retired, and in 1958 George Swindin arrived, after managing Peterborough. He made a bright beginning, Arsenal taking third place in the Championship in his first season.

He wouldn't do as well again. The club's League positions in his ensuing seasons would be 13th, 11th and 10th. This despite the arrival, in November 1961, of the highly talented blond inside-forward George Eastham, son of a pre-war Bolton star. After a long stand off Eastham won a major legal decision against his former club, Newcastle United, Justice Wilberforce decreeing that players' contracts were in restraint of trade.

Costing the Gunners £47,500, Eastham was a perfect provider for David Herd, who scored no fewer than 29 League goals that season; but was then, surprisingly, sold to Manchester United. And 1961 was the year when Ron Greenwood departed to manage West Ham United with such distinction and originality. Under Swindin's regime, there had been further embarrassment in the FA Cup, when the Gunners, at the third time of asking, went down in a second replay at Hillsborough to modest Rotherham United of the Second Division. In 1962, breaking at last the umbilical cord, Arsenal appointed as manager Billy Wright.

With hindsight, though he lasted four years, it is easy enough to say that Arsenal had gambled, that Wright, despite his 105 England caps, his exuberant captaincy of the international team, had no club managerial experience. Yet in future years, another famous international captain, Franz Beckenbauer, would be appointed by Germany, having managed no clubs. France did the same with their former star Michel Platini, and Germany appointed Jurgen Klinsmann, he, too, taking his first managerial role.

More to the point was Wright's personality. His previous job, running the England Under 23 team, suited him. Young players, indeed, were his speciality, and Arsenal owed him a debt for the string of them he left as legacy after he had been dismissed. There was also a strange lack of consistency in his published opinions. In the laudatory if comprehensive *Billy Wright: A Hero for All Seasons* compiled by Norman Giller, Wright pays abundant tribute both to Stanley Matthews and to Bobby Charlton. Yet in previous publications, he had made scathing criticisms of both of them.

As a club manager, his years at Arsenal evoked the chilling words of the American baseball manager, Leo Durocher, 'Nice guys finish last.' A view certainly implicit in the words of Frank McLintock, the Scottish international right-half brought to Highbury by Wright, later to become a dominant and influential centre-back. He is quoted in Giller's book. '[Wright] was too nice to be a manager,' thought McLintock, who said, of yet another FA Cup disaster in the club's defeat by Third Division Peterborough in the fourth round in 1965, 'This was when Billy should have brought down the iron fist, but it just was not in him. He was simply too kind, too nice. We needed a manager who could give us the kick up the backside that we deserved. I got so frustrated at our lack of success and what I saw as a lack of ambition that I asked for a transfer. Billy was terribly hurt by that. It was nothing against him personally. I always had a great affection for him. But I was hungry to win something and, to be honest, I could not see us doing it under Billy's management, and deep down I think Billy had the same feeling. He was not cut out to be a manager, but I have known few nicer human beings.'

In Billy Wright's first two seasons, Arsenal took reasonable if unexceptional seventh and eighth places in the League, but the following two seasons would see them drop to 13th and 14th. To his credit, Wright brought Joe Baker, the tough little centre-forward – a Scot who qualified by his Liverpool birth for England – back from Turin, where he and Denis Law had had a tumultuous season. He scored frequently, and in February 1964 in an FA Cup tie at Highbury surprisingly had the better of a flurry of punches with the far larger Liverpool centre-half, Ron Yeats. Both were sent off, Arsenal lost 1–0.

Wright survived the defeat at Peterborough, but he was plainly in choppy waters, and the events of the following season made his demise inevitable. In the second half of the season, he was at loggerheads with the most creative of his players, George Eastham, persistently and inexplicably using him not at inside forward but out on the left wing. Since Eastham, predictably, tended often to drift inside, large gaps were left on the flank, though no other player moved to fill them.

In April 1966, I wrote in the *Sunday Times*, under the heading 'What's Wrong With Arsenal?':

> The Arsenal crisis, week by week has taken on a moral complexity which might have intrigued Henry James. Whether the demonstrators who wait outside the sad stadium shouting, 'Wright must go!' might not as well be shouting, 'Hill-Wood must go!' must be an open question.

That Billy Wright sooner or later *will* go seems inevitable – one would have wished for his peace of mind and future career that the going need not have been made so painful and protracted. And here we reach the moral dilemma: has Mr Denis Hill-Wood, the Arsenal chairman, shown himself loyal, generous and consistent in sticking to Wright, against all criticism and catastrophe, or has he passed a point at which consistency becomes a self-indulgence?

More simply, in playing the game, in refusing to throw a victim to the *plebs*, has he been sacrificing both his club and his manager to his sense of abstract justice?

There are no villains in the piece. Mr Hill-Wood is a kind, straightforward, decent man, albeit something of a sentimentalist, whose family has a long and distinguished connection with Arsenal. Mr Wright is a hard-working enthusiast. Their mutual mistake was to suppose that a man with absolutely no managerial experience at club level could walk into a job as brutally difficult and highly publicised as Arsenal's, and expect to succeed.

If Mr Wright has failed, and his failure after all, is relative, Arsenal are still a First Division club – it is difficult to think of what manager would have succeeded. It can even be argued that the keel of the failure was laid in the last, balmy days of success under Tom Whittaker, a very great trainer and, up to a point, a successful manager, but a traditionalist whose strength was in handling men, rather than methods.

For a time, he was assisted by Alec Stock, on whom his mantle seemed likely to fall, but Mr Stock took only a few weeks to decide that it was wiser to return to Leyton. Two old Arsenal players followed Mr Whittaker: Jack Crayston and George Swindin.

Neither lasted, neither won Arsenal another Cup or Championship, though under Swindin, Arsenal belatedly discovered coaching, briefly practised at Highbury by Mr Ron Greenwood. By then, too, the tradition of the reserve player who stayed in the Combination side till he was old enough to retire or bow gracefully out of the League had also happily declined.

Billy Wright was the first Arsenal manager since the celebrated Herbert Chapman (1925–1934) to have no previous connection with the club. This in itself was an interesting step but, like patriotism, it was not enough. For all his 105 England caps, Wright has showed himself ingenuous both in his strange tactical approach and in his transfer ventures.

At a time when there were so many centre-halves at Arsenal that the man who tore one's ticket in two was, so to speak, a centre-half, he paid £62,500 for Scotland's Ian Ure. Making, despite his previous achievements, a disastrous start, Ure seems never to have reconciled his natural way of playing with the way he has been asked to play.

Later, £45,000 seemed a high price to pay for a full-back who, despite his impressive past, had for some time been notoriously slow on the turn. £80,000 was an even higher price to pay for a wing half who might have blended admirably into a specific pattern, switching with his inside-right for sudden thrusts, but was hardly the new Archie Macaulay that Arsenal needed.

In his handling of the Eastham question, Wright has been still more open to criticism. A couple of seasons ago he dropped him but had to bring him back, and saw him transform a lost cause at White Hart Lane, against the Spurs. This season, dropped again, with Baker, after the defeat at Blackburn in the Cup, Eastham went on the transfer list. The implication was that for some time he had not been giving his best.

But if a talented and possibly temperamental player (most talented forwards are) isn't giving his best, is this not to some extent a criticism of the way he's being handled? When, in the 1930s, Alex James was going through a poor spell, Herbert Chapman simply packed him off on a cargo boat. He came back cured.

The duplicated letter sent by Arsenal last February to their protesting fans seemed almost to gloat over the fact that 'more than a week after Eastham asked for a transfer, not one manager of any team had made an inquiry even to ascertain the amount of the transfer fee!' One would not have thought there was much basis for self-congratulation in thus devaluing a world class player.

Tactically, Mr Wright has been beating helplessly in the void, his policy of massive defence has been a confused, half-hearted application of what has been happening in the world game at large. One defends, as Feola of Brazil puts it, in order to attack. Arsenal have been defending in order to defend.

In Italy, the Arsenal affair must rouse the envy of almost every manager, accustomed as they are to be in serious danger of dismissal, after their club has lost two consecutive matches. This is destructive folly, but it can be equally dangerous to sacrifice a manager to a principle that has become irrelevant.

There is, I repeat, no disgrace in a young, inexperienced manager failing to do a job which would daunt a Herrera. It would be sad indeed were that manager's confidence harmed beyond the point of repair.

Soon after this, Billy and I found ourselves sitting side by side in a BBC studio in Bush House, in the Strand, participating in a broadcast. In between expostulatory noises of protest, he told me, petulantly, that he had reported what I'd written to the Chairman of Times Newspapers, Roy Thomson, a Canadian millionaire for whom soccer would have seemed an alien activity.

When, after yet another defeat away from home, disillusioned Arsenal fans would crowd around the players as they got off the train in London to shout, 'Wright must go!' Denis Hill-Wood would sturdily exclaim, 'Wright must stay!' But early in the subsequent close season, go Wright did, whatever Hill-Wood's assertions of support. Not only had results been poor, but the attendances at Highbury had been shrinking alarmingly. Even if the mere 4,554 spectators who turned up to watch the Gunners lose 3–0 at home to Leeds United on 5 May 1966 could be largely accounted for by the fact that Liverpool's European Cup Winners' Cup Final was being televised that evening, dismal previous attendances against Newcastle United, 13,979 and West Bromwich, 8,379, and the mere 16,435 who watched the last game of the season versus Leicester City, could hardly be explained away. Billy Wright had all too plainly been living on borrowed time.

So, for the first time since 1947, Arsenal elevated their trainer, or rather, in contemporary parlance, physiotherapist, to the purple. But Bertie Mee was a very different figure to Tom Whittaker.

Chapter 8

BERTIE MEE AND THE DOUBLE

THERE IS NO DOUBT THAT BERTIE MEE WAS AN OUTSTANDINGLY effective and successful Arsenal manager. Not only did he restore the team's fortunes after the four confusing years of the well-meaning but ineffectual Billy Wright, but he took the team to the coveted double of League and FA Cup, the first manager to do so since Bill Nicholson accomplished it with the Gunners' traditional rivals, Spurs, a decade earlier.

There would long be controversy over who deserved the greater credit for this feat; Bertie Mee or his accomplished coach and former full-back, Don Howe. It would probably be fair to say that each crucially needed the other. Mee, once such a well-qualified, effective physio-therapist, focused and authoritative, where Wright had been erratic, stabilised the regime. Equally certain was the fact that though before the Second World War he had briefly and somewhat anonymously played outside-left for Derby County, he was not, by his own ready admission, a talented player. Nor, in the estimation of many, was he, in the parlance of the game, 'a football man'.

As a physiotherapist, with a long, distinguished record before he ever came to Arsenal, he had been outstanding. But the Double could hardly have been won without the contribution of Howe, even though it would be quite wrong to assume that Howe's was the real credit.

The duality of the manager and the coach is an intriguing one. It should be remembered that the phenomenon of the coach was still a comparatively recent one in the history of football; Arsenal's first coach, in Ron Greenwood, having been appointed only in 1957. What would X be without Y, or Y without X? How much of the Gunners' double triumph was down to Mee, how much to Howe?

What I do know, because Howe himself told me so, is that his abrupt departure from Arsenal to manage his old club, as a player, West Bromwich Albion, was caused by a stupendous gaffe on the part of the club's Chairman, Denis Hill-Wood. At Arsenal's commemorative, celebratory dinner, he proceeded, in his chairman's speech, to thank Bertie Mee and a long roster of other people while failing inexplicably and tactlessly to mention Don Howe. That, for Howe, was enough. Away he went, taking with him Brian Whitehead, his assistant coach and George Wright, the physiotherapist who had followed Bertie Mee in that role.

As time passed, it became increasingly clear that Mee and Howe badly needed each other. Mee would remain in office for years to come, but Arsenal would never come close to repeating the successes of 1970–71, nor to winning the prize of all prizes, the European Cup. Yet by the same token, Howe without the umbrella and protection of Mee, as an actual manager, would never attain the heights he'd reached as the Arsenal coach. He had indifferent results at The Hawthorns, and when he eventually returned to Highbury as actual manager, it was the same story.

It could not be asserted that Mee grudged Howe his due. He was recorded as saying, 'Don Howe is the best coach in the business, and an ideal man.' But in any club, it is the manager who is always in the firing line, the manager who, though eulogised when things go well, will also take the brickbats. Working under him, the coach is protected from such slings and arrows. He is also often acceptable to his players because it is the manager, not he, who sometimes has to crack the whip – which Wright could never do – the manager who turns down requests for transfers – Frank McLintock wanted to go, in vain, in 1968 – the manager who refuses demands for more money, the manager who sells players who would rather stay where they are. It is ironic now to recall that when McLintock asked to go, it was because he thought Arsenal were insufficiently ambitious! Subsequently, and largely against his will, he was converted from right-half into an outstanding centre-back. Only, and eventually, to be unwisely sold to Queens Park Rangers when he had years of good football still in him.

Of Bertie Mee he wrote, in the preface to the autobiography of that supreme maverick, Charlie George, 'He didn't get on with our then manager, Bertie Mee, and that was clear enough to the rest of us. It meant Bertie didn't select him as often as he should have done for the good of the team. . . . It must have been devastating for him of all people to be shown the door at Highbury; though he wasn't the only one released too rashly by the club. [A clear reference to his own premature departure.] It was one of Bertie's misjudgements. It didn't do the club any favours, nor Charlie.'

Elsewhere, when I spoke to McLintock myself on the subject, he declared, 'Bertie had the sense not to interfere. He wasn't too good about football, he didn't know too much about football, but he let David Sexton [Howe's able predecessor, who left in 1967 to manage Chelsea] and Don get on with it. Bertie's presence was always about. He was a strict little bastard. He kept his distance all the time; he seldom gave us any praise. We didn't need such pats on the back: we just got on with our job.'

Bob Wilson, who would come to Arsenal as an amateur and mature into one of the finest goalkeepers of his time, a Scottish international, fluent and well educated, a future television pundit and the Gunners' able goalkeeping coach, observed, 'Bertie was a disciplinarian, almost to a fault. At times he was way over the top. But his skill was in surrounding himself with a brilliant group of coaching assistants, notably Don Howe, and Steve Burtenshaw with the reserve team.'

When, in a telephone conversation, I mentioned to Mee how distressed Don Howe had been at the Chairman's omission, and that this seemed to prompt him to go, his response was, perhaps predictably, one of scorn. Mee's speciality, one felt, was characterised by that depressing coinage, 'man management', but it emphatically had its limits, never more so than in the contentious case of Charlie George.

Certain odd if indicative memories return. Of phoning Bertie Mee in the hope of attaining an interview, at a time when the Gunners appeared to be in a trough. Mee simply refused. 'I know you've got your living to earn', he said. The sequel of it being that the following Saturday, a revitalised Arsenal team had a glittering and unexpected victory.

Then there was the story told me by Willis Hall, the playwright, screenwriter and satirist. Gossip, perhaps, but also indicative. Hall, though by then he lived in Hertfordshire, was a Leeds man, and when Bertie Mee came up to Leeds on business, he elected to show him around the city and stand him to a meal. Some weeks later, Hall made his way to Arsenal's Hertfordshire training ground, then on the playing fields of University College, London. There, he spotted Mee, a solitary figure, watching a juniors match from the touchline. Approaching him, he said, 'Hallo, Bertie!' at which Mee turned briefly to him, said curtly, 'I'm watching this match', and promptly turned his back on him.

In 1994, on the eve of the World Cup finals in the USA, Paul Elliott, the ex-Chelsea centre-half, had a High Court case, in which I was one of his supporters, against Dean Saunders, the Welsh international forward, whom he accused of culpably ending his playing career with a challenge at Anfield. Various figures in the game gave witness statements in Elliott's favour, among them Bertie Mee himself. But when it came to the day when he was due in court, he was unable to appear since his wife was ill. His statement, since he couldn't be cross-examined, was thus invalid. In the event, Elliott contentiously lost, but Mee sent in a bill for £2,000. Which was never paid.

His managerial appointment was a great surprise to the game at large, not least to Frank McLintock, 'To be honest,' he admitted, 'when he took over from Billy Wright, I wouldn't have put a bent penny on him making it. But we all overlooked his single-mindedness. He always had a feeling for Arsenal. I would say I've never known a man in football with so much sense of purpose as Bertie. He's not the sort of man you can get particularly close to. This annoys me because I like getting to know people.'

Mee's task, on his appointment, was hardly made easier by the departure of his most creative player, George Eastham, who would have an Indian summer with Stoke City. The traditional responsibility of the playmaking inside forward fell upon Jon Sammels, a competent rather than an inspirational player. There were, however, two significant acquisitions: Bob McNab, compact and quick, at full-back and George Graham from Chelsea, then a centre-forward.

To get McNab from Huddersfield Town, Arsenal had to face the competition of Bill Shankly, the idiosyncratic Scottish manager of Liverpool. McNab told the diverting story of how Shankly was continually on the telephone to him and when he heard that McNab was going to talk to Arsenal, he warned him, 'Dinna be blinded by the glamour of Highbury!' But when McNab phoned him to tell him he was joining the Gunners, Shankly snapped, 'You never were a footballer!' and slammed down the phone.

George Graham, a Scottish international, was a talented if somewhat casual attacker, with elegant ball control, the ability to strike and score with foot and head, though you could hardly call him one of the world's workers. Indeed, his nickname at Highbury was 'Stroller', and, strange though it may seem in retrospect, he had no time at all then for tactical discussions. Indeed, when they did take place among other players, he tended to pass them by with a dismissive comment. Yet, as we well know, a Damascene conversion would eventually take place. Graham, becoming a coach, at first with a minor Jewish club in North London's Wingate, would become more and more deeply involved in the game, fascinated almost to the point of obsession with the history of Arsenal, mutating, though he never lost his sense of humour, into a noted disciplinarian. Far from being known to the Arsenal players he subsequently managed as Stroller, he would be known as much harsher names.

Mee too, of course, was a down-to-earth disciplinarian, and he was determined not to be overawed by the formidable Chapman tradition, exemplified by the bronze bust in the imposing Highbury entrance hall. He was not, he announced, a 'showman' like Chapman, which seemed a little gratuitous, if not even disrespectful. If Arsenal ever had a manager who was a showman, it had surely been George Allison, whose forte this was, an accomplished publicist, even, as we can sometimes see on afternoon television, a convincing actor in that lame movie, *The Arsenal Stadium Mystery*.

There was surely nothing flamboyant about Chapman, that extraordinary innovator, whose ability to inspire and influence the players who loved him – they would hardly love Mee – made him an ideal father figure. A benign one. But if comparisons are odious, then any comparison between Mee and Chapman must surely be quite redundant.

Mee's first season in charge saw a modest improvement, a rise from 14th position to seventh. The tall, rangy, versatile defender Peter Simpson, destined to form, as left side centre-back such a formidable partnership in central defence with Frank McLintock, finally made regular appearances. Brisk little left-winger Geordie Armstrong, already a debutant in season 1961–62, continued to show what a true winger could do on the flanks. John Radford, who had made a spectacular beginning in January 1965 with a home hat trick against Wolves, led the line with power, in what you might call the Ted Drake tradition, though unlike Radford, Drake was never, into the bargain, an Alf Kirchen of an outside-right. Such a fine England international ambidextrous winger, his career was brought to a premature end by an injury late in the war.

Those were the days when the Football League Cup, its final mutating from an obscure, home and away affair, into a jamboree at Wembley, actually involved the full teams of the leading clubs. In season 1967–68, when they reached only ninth position in Division One, Arsenal won four of their League Cup ties at home, but lost 1–0 in a dull Final to Leeds United, to a goal by the attacking left-back, Terry Cooper.

The following season John Radford went back on the right wing, and the highly robust Bobby Gould arrived to play as a striker. Things went much better in the League, when fourth place was achieved, and once again the team reached the League Cup Final, which turned out to be a massive anticlimax. Especially as the Gunners' progress to it had been impressive, knocking out Liverpool at Highbury, where Peter Simpson scored a rare goal, and having the satisfaction of eliminating the traditional rivals, Spurs, in the semi-finals, winning 2–1 at Highbury and gaining a 1–1 draw at White Hart Lane.

When it was known that the opponents at Wembley would be Swindon Town, of the Third Division, victory may have seemed assured. In the event, it was a case of humiliation. On the way to Wembley, Arsenal's fans were patronising and dismissive to their counterparts, with much talk of milk and mangelwurzels. In the event, the Gunners could never master the pace, strength and penetration of the Swindon left-winger, Don Rogers.

True, the pitch was a wet and sandy horror, but it seemed no barrier to Rogers, who looked to have all the classical winger's talents and more, with the possible exception of application. Early on, he was clean through the Arsenal defence, only to be thwarted by a superb save with his feet by Bob Wilson, who had so impressively succeeded Jim Furnell late in the previous season. Swindon's opening goal was hardly Wilson's fault, Ian Ure's rash back pass bouncing off those same resourceful legs. Smart scored. Gould equalised, but in extra time, Don Rogers scored twice and the Cup was Swindon's.

Oddly enough, it would be against Swindon, in a pre-season friendly at Highbury, that Charlie George made his debut for Arsenal, remaining in the team to play his first League game for the Gunners on 9 August 1969, at home to Everton. He was sick before the match but then, by his own admission, he always was.

Of George's tremendous talents, there was never any doubt. Least of all in the case of Jimmy Robertson, who eulogised him: 'Charlie was a one-off, unorthodox, brilliant. You couldn't coach anyone to do what he did naturally. He could swivel, turn and hit a ball with ridiculous ease.' Robertson was a Scottish international winger who scored for Spurs in a Cup Final and briefly played for Arsenal. But Frank McLintock was still a more fervent admirer.

In his preface to George's autobiography, *My Story*, he wrote: 'An immense talent. . . .The ball would come to him head height and he would volley it over his shoulder into the top corner of the net. He would pass a ball forty, fifty yards with the outside of his foot just like Franz Beckenbauer and find his man. He was quick, he could head the ball, he was physically strong. There was not an aspect of his game that was missing. Charlie had terrific natural ability, he had the lot. He was without doubt the most talented footballer in his time at Arsenal. He could play up front with John Radford or behind the front two. He could shoot powerfully and accurately and from seemingly impossible distances, just like Sir Bobby Charlton.'

Which inevitably prompts the question, with such an array of qualities, why did George not achieve more? Why was his whole England career limited to one wretched appearance at Wembley in a September game against the Republic of Ireland? Don Revie picked him. Alf Ramsey, for whom eccentricity was something of a sin, and indiscipline intolerable, predictably never did.

At half time, Revie, to George's dismay, told him to play at outside-left. A decision that certainly made no sense at all, and to George simply meant that he was being lined up for substitution: which indeed occurred. As he came disconsolately off the field, Revie tried in vain to shake his hand. George pulled his own away and told him to eff himself. End of a pitifully brief England career.

George, alas, was one of the great lost English talents of his time: Rodney Marsh and Stan Bowles being two others. Yet even they had more of a chance than George. It was indeed a shocking waste, yet in English football, international football, what's new? The brilliant maverick has always been a luxury. From his schooldays at local Holloway School onwards, George was always a rebel. Later, by his own admission, he drank. On the field he was sometimes violent.

Yet as that extreme rarity, a local, Islington boy at Highbury, his huge commitment to Arsenal was passionate and undeniable. When eventually and reluctantly he left for Derby, McLintock was convinced that Bertie Mee had made a grave mistake. George himself would write bitterly of Mee. Yet what hope could there ever have been that any rapport could exist between the two? Mee, the implacable authoritarian, George, the eternal dissident? A Chapman, a Whittaker, a Wenger, perhaps a Graham, who at least played side by side with him, might have had a rapport: which after all did happen at Derby under Dave Mackay and Southampton with Lawrie McMenemy.

George himself wrote bitterly of Mee in his autobiography:

> As a player I know who influenced me most . . . Don [Howe] did his own thing to the satisfaction of the manager. And he did all of it in a way I understood and respected while Bertie hovered in the background, only occasionally to be seen at training in a tracksuit, which I thought made him look rather awkward . . . he never gave the impression he was genuinely interested in you. When he promoted Don to be the first team coach you had to believe he recognised his limitations in terms of working with the team.
>
> However for me it went deeper than that, so deep that eventually it would cause the break up of the double side before it had a proper chance to develop, mature and produce even more success.

George recalled that Bill Shankly when, having left Liverpool, he was working with Derby, once said to him of Mee, 'He's not a football man, is he, Charlie?' George, in his book, admits 'I know I can be awkward', which was perhaps putting it mildly. He called Mee 'a manager who cost me a lot and I believe virtually drove me out of the club I chose to play for and still remain loyal to.' Mee, he thought, should have resigned immediately after Arsenal won the double, but this surely would have made almost superhuman demands on a man who must, with some justification have thought he was at the peak of his career. 'Bertie', wrote George, 'is the only aspect of Arsenal I look back on and remember with disappointment and, less occasionally these days with rage.' Early in his first season, I interviewed Charlie George for the *Sunday Times*:

Tall and leggy, deceptively maladroit until the ball is at his clever feet, Charlie George may remind Arsenal's older fans of a young Charlie Buchan, that £100 a goal hero of their roaring twenties. He's a curiosity if only for the fact that he represents at last a local boy playing in the Arsenal first team; he went to Holloway school. [*From which, for all his football skills, he was expelled.*]

At eighteen and a half, an age which is unexceptional for a League player – 'It's not young is it, really?' – he still has a boyish, vulnerable air on the field, reinforced by a deceptively languid manner. This disguises an extreme combativity and a very quick footballing brain. As Don Howe, the club coach and his ecstatic admirer says, 'He's got this instinct for passing. He doesn't have to look. It's something you can't teach a player.' Moreover, 'He's got natural control. He can take a ball at any angle, control it and turn, beat a defender on the turn. He's always been able to do this. It isn't something he learned from us.'

Though there are times when he can look alone and palely loitering, rather after the fashion of Allan Clarke the comparison surprised him he can move very fast around the goal, get up well to the high balls, and beat a man with flowing grace. Howe also praises his maturity. 'He talks about football like people who've been in the game for a long, long time, he can take you back four passes to tell you what's happened,' but this one has to take on trust. On surface acquaintance, he is shy and laconic. He admits, however, that he prefers playing up front, where he should certainly be played, if anywhere. For the moment at least, he is essentially a striker, a potential scorer, even if, as Howe says, he is at present, 'trying to knock the cover off the ball'.

After such a bright beginning, George made only sporadic appearances, some as substitute, until he finally established himself the following

March; in time to play a leading part in Arsenal's progress to their first major success for so many years; and a European one to boot. Curiously, the Gunners slid down to 12th position in the League, and went out on a third-round replay at Blackpool in the FA Cup, succumbing at the first hurdle in the League Cup to Everton.

The Gunners hardly made a promising start in what was then still the Inter City Fairs Cup, beating the modest Ulstermen of Glentoran in Belfast, but inexplicably losing the return game 1–0 at home. But George was back in time to help them eliminate Rouen, a rare appearance in January, then scored twice in March at Highbury in the 7–1 thrashing of Dinamo Bacau, when Radford and Sammels also scored twice.

George then proceeded to score twice at home against by far the strongest of their European opponents yet, Ajax, inspired by Johan Cruyff, prince of Total Football, poised in the next three seasons to win the actual European Cup each time. Charlie would score twice, one a penalty, in a 3–0 win, and it was typical of him that he should subject Cruyff, when in fact he admired him, to a stream of badinage throughout the game. So much so that Cruyff, who actually swapped shirts with him, nicknamed him 'The Chairman'. Ajax won the return 3–1.

In the Final, the opposition also came from the Low Countries, in the shape of Anderlecht of Belgium; who had surprisingly beaten Milan in their semi-finals. Again, away from home, the Gunners went down 3–1. On a Wednesday evening, urged on by a fervent 52,000 crowd, the Gunners turned the tables with another 3–0 home win, with goals by Eddie Kelly, a gifted young Scottish newcomer in midfield, and Jon Sammels his goal decisive.

So to the triumphant double season of 1970–71. In retrospect, it must be fair to say that Mee couldn't have done it without Howe, Howe couldn't have done it without Mee. But they had to achieve it largely without Charlie George, badly injured in a feet first challenge by the Everton keeper Gordon West at Goodison Park in the first League match of the season. That was in August. He would not be back in the team till the following February. This should surely be borne in mind when, as we remember, Arsenal were so often criticised for being a dull, negative side. Who else had they with the flair of Charlie George?

When George, in agony, arrived with the rest of the team at Euston, to be met by his wife, Susan, Bertie Mee told her curtly that he had nothing to say about Charlie's injury. By way of some consolation, there was a new talent in attack in the forceful young Ray Kennedy, fiercely effective with left foot or head. But hardly a replacement for George. Frank McLintock had established himself in the previous season as a commanding centre-half, coolly supported by Simpson, as Ray Kennedy would combine so dangerously with John Radford.

Perhaps it was just as well that Charlie wasn't on the field when the Gunners met Lazio in Rome in the Fairs Cup first leg in September. It was after that game, drawn 2–2, at the post-match banquet at a Roman restaurant, that Lazio players, egged on by their Argentine manager Juan Carlos Lorenzo – remembering perhaps the torrid quarter-final of the 1966 World Cup against England at Wembley – viciously attacked the Arsenal men. It was a brawl in which Bertie Mee distinguished himself with his bravery, literally fighting for his team. Just in time, he managed to shepherd them all onto their coach; Lazio's pugnacious fans, I was once told by their centre-forward Giorgio Chinaglia, were rushing to the scene, armed to the teeth. Chinaglia himself, once a Swansea Town reserve, by then a local idol, stood aside from the fray.

In their first home League game, even George-less, Arsenal served notice of their serious intentions by thrashing Manchester United 4–0: three goals for an irresistible John Radford. Reporting the game for the *Sunday Times*, I wrote:

> Games between these teams at Highbury tend towards the dramatic and the unexpected. Yesterday's was well in the tradition. Arsenal, two up at half time when they might have been four, survived a brief aberration soon afterwards, and went on to a handsome victory. Even without several key players, they clearly have an excellent young team, one which played thoroughly enterprising football [*Boring Arsenal?*]. . . . To the already well established promise of Kelly, one may add that of another young star, the muscular Kennedy, who admirably complemented Radford . . . McLintock coolly marshalled an Arsenal defence more than equal to its task, with Wilson gloriously gymnastic in goal. Nor, among Arsenal's many assets, should one forget the determined running of Armstrong on the left.

When George eventually returned, Geordie Armstrong would largely operate on the right, though it was decisively on the left that, in the crucial last League game of the season at Tottenham. There was one major hiccough on the largely imperious way to the League Championship. On 26 September, the Gunners crashed 5–0 at Stoke. It's been pointed out, as a possible palliative, that the defeat came just three days after a 2–0 home victory against Lazio had taken Arsenal into the subsequent Fairs Cup round. It might have made more sense had the defeat taken place three days after the tumult in Rome.

Winning their last nine home games, though sometimes by narrow margins, the Gunners fought it out with a Leeds United team which, though evidently past its best – one even saw it knocked out of the FA Cup by little Colchester United – still doggedly set the pace at the top.

One of those narrow Highbury victories, coincided in early February with the belated return of Charlie George, of whom I wrote:

> One consolation for a dour afternoon was the form of Arsenal's George. He must surely resemble the late Charlie Buchan. His height and powerful physique, the delicacy of touch astonishing in one so large. To see him receive a ball amidst a ruck of defenders and escape them with the skill of a Houdini is delightful.
>
> With his short stride, the curtain of hair flapping at his neck, his air of apparent distraction, his evasiveness, the frequent originality of his passing, continually surprise. Above all, he has what the Samurai deplored in feudal times: he always does the unexpected.

The Gunners then proceeded to knock Manchester City out of the FA Cup at Maine Road, with a couple of goals by George, who then contrived to score the goal at Highbury which gave a hard won success against Leicester City in the next round. The semi-final gave the chance of a revenge on Stoke City, who had never won the FA Cup, for that 5–0 rout. Yet in the first game in Sheffield, how close Arsenal came to defeat. Two–nil down, frustrated by the superb goalkeeping of Gordon Banks, they equalised only through a penalty in extra time by Peter Storey; winning the replay at Villa Park 1–0. As well for Charlie George, whose sudden aberration, rolling a lethally short pass back to Bob Wilson, had given Ritchie a goal.

Yet does distance lend enchantment? For I find that in early April 1971, with Arsenal still in contention for Cup and League, this was what I wrote in the *Sunday Times*:

One thing above all characterises this season's First Division Championship: its mediocrity. The fact that two teams as moderate as Arsenal and Leeds United have been able to scatter the field, making it the most flagrant of two horse races, speaks for itself.

In recent weeks, both have been tottering badly. Leeds slid out of the Cup at Colchester. . . . Arsenal, though they duly accounted for Stoke last Wednesday, were lucky to get off the hook at Sheffield, while when they recently met Blackpool, the bottom team of the division, at Highbury, they scraped through thanks to an absurdly lucky goal and a catalogue of marvellous saves by Bob Wilson.

Let us be fair. In the first place, it is not Leeds and Arsenal's fault if everybody else has been so bad. Indeed, Arsenal are to be warmly thanked and congratulated for having the grace and stamina to keep in the race. As Bertie Mee, their logical and eminently reasonable manager says, they are well on the way to achieving that consistency which Leeds have, and without which championships cannot be won.

Secondly, there are extenuating circumstances for both Leeds and Arsenal. . . . Arsenal, as Mee concedes, have not yet, despite the fine improvement of these two seasons, reached their full potential. He is at pains to emphasise how young the team is, including as it does such newcomers as Kennedy, 19, and 20-year-old Charlie George. . . . Arsenal, meanwhile, lack the courage of their convictions, are obsessed by 'work rate' at the expense of talent, and have hedged their bets by playing a full-back, Peter Storey, when they have four of the best linkmen in the First Division. Of Storey's value in the harder, counter-punching matches, there is no question, while his newfound flair for scoring goals is priceless to his team. Yet he has kept out more creative players in matches where their talents were clearly needed, while a virtuoso such as Graham has been encouraged to subdue his natural instincts in the interests of hard labour. Mee praises Graham's self-sacrifice, but at Sheffield [*in the semi-final*] it had the effect of rendering him neither fish or fowl.

As for the defence, traditionally the source of Arsenal's strength, I'm still not sure. There are times when it seems to me a modern Maginot Line, formidable in aspect, vulnerable when challenged.

Roll back the years. Similar criticisms, as we know, might have been made even of Herbert Chapman's team in so far as negative tactics were concerned, though there was little wrong with Chapman's Third Back defence. And even Chapman's teams never achieved the double. In their last home League match, yet again versus Stoke, only the surprising appearance of a striker, John Radford, to clear from the goal line in the final seconds, preserved a vital 1–0 win: against a side packed with reserves. 'Arsenal', I wrote, 'looked once more tediously functional, dully unimaginative.'

So the team was faced, quite unfairly, with two vital games in the space of Monday to Saturday. Monday, most taxing of League games, a match that had to be won to take the title, at White Hart Lane, against a Spurs team hell bent on preventing their historic rivals from matching their own League and Cup double of a decade before.

The streets around Tottenham's ground were blocked with traffic, so much so that at one stage Frank McLintock, defying Bertie Mee, had the Arsenal coach stopped to take his wife and Geordie Armstrong's, standing among the throng, on board. As many as 40,000 fans were locked out of the ground. And Geordie Armstrong it was who would fashion the only goal, beating the Tottenham right-back Joe Kinnear, out on the left, and crossing a ball which Ray Kennedy headed in off the underside of the crossbar.

So to Wembley and the Cup Final, against Liverpool. Doing his best to undermine Bob Wilson, Bill Shankly, Liverpool's manager, publicly warned him that it was 'a nightmare pitch for goalkeepers'. There was some truth in this. Eddie Hapgood, in his autobiography, had opined, 'no wonder it's called the goalkeeper's graveyard', when describing how a shot from Bryn Jones – never his favourite player – had squirmed its way through the hands of the England and Charlton keeper, Sam Bartram, to give Wales a 1–0 victory in a 1940 wartime international. You might say that Shankly was in some sense prophetic, for Wilson would give away untypically Liverpool's opening goal.

Overall, Wilson had an excellent game, as did his counterpart, Ray Clemence, in the Liverpool goal. But after only a couple of minutes of extra time, when Liverpool hardly deserved to be on level terms, Steve Heighway, the exuberant left-winger, who had turned professional with Liverpool only that season, cut in from the left and beat Wilson, who had come forward evidently expecting a cross, inside his near post. A cruel setback for an Arsenal team whose best had arguably come earlier, and even by full time they'd largely out-played Liverpool.

George Graham's soaring headers, one of which came back from the bar, John Radford, in dynamic form after recent failings, Charlie George, with his masterly passing, had given a ponderous Liverpool defence a torrid time. But now Arsenal rallied and with Eddie Kelly, so much more adventurous and fluent, having replaced Peter Storey on 63 minutes, they responded with an equaliser 11 minutes into the extra period.

Graham, who to be fair did deserve a goal, claimed it, deceiving many of us, but it was actually Kelly who scored. Kennedy and Radford forcefully set Kelly up, his persistence gave him the chance to turn the ball for goal, and though Graham seemed to get a foot to it before it beat Clemence, Kelly it was who actually scored.

The spectacular winner, six minutes into the second extra period, so suitably went to George, the local hero and impassioned Arsenal fan, George neatly headed the ball to Radford on his left and when the return pass came, struck a tremendous right-footed drive past Clemence, then falling flat on his back with arms raised in the air waiting to be pulled up by his joyful colleagues.

So Arsenal, crowned with double glory, faced a future without Don Howe. In training, he had worked the players very hard, but they appreciated his methods. Mee made light of it all, saying he had always hoped that Howe would strike out for himself. Steve Burtenshaw would move up from the reserve team to take over, a competent coach, but not as forceful as Howe, who spoke well of him. 'I think he'll do well. He's come on in leaps and bounds. He's a zonal man, same as me. He likes certain players in midfield to attack, and certain players to defend . . . and it's the old, old story. The coaching staff takes the lead from the top man.' Unlike Howe, Burtenshaw had never been a leading player, having played at wing half for Brighton. But as he emphasised, playing was one thing, coaching another.

How would things go without Howe and the greatly influential George Wright, who had followed Howe to the Hawthorns? Howe thought a lot would depend on Frank McLintock, who admitted, 'I was very disappointed at the time, even more than when Dave Sexton left, but I think we're better equipped to look after ourselves now. If you'd asked me a couple of weeks ago, I'd probably have given you a different answer, but the way Steve has settled in very quietly and smoothly, I think we've got just as good a chance of doing well this season [1971–72] as last season. One good thing about it all, the young lads, who can be quite awkward players if you don't handle them properly, think very highly of him.'

For Charlie George, it was another ill-starred start to the season. This time, it was a pre-season collision with Sammy Nelson, the Irish left-back, which severely injured his knee. On this occasion, he wouldn't be out quite as long as before, returning in early October.

Three days before Christmas 1971, Arsenal controversially paid Everton £220,000 for Alan Ball, a hero of the 1966 World Cup Final. A development exacerbated, as far as the other players were concerned, when it quickly became clear that Arsenal had radically broken their wage structure to accommodate him. Bertie Mee justified the deal on the grounds that the club had sold Jon Sammels, but this made scant sense, since Sammels had not figured in the double team in the latter stages of the previous season. Of Ball's arrival, George wrote in his book, 'The older players were furious and younger ones like myself weren't exactly delighted.'

The Championship slipped away, the Gunners finishing a mere fifth. In their first foray into the European Cup, they were unlucky to encounter an Ajax team at the peak of its Total Football form, losing by a flattering 2–1 in Amsterdam, 1–0 at home, where Graham put through his own goal.

But there was consolation in the Cup, where Arsenal again reached the Final, again beat Stoke in a semi-final replay, and previously edged out Derby County in the third of three games. In the Wembley Final, Leeds United, who had already beaten the Gunners comfortably at Elland Road, won deservedly 1–0, repeating their previous League Cup Final success. The winning goal was splendidly headed by a refulgent Allan Clarke, though Alan Ball, largely marginal, did have a fine volley kicked off the line. While Charlie George, used as a striker, couldn't repeat his exploit in the previous Cup Final.

Season 1972–73 saw an honourable performance, runners up in the League, beaten semi-finalists by Sunderland in the FA Cup, though there were what you might call several blips. A 3–0 home defeat by Norwich City in the League Cup, a 5–0 thrashing at Derby and a 6–1 disaster at Leeds: the last game of the Championship. Little, lively Peter Marinello, the gifted Scottish outside-right who'd somehow failed to make his mark in the couple of years since he'd been bought by the Gunners from Hibernian, made 13 League appearances and paid tribute to the encouragement of Steve Burtenshaw who would, surprisingly, be ejected at the end of the season.

Bertie Mee explained it and the advent of Bobby Campbell like this: 'The most difficult decision I have had to make in football was in parting company with Steve. It was so difficult to accept because of the close relationship I had with him. He had said that he had reached the point where the players would not respond to him. . . . He was more intimately concerned with the players than I had to be.' As for Bobby Campbell, 'I wanted someone who was the opposite to me. Bobby is the extrovert. He's verbally aggressive. We complement each other. I'm sure that I've made the right decision in appointing him. He has a tremendous way with players.'

Though not with Charlie George who remarked, in his book, 'He spent a lot of time screaming and shouting.' But why, in the name of logic, was Frank McLintock, defensive bulwark and ideal skipper, allowed at the same time to go? Go, for a derisory £25,000, across London to Queens Park Rangers, where he proceeded to flourish. Jeff Blockley, the young stopper who had come from Coventry City, never really settled at Highbury, and left at his own request early in the following season; as later, more dramatically and controversially, did Charlie George.

Season 1973–74, after a fatuously superfluous so-called third place FA Cup match, lost with a weakened team at Highbury to Wolves, began with the promise of an easy 3–0 home win against a waning Manchester United. Alas, it proved illusory. The team, with Campbell rather than Burtenshaw coaching, slumped from second place in the League to 10th, were humiliatingly knocked out of the League Cup at home by humble Tranmere Rovers, quickly eliminated from the FA Cup in a replay by Aston Villa.

Given his icy relationship with Bertie Mee who, he asserted, never talked to him – though George himself never hid his own hostility – it was inevitable that Charlie would leave. Mee put as good a gloss on it as he could, asserting, 'So far as Charlie George is concerned, he feels he will benefit from a move to another club and a complete change of scene.'

It would perhaps have been more exact to say, 'a complete change of manager'. For there was never any doubt that whatever his intransigence, his drinking, his gambling, George's heart was ineluctably at

Highbury. So much became all the more plain when, retiring from the game, he worked there as a tour guide. In August, George figured in the team which thrashed Manchester City 4–0 at Highbury, when Brian Kidd, arriving from Manchester United, scored a couple of goals. George did reappear transiently in the team on the last day of November, contributing to a 2–0 win against Middlesbrough, but that was that.

In the close season, Tottenham came in for him and Mee seemed surprisingly ready to let him go there. But Tottenham dallied, and it was for Derby County that George would sign. Somewhat ironic in that, after the 5–0 defeat at The Baseball Ground, Mee had made George and left-back Sammy Nelson the culprits, to George's fury, and that when he had scored a spectacular goal there against Derby, he provocatively put two fingers up at the crowd.

Dave Mackay, then managing Derby, could hardly believe that he had captured George for a mere £100,000. As for George, perhaps typically, perhaps ominously, he crashed his car on the way up to Derby, but escaped unscathed. At least he would be happy there: as indeed he would be at Southampton. As for Bertie Mee, it is hard not to feel that the departure of George was arguably a confession of failure.

1974–75 was in fact a wretched season for Arsenal, as reflected in the 16th position they had occupied in the League. In the FA Cup, they did at least get through their first three rounds, before going down in a London derby 2–0 at home to West Ham United. In the League Cup, they quickly went out on a replay at Leicester City.

There was some consolation in the bright emergence of Liam 'Chippy' Brady who made his debut at the age of 17. This splendid left-footed player, a supreme strategist and at times a goalscorer as well, had been coming to Highbury in his school holidays from the age of 13, having been discovered felicitously by the Gunners Welsh scout, who happened to be visiting Dublin. Brady began out on the left wing, where he fared well enough, but it was when he moved subsequently to his natural position of inside-left that one would see the best of him, a playmaker in the Arsenal tradition exemplified by Alex James.

Other stars had gone. George Graham joined Manchester United for season 1973–74 and in the opening League game at Highbury, when United were well beaten 3–0, with Charlie George exceptional in the heat, Graham headed against the Arsenal bar. A year later, Ray

Kennedy was surprisingly allowed to go to Liverpool where, dropping back into a left-half position, he would flourish anew. Condemned, alas, to a crippling disease in later years. As for George, when he returned to Highbury with Derby County, he was presented with a bouquet of flowers by a supporter who ran on from the terraces. Well might Bob Wilson generously say that the Gunners could never have done the double without him.

It was Wilson himself, however, a mature and well-educated figure, who ominously sounded the alarm before that unhappy [1975–76] season began. 'Every club has problems,' he said, 'even the successful ones, and I fear Arsenal's are going to be bigger than last season's. Most of the experienced players have gone and have not been replaced. Alan Ball wants to get away [he changed his mind]. . . and to me the signs over Highbury don't look good. I think Bertie Mee genuinely believed the team needed changing [after the double] if Arsenal were to remain successful, but it hasn't worked out. Frank McLintock, George Graham and Ray Kennedy were all excellent players when they left Arsenal, and although Brian Kidd came off as a goalscorer, the team as a whole slipped back last season.

'None of us felt his place was safe after "double" year. Now Bob McNab has gone. I can see him being a great success at Wolves. He is still one of the best defenders in the country.'

Though Wilson opined that Bertie Mee 'had no option' but to release Charlie George – whom he himself, as we know, admired – he was, in fact, bringing a serious indictment on Mee's aegis. And indeed, things could hardly be said to improve in the ensuing season; a wretched 17th position in the Championship, early elimination in both the domestic cups.

After almost a decade in charge, and the indelible achievement of the double, Mee's time had plainly run its course. In March 1976, he announced that he would retire at the end of the season. At the resulting Press Conference, he declared, 'I've run out of time. I haven't had eight hours' unbroken sleep for years.' But it was when he was asked which was his greatest memory, outside the field of play, he unexpectedly answered that it was when the players sang on the team bus when on tour in Cyprus. Then he broke down in tears.

The final game of the season at Highbury saw him applauded by the supporters. Some of them presented him with a bottle of wine and draped a scarf around his neck. Another kneeled in front of him, begging him to stay. Ipswich somewhat spoiled the party by winning 2–1, with an own goal by, of all people, Alan Ball. 'At least it was a lovely sunny afternoon', said Mee, philosophically. But he left behind a splendid Irish legacy. Not only Liam Brady, but the precociously cool centre-half, 17-year-old David O'Leary, and the powerful, incisive centre-forward, Frank Stapleton, a tribute to the scouting system, none of whom cost a penny.

Chapter 9

THE YEARS OF TERRY NEILL

MEE'S SUCCESSOR WOULD BE TERRY NEILL, A TOTAL CONTRAST in character. Where Mee was reserved, detached, essentially an organisation man, Neill, an Arsenal player for almost a decade, was humorous, expansive, even charming. He had begun playing for the Gunners, either as a solid right-half or an equally solid centre-back, as an 18-year-old in 1961 when he also won the first of his 59 caps for Northern Ireland. In those years before he left the club for Hull City in 1970, where he'd become player-manager then manager, he would sustain runs in Arsenal's first team, alternating with periods when he was sidelined.

For Northern Ireland, he even scored the only goal of the match against England at Wembley in 1972. From Hull, he returned to North London, to manage, initially, not Arsenal but Spurs, with moderate success. And thence, in 1976, back to Highbury.

Arsenal plainly needed rebuilding, and Neill immediately showed his enterprise in the transfer market, weaning Malcolm Macdonald away from Newcastle United, where he had been idolised. A prolific goalscorer, with his strength, pace and powerful left foot, he had become almost as great a hero on Tyneside as his predecessor Jackie Milburn, though Milburn of course was a Geordie and Macdonald a West Londoner.

His career had been an unusual one. Starting with Fulham as an unexceptional left-back, he had been sold to Luton Town, who with great percipience, and huge success, turned him into a centre-forward. A prolific one. Thence the long journey northeast to Gallowgate. Goals were his *raison d'être*. He was sometimes accused of seeking them at the expense of team play. But as has often enough been pointed out, natural goalscorers tend to be egotists on the field, consumed by their eagerness to score.

He didn't do so on his League debut for the Gunners at Highbury in August 1976. Indeed, it was a disastrous day for Arsenal, beaten 1–0 by newly promoted Bristol City. 'Will Malcolm Macdonald succeed at Highbury?' I asked in my match report, pursuing, 'Where City, after a gauche beginning, were efficient, quick, lively, methodical, Arsenal were inept. Without a goalkeeper as brilliant as Jimmy Rimmer, they must have lost by four or five, not one. . . . Macdonald had to do what little he could with a pathetic service. Brady, it is true, did not play, but he has the task of an Atlas awaiting him.' Another formidable Irishman, Frank Stapleton, wasn't playing that afternoon, either, but when he returned he hit it off well enough with Macdonald.

One saw the Gunners again in late September when they went down 3–1 at Ipswich and was equally unimpressed, though home form had substantially improved. 'Fine words butter no parsnips,' I wrote, 'and all Mr Terry Neill's promises that Arsenal would play attacking football seemed quite irrelevant yesterday.' Arsenal, one felt, were playing dourly for a draw; and didn't get it.

Eighth place in the League was at least a substantial improvement on the previous season, and if Neill was no master strategist or coach, at least he was a shrewd operator in the transfer market. Malcolm Macdonald was a conspicuous success, missing but one of the 42 Championship games and scoring no fewer than 25 goals; 13 more than anybody else. Especially inspired was the acquisition of Alan Hudson, arguably one more of the great, lost English creative talents, who came from Stoke at the turn of the year. A precocious teenager with Chelsea – from whose stadium he had been brought up in a prefab just down the road – Hudson was a supreme ball player and passer, right-footed to Liam Brady's left. To that extent they at least complemented one another, though it was bold of Neill to use the two of them, essentially constructive attackers, in midfield.

At Chelsea, Hudson, and his fellow, homegrown star, Peter Osgood, had fallen out severely with their manager, Dave Sexton, both being cast out of the club. Hudson arrived at Highbury at the turn of the year. Willie Young, a big, blond, uncompromising Scottish centre-back, came from nearby Spurs, in March. The Gunners went out in the fourth round of the FA Cup, but survived four rounds of a League Cup which they still took seriously, beating Chelsea in the fourth game 2–1 at home, before a crowd of 52, 305; the largest of the season.

New order, purpose and organisation would be given to the team with the return as coach of Don Howe, following his disappointing spell as manager of West Bromwich Albion. Credit, however, had to go to Terry Neill for the continuing success of his transfer policy. It was a coup indeed, and an extraordinary bargain, to acquire Pat Jennings in 1977 from Spurs, eternal rivals, for a derisory £40,000. Beyond doubt one of the world's finest goalkeepers, big, powerful, brave and agile, adept at saving with his legs, Jennings had been in the public eye, and London's, ever since he excelled for Northern Ireland at Wembley, in a youth international tournament.

From Wolves came the swift, incisive scorer Alan Sunderland, a Yorkshire born inside-right who, by his own account, was determined to play professional football as an escape from the coal mine, where his father had worked. And there was a new, effective home produced figure on the left wing – no Armstrong, now – in Graham Rix. He was perhaps an inside-left rather than a natural winger – a role emphatically occupied by Liam Brady – lacking an essential change of pace, but his left foot was a precise and productive weapon.

This time, fifth position was taken in the League, in the League Cup, four rounds were negotiated before defeat by Liverpool in a replay. But in the FA Cup the team reached the Final at Wembley for the first of what would be a remarkable three consecutive times. Wolves and Walsall were beaten en route to Wembley, at Highbury, Leyton Orient easily accounted for in the semi-final at Chelsea. This left the Gunners strong favourites for the Final, but in the event, they failed to perform.

Ipswich Town, instead, rose far above their usual form, dominated most of the game, and fully deserved the 77th-minute goal by Osborne with which they won. Previously, Ipswich had three times hit the woodwork, while Jennings had made a stupendous save from George Burley, the Ipswich right-back and future manager. Macdonald was seldom seen, but a crucial factor was probably the condition of Liam Brady, carrying an injury.

A year later, Arsenal were back at Wembley again and this time, with Liam Brady in exceptional form, they beat Manchester United in the FA Cup Final, in a dramatic late finish. Fifth position was reached in the Championship, in a team which now functioned without Malcolm Macdonald, who played in the opening League game at Highbury but then was marginalised, once coming on as a UEFA Cup substitute in December, and without Alan Hudson. Neill had sent both of them home from Adelaide on a summer tour, when they'd stayed out late at night drinking, taken sleeping pills and missed the next day's training. Though late in his managership, Neill did consider taking Hudson back.

In Macdonald's absence, Sunderland, a very different kind of attacker, more perhaps of a natural inside-right than a centre-forward, worked harmoniously alongside Stapleton, whose clever, subtle positioning at a corner enabled the Gunners to gain, with his headed goal, a notable FA Cup victory at Nottingham Forest, then a power in the land. It took two replays earlier to get the better of Sheffield Wednesday; Wolves, in the semi-final at Villa Park (2–0) were less of a problem.

Somewhat ironically, Brian Talbot, who'd played a key role in Ipswich Town's victory in the previous Final, had joined the club in January and, a natural right-half, adept at right-footed free kicks on the edge of the box, had strengthened the midfield. And Talbot it was who put Arsenal ahead against Manchester United, Stapleton doubling the lead before half time. All seemed done and dusted till, with just three minutes of normal time to go, United suddenly and vigorously came to life, scoring not once, but twice, first with a header by their big, blond Scottish centre-back, Gordon McQueen, then equalising through their Northern Irish international, Sammy McIlroy.

A game which had seemed well won was slipping into extra time. But to their huge credit Arsenal, in the 89th minute, came away and won the game. A characteristic, outswinging cross from the left by Graham Rix, swerved away to Alan Sunderland, who drove it home to give Arsenal a Cup they surely deserved, Liam Brady this time playing a salient part. Having scored, Sunderland, by his own subsequent admission, rushed back upfield, emitting a stream of triumphant obscenity.

In May 1980, the Gunners were at Wembley again, strong favourites to beat another London side in West Ham United; but it didn't happen. Their display, indeed, in its strange inhibition, far more resembled that against Ipswich Town than that against Manchester United.

Ten days earlier, in the second leg of the European Cup Winners' Cup semi-final, in Turin, Arsenal had beaten, as one saw, a bizarrely defensive Juventus side. The goal was scored with a spectacular jump and header by the teenaged attacker, Paul Vaessen, from Rix's cross. The future seemed bright for Vaessen, but alas, his career would be abruptly ended by a grave knee injury, he would drift into drugs, and die wretchedly young.

At Highbury, in the first leg, David O'Leary in dominating form in Turin, splendidly abetted by Willie Young, was painfully kicked by Roberto Bettega, usually the essence of sophisticated elegance. No wonder O'Leary was not only hurt but surprised. Bettega was not sent off; Marco Tardelli, destined to score for Italy in the 1982 World Cup Final, was.

To reach the Cup Final, the Gunners had had to face Liverpool no fewer than four times. Once at Hillsborough, twice at Villa Park and finally at Coventry, where another of Brian Talbot's invaluable goals took them through at last. 'If people think we're doing it in training,' said Don Howe, at Coventry, 'they're kidding themselves. It's character, it's the individual character. They've ability. They want to win, they want to graft, and when you've got that, you've got a chance.'

Yet perhaps, at Wembley, the alarming burden of matches took its toll; and absurdly enough, the Cup Winners' Cup Final against Valencia was imminently due in Brussels. One more game which went to extra time four days later. The FA Cup Final didn't. This time, the wheels were simply not turning; legs were surely heavy. 'The virtue, after all those endless games,' I wrote, 'seemed to have gone out of them.' A header by, of all unlikely people, Trevor Brooking, in transcendent form, decided the game on 14 minutes. West Ham might even have had, and deserved, a second goal near the end, when the 17-year-old Paul Allen, served cleverly by Brooking, went by Rix, only to be crudely and cynically brought down by Willie Young. Whose yellow card might well, under later dispensations, have been a red.

So, wearily but resiliently, to Brussels, where the Gunners after all their previous exertions, were forced goallessly by Valencia into extra time; followed by penalties. The two left-footers, Liam Brady, followed by Graham Rix, both missed, and another cup had slipped away.

In the summer, Liam Brady himself slipped away, to try his luck, most successfully, in Italy, with Juventus of Turin.

Not until late in the ensuing season did the teenaged Paul Davis begin to make regular appearances for the Gunners, a natural born creative inside forward with precocious technique and poise, and a fine passing range. He had been training at Highbury from the age of 13, the first of three fine black players from South London to come through the club's training scheme. Johnny Hollins, the English international right-half, arrived from Queens Park Rangers. And, in a bizarre transfer scenario, the £1 million Kenny Sansom crossed London from Crystal Palace.

A solidly built, adventurous left-back who would play many games for England, though plagued by his gambling habit, Sansom was swapped with another £1 million player in the striker, Clive Allen, who came, like Hollins, from Queens Park Rangers but departed without kicking a ball in anger. It would be explained that the Gunners had made such high profits in the previous season that they would have had to pay £400,000 in Corporation Tax had they not spent it. As it transpired, Sansom, for all his extra curricular problems, by and large would justify his fee.

Arsenal in the League took an honourable third position, their best for some years, though they lost away to Everton in the FA Cup, to Spurs in the League Cup.

Alas, in the close season they lost, arguably, something still more important to them: Frank Stapleton, so eager to join Manchester United. 'You're just a greedy——, Stapleton, Stapleton!' the North Bank would bitterly serenade him on those occasions when he returned to Highbury. Who would replace him? Certainly not John Hawley, a moderate striker picked up on the cheap from Sunderland. And Arsenal's own Sunderland struggled without Stapleton.

There was at least some consolation in the precocious midfield form of young Paul Davis. Of him, I wrote, after a dull September draw at Highbury with Sunderland, 'Young Davis is confirming all the ebullient promise he showed towards the end of last season, a delightfully gifted player with exquisite control, a pleasing refusal to be hurried or shaken off the ball, a very shrewd way with a pass.'

But by late February, when Swansea came to Highbury to beat a pedestrian Arsenal team 2–0 – Ray Kennedy, now Swansea's, scoring one of the goals – even Davis had been drawn into the general Stygian gloom. In the match programme, Terry Neill insisted that Arsenal were not prepared to pay vast transfer fees. Which simply reminded me how he himself, just after the 1978 World Cup in Argentina, having phoned me so frequently about the merits of that country's Ossie Ardiles and Ricky Villa, suddenly and embarrassingly found that Keith Burkinshaw, Tottenham's seemingly parochial manager, had stolen a march on him, flown out to Buenos Aires, and bought them both instead.

An eventual fifth place in the Championship was no disgrace, but as one official of a more successful club had observed to me, it was strange that Arsenal had let Stapleton go. Given that his departure had so long been on the cards, without making provision to replace him. With scant success in three Cups, including UEFA's, it was hardly surprising but surely alarming that attendances at Highbury should fall so low, at the start of the year: a mere 15,000 odd to see Wolves beaten 2–1, 13,738 watching the 1–0 defeat of Middlesbrough.

New faces arrived the following 1982–83 season. Far and away the most famous of them belonged to the left-footed England striker Tony Woodcock, bought from Cologne, though he made his name under Brian Clough at Nottingham Forest. He'd make an ideal partner for Sunderland though neither was a natural centre-forward. Big blond Lee Chapman was; he cost an excessive £500,000 from Stoke City but proved irredeemably static. Later the clever blond winger Petrovic, a Yugoslav international, came from Red Star Belgrade; gifted but sporadic. Big, blond Scottish George Wood complemented Pat Jennings in goal, the talented but unpredictable Chris Whyte now partnered O'Leary at centre-back; the strong young Stewart Robson would prove a force, and a home bred one, in midfield.

Tenth position in the League was no more than mediocre. A shocking 5–2 defeat at Highbury by Spartak Moscow – shades of the

Logie affair – in the first round of the UEFA Cup prompted Neill to concede, 'They murdered us. A bit of a shock to the system. But the good old Arsenal fans recognised a good performance.' Just as they surely recognised such an inept one. But better things were ultimately in store, notably a strong FA Cup run to the semi-final, where, without Sunderland, the Gunners narrowly went down 2–1 to Manchester United. Bolton, Leeds, Middlesbrough and Aston Villa were beaten on the way.

Terry Neill would not survive the following season; and the bleak humiliation of his team being knocked out 2–1 in the second round of the League Cup by Third Division Walsall. 1933 and all that; but this time, the match was not in Walsall but at home.

In the close season, Neill had made what he hoped would be a major acquisition, in the shape of Celtic's *fantasista*, Charlie Nicholas. An inside-forward of outstanding skills but uncertain temperament and erratic tendencies, both on and off the field, Nicholas couldn't, as he later regretted, score the goals which might have saved a manager whom he liked and to whom he responded. There was no doubt that on his day, he could do exceptional things. When they lost 1–0 to Liverpool in their third home match, I wrote: 'Nicholas was terribly unlucky not to be rewarded with a spectacular goal after 13 minutes of the first half. . . . Nicholas brought the flighted ball down to his chest and volleyed a fine shot which absolutely beat Grobbelaar, but rebounded from the bar.'

Before their League Cup debacle against Walsall, Arsenal had knocked Spurs out of the competition at White Hart Lane, but the storm clouds were gathering round Neill. A dissident, highly vocal group of fans, calling themselves the Arsenal Action Group, who would later bay for the head of Don Howe, demanded Neill's dismissal and were given audience by Peter Hill-Wood. Ominously, too, Neill had crossed swords with David Dein, the rising influence at Highbury, disliking the way Dein popped up in the dressing room before kick off to exhort the team, and his habit of taking favoured players off to a night club.

As things grew steadily worse and the team slipped down the League, Neill's post-match mantra, rather like that of Boxer, the loyal cart horse in Orwell's *Animal Farm*, was, 'We must work harder; we've got to work harder.' Finally, in December, the axe fell. Neill, you might say facetiously, was the victim of the seven-year glitch, for how many leading managers in these turbulent times could hope to last as long?

Later, Hill-Wood would disclose that he thought of sacking Don Howe, at the same time, only to change his mind and make him manager. With hindsight, it might well have been better had he made a clean sweep, or perhaps kept Howe as coach, while bringing in another manager. Howe, after all, for all his coaching prowess, had failed as a manager at West Bromwich.

In the event, Howe steadied the ship, using Tommy Caton, whom Neill had bought from Manchester City for half a million pounds, at centre-half, and buying Paul Mariner, a late developing but successful centre-forward, from Ipswich Town. To finish sixth in the League, after so much *sturm und drang*, was hardly a disgrace. But Howe would have no easy ride.

Chapter 10

HERE'S HOWE

THOUGH DON HOWE, STILL COACHING THE ENGLAND TEAM AT internationals, was installed after Neill's demise in 1983 as temporary manager, he had to wait until late the following April before he was finally confirmed in office. Initially, he called his players together in 'a little room at Highbury situated between the dressing rooms and the pitch. We call it "Halfway House". That's where I went through the lot of them with no holds barred. . . . I went through them all one by one. I wanted them to know exactly where they stood. The message was simple enough. What they had been doing in the name of Arsenal was just not good enough.'

When Neill went, Howe later admitted, 'I thought I would be sacked.' The players certainly wanted him but then, when it comes to coaches, players usually do. The coach tends to be their friend; the harder decisions are taken by the manager. But if and when the coach moves up to manager, he finds he cannot be all things to all men. The Arsenal fans, it seemed, by and large hadn't wanted him. Just how significant and accurate a poll among them by the *News Of The World* in December 1983 might have been was doubtless open to question. But it must have meant something when, asked whom they would like to take over permanently, Howe came bottom of a poll of 10 with a miserable 2 per cent. Twenty-two per cent less than the former centre-forward, Malcolm Macdonald, by then the manager of Fulham. But Peter Hill-Wood made it clear that Macdonald was not under consideration.

In an interview at the beginning of January 1984, Howe bridled at the suggestion that some were coaches, some managers. 'It's a load of bull. All this talk of man management when, as a coach, that's what you're up to your neck in, all the time. You must get the players to believe you want to win as much as them. You share their sadness and anger and excitement. You are as deeply involved as they are and you are with them, all the time you can, to prove it.'

Such a philosophy perhaps goes some way to explaining why Howe would find it difficult to be a manager. Indeed, he was eventually obliged to bring in a coach in the shape of John Cartwright, who had won high praise as an innovative coach of young players, and to this day remains a refreshingly original thinker on the game. But at Highbury, the partnership would not bear full fruit.

Week by week, in the earlier days of his provisional managership, newspapers gave this game and that as the one which might decide whether or not Howe would be promoted to the purple. I covered some of them myself, notably in the New Year a well-deserved victory at Nottingham Forest, and an embarrassing 4–0 defeat by Manchester United at Old Trafford. Howe had surmounted his first major hurdle when on Boxing Day 1983, Arsenal had gone to White Hart Lane and beaten their traditional foes, Tottenham. But when it came early in 1984 to the FA Cup, they went out at once to Malcolm Allison's Middlesbrough, away.

Consistency was hardly the team's strong point. However good they'd looked at Nottingham, they were overwhelmed at Old Trafford, where huge spaces were left in defence, Tommy Caton was sent off and Charlie Nicholas was negligible. So much so that I wrote: 'Nicholas has become almost a pathetic figure. As things are, the best course Nicholas could follow is surely to go back to Scotland and rebuild his reputation.'

This he didn't do. Howe moved him back into midfield with fleeting success and spoke of him now with admiration, now with frustration. But Nicholas, for all his great potential, would never find consistency.

Neill, when he left Highbury in bitterness, forecast that despite the team's catastrophic League position at the time it would still attain sixth place. In fact it did indeed, with the marginal decline of two places, in the following two seasons.

That Howe, even in his early managerial spell, was wont at times to clutch at straws was shown when, after the debacle at Old Trafford, he contentedly announced, 'The confidence of the team hasn't been affected one bit. That showed in midweek with the will to win they showed in a friendly at Isthmian League Windsor.'

Overall, Howe's transfer policy was successful. Paul Mariner had done well. Now John Lukic, who had come from Leeds the previous season, would in due course succeed the veteran Jennings in goal. And in the summer, Viv Anderson, an adventurous right-back, the first black footballer to play for England, arrived from Nottingham Forest.

No trees were pulled up, though the Gunners lost only a couple of League matches at home, though the first of them on New Year's Day was against the local rivals Spurs: 1–0. Manchester United beat them in February by the same margin.

Away from home, there was no such consistency, so that the latter part of the season, a victory at Spurs aside, was punctuated by Don Howe's lamentations, expostulations and imprecations. Signs, it all too alarmingly seemed, of a manager who was losing the plot. Ominously, come the spring, the notorious Arsenal Action Group made its raucous voice heard again. It had two meetings with Chairman Hill-Wood, who refused it a third, and three with David Dein. Something of a rarity in England, but common enough when things went wrong in Italy, where supporters were so replete with self importance.

The third round of the FA Cup saw the Gunners held to a draw at little Hereford United, but at least Hereford were renowned Cup fighters and Arsenal thrashed them 7–2 at Highbury in the replay. Only to go down in the fourth round away to Third Division York City. A defeat substantially worse than that suffered previously in the Milk Cup at Second Division Oxford City. The 1–0 defeat at York was followed by a 3–0 defeat at Liverpool, who had been comfortably beaten 3–1 early in the season at Highbury. A season in which Arsenal at this point were riding as high as fourth in the League.

Howe publicly expostulated, 'There is no crisis here. It is absolutely ridiculous to suggest there is. . . . All that has happened is that we

WOOLWICH ARSENAL LEAGUE TEAM, 1908–9.

Dick, Greenaway, McEachrane, Curle,
Mr. G. Morrell (*Manager*), Gray, McDonald, Shaw, Ducat, Cross, Raybould, Sands, R. Dunmore (*Trainer*).
Lewis, Satterthwaite, Lee, Neave.

A postcard of the Woolwich Arsenal League Team of 1908-9, four years before Sir Henry Norris moved the club north of the Thames to Highbury.

The front page of the *Daily Mail*, 23 April 1927, showing headshots of the FA Cup finalists from Cardiff City (left) and Arsenal (right). The headline was 'Stage Set For Today's Cup Final'. Arsenal suffered a 1–0 defeat.

The legendary manager Herbert Chapman with his captain, Alex James (right), and the talented Welsh player and coach, Bob John.

David Jack (left) was a renowned international player for whom Chapman paid an unprecedented £10,890. Here he prepares a schoolboy for coaching with Tom Whittaker (right), a former player who became Arsenal's first trainer.

Tough little Alex James holds the FA Cup aloft after Arsenal beat Sheffield United 1-0 in the FA Cup Final at Wembley, 1936.

Arsenal's international players: (from left to right) Jack Crayston, George Male, Eddie Hapgood and Cliff Bastin.

Ronnie Rooke (right) battles with Manchester United player Chilton for the ball. In 1947, the year after he joined Arsenal, Rooke led the club to victory in the First Division, scoring a club record of 33 League goals.

Arthur Milton (left) training with his team-mates Cliff Holton (right) and Jimmy Logie. Logie initially joined Arsenal in 1939 but was called up to the Navy shortly afterwards. As a creative inside-forward, he played an important part in the team's post-war successes.

Reg Lewis heads a goal at Brunton Park. Lewis was a fluent player who scored 100 goals in three wartime seasons. He was a great asset to Arsenal, spending his entire career with the club.

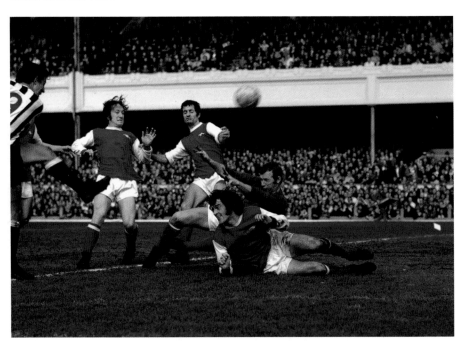

Playing in the English Football League Division One against Newcastle United. Keith Dyson shoots as George Armstrong, Frank McLintock, Peter Storey and goalkeeper Bob Wilson make a tackle, 17 April 1971.

The prolific goalscorer Malcolm Macdonald, who Terry Neill transferred from Newcastle United in 1976 for over £330,000.

Arsenal players: (from left to right) Willie Young, Pat Rice, Frank Stapleton and David O'Leary at the FA Cup Final against Manchester United at Wembley Stadium, 1979. This match is known as the 'five minute final', as Manchester United scored two equalising goals in the 86th minute, followed by Alan Sunderland's last-second winner.

David O'Leary lifting the trophy for Arsenal after beating Sheffield Wednesday in the Coca-Cola Cup Final, 19 April 1993. Apprenticed by the club in 1973, he played as a cool and collected centre-half for 10 years.

As a player, George Graham was a gifted though rather laid back attacker, who earned the nickname 'Stroller'. He went onto become a strict coach.

Ian Wright was a latecomer to football, signing for Crystal Palace just before his 22nd birthday. He was bought for the then club record fee of £2.5 million and became a legendary scorer, known for the electric pace he set.

David Dein, the director who brought Arsene Wenger to Highbury. He holds the trophies for both the League Cup and the FA Cup after Arsenal won the Double in 1998.

Thierry Henry signs for Arsenal at the Highbury Stadium, August 1999. He would play with them for eight years and become Arsenal's all-time leading scorer, with 226 goals.

Arsenal's manager Arsene Wenger celebrates with captain Patrick Vieira after winning the FA Cup final against Manchester United at the Millennium Stadium in Cardiff, 21 May 2005.

Goalkeeper Jens Lehmann is sent off in the Arsenal Champions League Final against Barcelona in Paris, 17 May 2006.

The east facade of the Highbury Stadium, London. Arsenal moved here in September 1913 and the last game was between Arsenal and Wigan Athletic in May 2006.

The Emirates Stadium, Islington, London. It was built at a cost of £430 million and opened in July 2006.

Jack Wilshere, Arsenal's new boy wonder, during the Emirates Cup match against Juventus at the Emirates Stadium, 2008. Wilshere rose through the ranks of the Arsenal youth scheme, debuting at age 16, a club record previously held by Cesc Fabregas.

Cesc Fabregas and Alex Song in 2009. Fabregas was whisked away from Barcelona as a 16-year-old and proved to be an exciting talent.

have lost on the ground of the European champions. . . . It was a brilliant game which we might have won, and even the Liverpool people agreed with that. . . . It is the penalty of being the Arsenal. The standards we have set ourselves and the sort of football we have played at times this season means that people have a go at us when we do less well.'

At this point, Tony Woodcock had been dropped into the reserves, but the acquisition for another half million pounds of the Southampton right-half, Steve Williams, a somewhat malcontent but unquestionably effective player, had been another of Howe's shrewd acquisitions. And the coolly precocious teenaged centre-half Tony Adams, from Romford, who had made his debut the previous season, began to figure more often in the side.

But things continued to fall apart. There was a 2–0 defeat at Stoke, who were all but relegated, in early April. 'Unless we can achieve consistency each week,' declared Howe, somewhat superfluously, 'I shall have to do something about it. Sometimes the team have lifted me this season with delightful football, sometimes they've been hopeless, like they were at Stoke. . . . We can beat anyone on paper, but we don't play on paper. The title has slipped away. The reasons? A complete lack of consistency and attitude has got to come into it. That's why I've been chasing the players, getting at 'em, pushing them hard in training. . . . Sometimes I've got a burning desire to go crash, bang wallop with the players. But really, I've got to get things straightened out; find the best way of going forward.' But he searched in vain.

Consistency was no more than a tantalising mirage. Victory in one London derby at Tottenham was followed by an abject display and 1–0 defeat at Queens Park Rangers, in another. Worse still, in early May, was the performance at Luton Town, where Arsenal were brushed aside, 3–1. After haranguing his team in the dressing room, Howe emerged and told the Press, 'We could have turned round four down, but their finishing let us off. Our attitude was diabolical, and I have to find out why. It is something that keeps rearing its head. We go to Spurs and scrap and fight and win and then we go to QPR and lie down. I have to get to the bottom of it. . . . I have had a blast at them. . . . I don't throw cups of tea at the dressing room wall. I try to make the point that it is embarrassing and degrading when they play like this. I think it hurts me more than it hurts them and that is not just because my job is on the line. . . . They should be ashamed to collect their wages on Thursday, they did not earn them. I will be ashamed to collect mine, because I line up alongside them. People should stop asking them about their contracts and ask them how they are playing. The players never looked like performing yesterday.'

To pile Pelion on Ossa, come July, Graham Rix became the fourth Arsenal player to be convicted of drink driving and, to his chagrin, was promptly deprived of the captaincy by Howe. At the annual share-holders meeting late in August, when he came under criticism, Howe admitted that he should have punished the first of the offenders, a year and a half earlier, more severely. 'But you hope players will learn their lesson,' he said, 'then all of a sudden you find the same thing happening over and over again.' As indeed it would, a great deal more insidiously, with the drinking culture which would come when he himself had gone. But already he was hanging by a thread, though it would not snap until the following year. In the meantime, Arsenal officially denied that Howe was under threat. At least this wasn't the usual, minatory, vote of confidence.

Early in September, Howe and his team came under scathing criticism for the highly controversial long-ball tactics they had used when winning an abysmally dull game 1–0 at Queens Park Rangers. Watford had been successfully but contentiously using such tactics in their rise from the Fourth Division to the First, but though Arsenal under Chapman may have perfected the strategy of counter attack, this was hardly something to be expected of them.

Howe defended the methods which turned out to have been imposed by John Cartwright, the new coach. 'We met before the season started and the style was agreed upon', he said. 'The players like it because it gets results. We decided to go for percentage rather than perfection, that's all. We knew we would get some criticism. But results are the important thing for the club at the moment. Hopefully, we can try to refine our style at a later stage.'

A style which, later in September, not only contributed to another dreary game but, at Highbury, brought no better than a goalless draw with Newcastle United. Crowds at Highbury, except for the most attractive fixtures, would steadily diminish. Half of the first 10 League fixtures at Highbury had attendances of fewer than 20,000. And when Hereford United, opponents once again in the first round of the

League Cup, lost 2–1 in an embarrassing replay at Highbury, only 15,789 were there, in contrast with the previous season's FA Cup replay, watched by 26,023.

Three days before Christmas, there was a sudden shaft of light when Niall Quinn, 19 years old, a tall Irish centre-forward, made a splendid debut against Liverpool, who were beaten 2–0. Quinn himself, ubiquitous despite his size, thumped in Arsenal's second goal in a much needed win, doing most of the things which another big centre-forward, Paul Mariner, had been bought to do. A fellow Irishman, David O'Leary, praised him. O'Leary's partner in central defence was another confident teenager in Martin Keown, who had been on loan at Brighton, and would eventually leave Highbury contentiously for Everton, but return to play there, again.

It was perhaps too good to last. Things fell apart again when Luton Town, who'd been beaten in the League at Highbury, were met in the fifth round of the FA Cup, on their plastic pitch. In biting cold, Arsenal drew 2–2, one of their goals being scored by another splendid new teenager in the right-winger, David Rocastle. The replay was drawn 0–0 at Highbury in March, but the Gunners crashed 3–0 in the third tie at Kenilworth Road, and Howe at last was on his way; in some confusion. Howe insisted that he had resigned, just before managing the Gunners to a 3–0 home win over Coventry, which left them in an honourable fifth place. He had learned that Arsenal had been talking to Terry Venables, then the manager of Barcelona. But Peter Hill-Wood contradicted him, declaring that he had told Howe a couple of weeks earlier that his contract would not be renewed.

The irony of it all was that the victory over Coventry was the fourth in succession. In sharp contrast with the previous campaign against Howe by the 'activist' minority of fans, over a thousand supporters gathered outside the main entrance to the stadium in Avenell Road to abuse Hill-Wood and chant for Howe, after they had seen Arsenal go down 2–0 to Watford. Hill-Wood declared that the demonstration would make no difference. It transpired that he had wanted Howe to stay on to the end of the season, but both Howe and his coach, Cartwright, walked out. They were succeeded temporarily by Steve Burtenshaw, an experienced manager and coach, at this time the chief scout. Terry Neill, ever good for a quote, and Hill-Wood exchanged barbs.

'It seems,' said Howe, 'the directors decided last summer they wanted a change. But they certainly didn't tell me at that stage.'

Terry Venables expressed no interest in the job. It would go to George Graham.

Chapter 11

George Graham:
Triumphs and Disaster

'I WOULDN'T JOIN A CLUB THAT WOULD HAVE ME AS A MEMBER', were the famous words of Groucho Marx. Broadly speaking George Graham, appointed Arsenal manager in the summer of 1986, though more than happy to rejoin his old club, would make it clear that he wasn't looking for the kind of player he had been. Implicit in the nickname 'Stroller' was his almost nonchalant attitude to the game drifting, as an attacker, into the right positions, controlling the ball with practised ease, scoring frequently with foot or head. In time, he would even break with the long established Arsenal tradition of having a general, a schemer, a playmaker – in current parlance – operating in midfield. Though in Paul Davis he would find one of exceptional ability.

Almost contemporaneously with Graham's arrival from Millwall, where he had worked effectively with a far less fashionable London club, Spurs, the rivals, appointed David Pleat from Luton Town, where his profile had been higher. This was what I wrote in the *Sunday Times*:

On the face of it, Tottenham Hotspur appear to have won the managerial derby against Arsenal. David Pleat was surely the supreme prize, the outstanding young British manager still occupying a job – however pleasant – below his full, large potential. . . . This is in no way to show disrespect for George Graham. . . . Graham, like Pleat, is young, and although he has not remotely had Pleat's degree of success, his period at Millwall has been an impressive one. All in all, it looks like the first truly sensible and productive managerial appointment Arsenal's much criticised board has made for a very long time.

Both these great clubs have been, in the business sense, ripe for managerial takeover in that neither, over recent years, has remotely fulfilled its immense potential. The point is not lost on their fans – a combined fall of 324,000 in attendances – this season – with Spurs doing marginally the worse – has raised the defections of recent years to the proportion of crisis.

Each seemed to make the same mistake: that of promoting a coach to the managerial position. Sometimes it works, usually it doesn't. When Arsenal won the double in 1971, the combination of Don Howe as coach and Bertie Mee as his managerial umbrella functioned splendidly. When Howe went off to manage West Bromwich his deficiencies and those of Mee lay exposed.

Both clubs subsequently appointed the same fluent but disappointing Terry Neill. And when Neill was kicked out by Arsenal, their divided board, most contentiously, appointed Howe, whose protests that he had really had nothing crucial to do with club policy may have convinced some of the directors, but surely did not convince the football world at large. . . .

Will Graham be able to get his fellow Scot, Charlie Nicholas, truly to exert himself and show his proper potential? Will he find, as the temporary manager and former youth coach, Steve Burtenshaw, promises, a remarkable seam of young players (Quinn, Adams, Keown)? It's a difficult task, but could well be a wonderfully rewarding one.

There were early season signs that Nicholas might indeed respond. On a late August afternoon at Highbury, Nicholas it was who scored the late goal which beat Manchester United, 1–0, even if, one observed, 'We had not till then seen anything of Nicholas for some time, but now, characteristically, perhaps, he produced a powerful, left foot shot which Turner dived in vain to save.' It was Paul Davis, 'who had been playing with great bite, energy and versatility, all afternoon, who forced the ball through, allowing Nicholas to nip in and score.' But even Davis was surpassed on the afternoon by his fellow South East Londoner David Rocastle on the right wing. 'He can tackle,' one reported, 'he can use the ball, he can go past full-backs like a winger.'

But just a week later, when the Gunners unluckily lost to Liverpool 2–1 at Anfield, 'What we saw,' I reported, 'was an enormously effective and elusive Charlie Nicholas who might, but for the excellence of Hooper in the Liverpool goal, have had two or three goals to his name.'

The new revelation, however, was surely David Rocastle, even if David O'Leary believed that his ideal role was not on the right flank but in his original position in central midfield. 'With his pace,' one heard from O'Leary, 'what they're trying to do is make him go at people, but knowing the position can only come from experience. When you play wide, you play on the touchline, and that's another thing he's trying to learn.'

When, almost five months later, the exceptional 22-match unbeaten run which Arsenal achieved under Graham came to an end at Old Trafford, 2–0, Rocastle alas got himself sent off for a second booking. The player he fouled, Manchester United's aggressive young striker Norman Whiteside, had, in the vernacular, been putting himself about from the first; Rocastle himself and Davis being two of his early victims. Rancour was in the air throughout.

In the previous month Arsenal, so much improved under Graham, celebrated their centenary, having been formed as Dial Square in the Woolwich Arsenal in 1886. And Graham himself, of course, had been a talented member of the team which won the double in 1970–71.

The centenary was fittingly celebrated at Highbury, with the Gunners actually top of the Championship, though Graham cautiously and presciently declared that they would not ultimately stay there. A host of red and white balloons soared up to the sky, old heroes such as Ted Drake, George Male and Joe Mercer were paraded. Southampton were beaten 1–0.

Perhaps the Championship could indeed have been within Arsenal's grasp – they'd finish an honourable fourth – had Paul Davis, the fulcrum of attack, not been badly injured in a clash with Clive Allen, the striker who so nearly played for Arsenal, in the third of three demanding League Cup ties against Spurs. Tottenham's manager, David Pleat, would not, eventually, enjoy as much success as Graham. In the sixth round of the FA Cup, a team still without Paul Davis went down 3–1 at Highbury to Watford.

February saw the well-deserved debut as England centre-half, in Madrid, of the 20-year-old Tony Adams, the first Arsenal man to be capped in the position since the 38-year-old Leslie Compton, in 1950. Till that point, in 1987, England's centre-backs had been a sorry lot, being regularly taken to the cleaners by quick Continentals. 'No wonder, then,' I wrote, 'that everyone is raving about Tony Adams, the 6 foot 3 inch [1.9m] 20-year-old from Essex who, in his first full season with Arsenal, has been stopping strikers, scoring goals and winning applause from almost every quarter. "He's a natural leader," says George Graham, Arsenal's manager. "He's a pleasure to train. He's everything a centre-half should be."

'David O'Leary, who was a mere 17 when he established himself in club and international football, and now plays side by side with Adams, says, "I don't think there's a better young prospect in the country. Tremendous. He needs experience, but you only get that with playing games, and I think it must be great to have somebody like that coming through."

'Adams, very quick himself, seems to have the edge on most of them. He's mature. He both plays and talks an impressive game. He is particularly interesting on the difference between British and Continental football: "The technical side of players, the touch, is killed in this country because of our competitive nature. You've probably heard it time and time again. They seem to have more time on the ball. Their first touch is better, because we play so competitive in this country. The main difference is, we're running around and they're laying it off first time."'

He did well against Spain, where England won encouragingly, 4–2, although he was up against as elusive and sophisticated a striker as Emilio Butragueno. Gary Lineker, who scored all four England goals, praised him: 'I thought Tony looked very impressive. I couldn't believe how clever he was, and some of his passes were excellent.'

Adams himself admitted that he had to concentrate so much more than in a club game that he finished with a headache. It was a shock to learn, years later, that even then, he was on his way to alcoholism.

In April 1987, the Gunners at long last won what was then still a major trophy: the Football League Cup, at Wembley, against old, familiar foes in Liverpool. On the way there, besides beating Spurs, the Gunners had knocked out Doncaster Rovers, Bournemouth, Stoke City and Everton.

The team which won at Wembley included several new or relatively new faces. Martin Hayes, a competent and economical figure, Walthamstow born, now figured on the left wing. There were two substitutes in the red-haired Perry Groves, who'd come from Colchester though a Londoner, and whose characteristic dash through the Liverpool defence, seven minutes from time would set up Nicholas' winning goal, and on 85 minutes Michael Thomas, like Davis and Rocastle, a South East Londoner, who was destined to score one of the most important and dramatic goals in the history of the club. He replaced Hayes, Groves substituted Quinn.

When Ian Rush put Liverpool ahead after 23 minutes, the omens looked bleak. Liverpool had yet to lose a game in which Rush scored the opening goal. But on the half hour, with Arsenal now well in command, Nicholas knocked in the equaliser. Groves finished his late burst with a pass to Nicholas, whose shot was unexceptional. But it took a deadly deflection, and spun past Bruce Grobbelaar in the Liverpool goal. George Graham spoke modestly of 'a couple of scruffy goals', but they were enough to win him his first Arsenal trophy.

Graham meanwhile had signed an accomplished centre-forward from Leicester City in Alan Smith, adept in the air and in holding the ball up, and a frequent scorer. He had actually had to play against Arsenal in a League game at Highbury after his transfer to them had been agreed. Kevin Richardson, in essence a right-footed midfielder, once at Everton, arrived from Watford, and would play on the left wing. Tactically it worked, though something was plainly lost. In January, Nigel Winterburn, a left-footed full-back, arrived from Wimbledon, though he would play at right-back, relieving Michael Thomas who had succeeded Viv Anderson in the role. In time, he would move forward to his ideal position in central midfield where his power and drive would find full scope.

Winterburn it was who would miss a crucial and arguably decisive penalty against Luton in the League Cup Final, which the Gunners reached again, only to lose. A promising run in the FA Cup, which featured victory over Manchester United, was brought to an end at Highbury by Nottingham Forest, while the team slipped two places in the Championship to sixth.

The FA Cup looked a tempting target when, in late February, a little over a month since Manchester United had won by the odd goal of a League match at Highbury, they came there again to be knocked out of the Cup 2–1 in the fifth round. 'The quality of the football may seldom have been very high,' I wrote, 'but the drama, particularly in the second half, was remarkable.'

Arsenal dominated the first half against a curiously dazed, even demoralised, United team, scoring twice, once through an own goal. But the pendulum swung drastically in the second half, United calling the tune, but missing what could have been an equalising penalty four minutes from time when Brian McClair blazed the ball over Lukic's bar. It was Michael Thomas, moved up from right-back into centre midfield in the absence of Williams and Davis, who gave the spot kick away, Thomas who had fallen over a perfect ball from Rocastle when he should have made matters safe. But, as we know, better things were in prospect. But in the sixth round, Nottingham Forest came to Highbury; and won. This time, Davis did play, if only as a substitute, but the star of the game was Forest's clever, versatile centre-forward, Nigel Clough. He was such a contrast in both style and personality with his father and manager, Brian, an exceptional goalscorer and centre-forward in his time, before a shocking injury at Sunderland put a cruelly premature end to his career. Nigel would look even better the following year; Nottingham Forest came to Highbury and won again, 3–1.

In the League Cup, the Gunners came strongly through to the Final, beating Everton both home and away in the semi-finals. When it came to the Final at Wembley, David O'Leary dropped out, an expensive absence at any time, but positively disastrous when Graham played in his place the young centre-half Gus Caesar, whose ultimate error, when he stumbled over the ball, let Luton in to score their third, decisive goal.

Yet had Winterburn not had his penalty saved by Luton's inspired reserve goalkeeper, Andy Dibble, which would have made it 3–1, Caesar would surely have been spared his ordeal. Brian Stein had given Luton a half-time lead, Martin Hayes, who came on as a substitute, equalised, Alan Smith made it 2–1, but Luton fought back bravely to win. In those distant years, as we have seen, they were well capable of holding their own and more with the Gunners. Their recent demise has been very sad to see.

The next 1988–89 season saw Graham and Arsenal achieve their first major success; at last regaining the Championship, in a remarkable switchback of a League season, in which the Gunners' form was oddly unpredictable, in which they seemed to have thrown away their chances near the end, only to win at the last gasp in an unforgettably dramatic match at Anfield. Well might Peter Hill-Wood call it, 'Without question, the most dramatic ending to a domestic League campaign in history.'

Arsenal could scarcely have made a better beginning, thrashing Wimbledon 5–0 in their fortress of Plough Lane; a team normally so hard to beat, with its notorious use of the long ball, and its notoriously physical challenge. Up front, Alan Smith was in irresistible form, as indeed he would be, though less prolific, in the decisive match at Liverpool.

This, after the 4–0 trouncing of Spurs at Wembley, in one of those mini-tournaments, was watched by a mere 30,000. They saw a game hectic rather than distinguished, which featured two new, blond figures in the Arsenal team: Lee Dixon, a lively right-back bought from Stoke, and a fast and penetrative all round attacker in Paul Merson, a 20-year-old West Londoner. Both would come fully into their own in the following season, both would be capped for England, but drinking and gambling would almost put an end to Merson's initially buoyant career.

But there were early shocks in store. The first home League game, against Aston Villa, was lost 3–2. A fortnight later came the shock and surprise of a punch by Paul Davis which would have him suspended for nine whole games, thus robbing the Arsenal attack of its most creative player, the latest and by no means the least in the tradition established by Alex James.

Playing against Southampton, Davis, usually the mildest of men, shy, modest and discreet, suddenly caught the Southampton inside forward, Glenn Cockerill, with a left hook from behind, breaking his jaw. The Football Association, examining the television evidence, decided to impose their draconian ban and to fine Davis £3,000 into the bargain. There was scant consolation for Davis from an outburst in his favour from the ever quotable Terry Neill, who emphasised what a decent and likeable fellow Davis was; an opinion which, as one who has known and liked Davis for so many years, I would readily concur. But his offence was hardly a trivial one, even if one assumed that he must surely have been greatly provoked.

This left Arsenal and Graham without a midfield strategist, but the wonder of it was that they contrived to win the Championship, just the same. With the hefty Steve Bould, like Dixon acquired from Stoke City, now there to bolster the defence, which, with Adams and O'Leary both available, could if required play in a sweeper formation, the Gunners substituted Davis with Richardson, against Southampton, with whom they drew 2–2, in the evident hope that his energy would compensate for the lack of a general.

And so, by and large, it did, Arsenal remaining unbeaten in the League at home until, in March, Nigel Clough and Nottingham Forest played havoc with their defence. Davis, alas, would largely become an un-person, making a fleeting appearance as substitute for Rocastle in January, when the Gunners went out of the FA Cup at Highbury in the third round, 1–0, to West Ham United. The following season he would be surplus to requirements until January, but he was back in favour at last the season after that.

Meanwhile, even without him, the Gunners made a strong challenge for the League. They may have lost to West Ham in the Cup, but later in the month, they went up to Everton for an impressive 3–1 win. But Liverpool, making up a 19-point difference with an astonishing 28-match unbeaten run, would breathe down Arsenal's neck, although their first victory on Merseyside would put them in first place. Ironically enough, Davis would be given another run out at the end of March against of all clubs, Southampton, when the Gunners won well, 3–1, at the Dell. And who should score Southampton's goal with a powerful cross shot but . . . Glenn Cockerill.

During this period, Arsenal were reported to be keen on signing the Scottish international centre-forward Frank McAvennie, unsettled at West Ham United, though to some of us, their problems in the latter stages of the season lay in defence rather than attack. Especially when Graham's attempt to play with a sweeper had arguably backfired. Such tactics had looked clumsy at Old Trafford, where Adams of all people had sliced at a ball to give Manchester United a goal and a 1–1 draw. It didn't look much better when one saw them a week later at home in the return with Everton. This time Bould sliced but got away with it.

Writing in the match programme, Graham meditated on whether a sweeper system ought to be valid at home as well as away, arguing that it need not be negative. Unarguable, I wrote, if you had a Franz Beckenbauer but David O'Leary, for all his undoubted talents – and his determination to play football from the back would cost him his role with Ireland under Jack Charlton – was not that kind of player. Still, when Graham belatedly saw the light and put on Merson with his speed early in the second half, things predictably improved and Arsenal won 2–0. Liverpool earlier that day had won 5–0 and seemed to be in pole position.

All the more so when the Gunners suddenly and alarmingly faltered at home, within the space of four days in May losing 2–1 to Derby County and drawing 2–2 with Wimbledon. So it would all come down to the final game at Anfield, where the Gunners had not won for 15 years. Now three points behind they not only needed to win but to win by at least a two-goal margin were they to take that title; Liverpool had only lost at home by such a margin nine times in 20 years.

Still, the sweeper system was working better now, enabling Dixon and Winterburn, the full-backs, to come flying down the flanks. That the game was played so late in May was the consequence of the appalling disaster of Hillsborough, where 95 Liverpool fans had been cruelly crushed to death before the FA Cup semi-final. Liverpool were permitted to postpone their game, while Arsenal, defying pressure from the Football League, went 16 days without a match. They were without the shrewd and influential Brian Marwood on the left flank, but a lively display at home to Norwich City showed their potential, though the subsequent results against Derby County and Wimbledon were cause for some alarm.

Certainly it was not shared by George Graham, who seemed to relish the challenge. 'I hope we get this sort of pressure every year', he declared. 'This is enjoyable pressure. I don't know whether we will win. Any team can win one game, particularly with an away record like we've got.'

And win they did, having, before the start, presented a cheque for £30,000 to the Hillsborough Disaster Fund, and, in Continental style – just as the Moscow Dynamos had done, to general surprise, before they met Chelsea at Stamford Bridge in 1945 – handing bouquets of flowers to the fans. But that would be the extent of their generosity.

Six hundred million viewers were said to be watching the game globally on television, and they saw Arsenal, far from relying on breakaways, take the game to Liverpool from the first. In midfield, Richardson, Thomas and Rocastle were in command, while Steve Bould largely eclipsed the Irish international striker John Aldridge. Ian Rush, his partner, did have Liverpool's one significant shot of the first half, but he did not survive it, giving way to the quicksilver little Peter Beardsley.

Six minutes after the break, the Gunners took the lead. Steve Nicol committed a foul on the left-hand edge of the Liverpool penalty box. Nigel Winterburn sent the free kick to the far post where Alan Smith, in exuberant form, rose to head his 23rd goal of an outstanding season. Liverpool protested vigorously, insisting that the linesman had momentarily raised his flag, indicating either a presumed foul, or the fact that the ball had curled into the net untouched by Smith, thereby, since the free kick was indirect, rendering the goal invalid. All in vain; the goal stood and Arsenal were ahead.

But a second goal was essential. On 74 minutes, Michael Thomas seemed to have the chance to score it when Kevin Richardson found him, a mere dozen yards from goal. But Bruce Grobbelaar, Liverpool's resourcefully flamboyant keeper, saved without difficulty.

The game had reached the 89th minute when John Lukic cleared a ball, Lee Dixon controlled it, and sent it, long but accurate, to Alan Smith. He in turn coolly controlled it, then sent an inspired 30 yard pass through to Michael Thomas. Thomas raced on to the ball, Nicol moved to challenge him, but luck was against him; the ball bounced off him to give Thomas a free run. Nicol and Ray Houghton did their desperate best to stop him, Grobbelaar dashed out of his goal with an equally desperate dive but Thomas, cool and calm, actually took his time before flicking the ball over Grobbelaar's body into the right-hand corner of the goal. There were just 30 seconds left to play, and the Championship was Arsenal's.

'We have laid a foundation of belief at Highbury', said George Graham. 'If you lose hope or lose belief, you may as well get out of football. Tonight was the fairy tale, the unpredictable that makes us all love football.' North London went wild. When the team travelled subsequently through Islington in the traditional open top bus, tens of thousands of their fans applauded them.

The new season began in 'after the Lord Mayor's show' mode. Liverpool were met again at Wembley in the curtain raising Charity Shield, but this time, they would deservedly win, even if the margin was merely 1–0. Again, the Gunners deployed a sweeper system which seemed imperfectly understood. In the absence of the injured Bould, it included the hapless Caesar, who once more alas looked out of his depth.

Worse was to come in the opening League game where one saw the Gunners swept aside at Old Trafford, a match preceded by an extraordinary display in front of the Stretford End by the new owner of Manchester United, Michael Knighton, dressed in a track suit, playing keepy-uppy with a football.

Inspired, perhaps, by his performance, United proceeded to overwhelm Arsenal 4–1. Yet it proved to be a false dawn, the team falling on such hard times that for a while, it even seemed that their manager, none other than Alex Ferguson, might lose his job.

Arsenal's own form was curiously erratic, never more clearly shown than in their four meetings with Queens Park Rangers, now managed by Don Howe, two in the League, two in the FA Cup. In November, they won the first, League, game at Highbury comfortably, 3–0. Niall Quinn led the attack that day, but his days at Highbury were limited and strictly numbered.

By the end of the season, the tall young Irish centre-forward was playing for Manchester City but, like Kenny Sansom, who would oppose the Gunners in their games against Queens Park Rangers, he left without rancour. 'On just his second or third day at Highbury,' Quinn recalled, Graham 'called me into his office and said if I didn't do it for him, I'd be out of the club. He still gave me a new contract; more or less against his better judgement, he called it. But over the next three years, I hardly got a game, and he got so fed up with fining me for some reason or another that he delivered the ultimate insult. He dropped me from the reserves for being overweight.' At 6 foot 4 inches (1.93m) tall and 12 stone 4 (78kg)! You imagine your first chat with the new boss is going to be nice and friendly. But he was ruthless.

'I'd only been in the team six months, and because I was a kid, I'd been pampered. George just said, "I'm not sure about you, but I'll give you a chance to prove me wrong. Show me you can play or else I'll show you the door."' Which, in due time, he did; to a man who would eventually become the benign and respected Chairman of Sunderland.

As for Sansom, he had crossed swords with Graham in March 1988 over his contractual demands. Graham took away his captaincy, handing it to Tony Adams, and, the following season, dropped him to the reserves and never again put him in the first team.

Sansom, however, said how delighted he was in January 1990 to be back at Highbury, playing for QPR in an FA Cup replay. Indeed his affection for Arsenal was such that well into the 21st century, he would be seen at Highbury, officiating in the club's museum. 'I certainly don't look back now,' he pursued, 'and think, if only, because I am proud of my career at club and international level. I like to think, however, I am big enough to admit, George, you were right.'

A week before that Cup tie, in which superb goalkeeping and three fine saves by QPR's David Seaman, who'd missed the first encounter, and who had been pursued by the Gunners in the summer, torrid scenes had marred a 1–0 win against Spurs. Thousands of frustrated fans had milled about in the street, unable to get into a match which, absurdly, had not been made all ticket.

Though Arsenal's form in a 0–0 draw had been unimpressive, QPR had shown little sign of emerging from a packed defence to take the return game at Loftus Road. Yet as it transpired, they did, going through by 2–0. It meant the Arsenal team had scored just twice in their last five games; while they'd already lost at modest Oldham in the League Cup. Graham said, 'I can't understand the reasons for it. We're solid at the back and then creating chances and missing them.'

But when Arsenal went back to Shepherd's Bush in March for their return League fixture, what should QPR do but beat them again: once more by 2–0. Arsenal had sufficient chances to win but again found David Seaman a major obstacle. The much-travelled England international Ray Wilkins struck a fine first goal for Rangers. Ironically an error by Richardson, previously in excellent form, gave away a second.

Though they did at one point head the League, Arsenal were simply too inconsistent to win it, and had to settle for fourth place. Bleakly remembered were the 3–1 League Cup defeat at Oldham, a huge anticlimax after the 1–0 defeat at Highbury of Liverpool in the previous round; and the November brawl with Norwich. This took place beneath the North Bank and resulted in a £20,000 FA fine for Arsenal, a £50,000 fine for Norwich. It would, alas, have its violent sequel the following season at Old Trafford. But worse still would be the imprisonment of Tony Adams for drunken driving.

Two significant signings were made in the close season. The supremely reliable David Seaman, an amalgam of powerful physique, splendid agility and cool courage, a late but spectacular developer, came for £1.3 million, and a disenchanted John Lukic returned to Leeds United for as much as £1 million. From the unfashionable Italian club of Cremonese came the volatile Anders Limpar, a left-winger of prodigious skill and pace and combative personality. He cost £1 million and was a current Swedish international, though of Hungarian descent.

It did not take long for Limpar to cross swords with Graham. In October, he defied Graham, who'd successfully converted him from an inside forward to a winger, by going off to Stockholm to play for Sweden when Graham believed he wasn't fit. As it transpired, he hurt himself in training and didn't turn out for his country. In the meantime Arsenal had demanded £3,000 from the Swedish Federation for every game Limpar missed, after international involvement.

Limpar hardly minced his words, which were duly reported in England. 'Probably my hair will fly off when he starts shouting at me. He believes I should not think that I'm bigger than Arsenal. But I always behave. I never visit night clubs like some players, but that doesn't seem to matter to him. Mr Graham wants control over everything you say. When I was in Italy, playing for Cremonese, you didn't eat bananas and ice cream. In England they don't worry about what you eat, only about what you say! [*The tide would turn with Wenger.*] George Graham is never satisfied and is always shouting at everyone. We won 2–0 against Norwich last week and all he said was, "Why didn't we score more?" The other day, George Graham and Michael Thomas had a terrible row. They stood and shouted at each other. Michael was going to the toilet, and George shouted, "Get back here." Michael's reply was, "Can't you even go to the toilet at this club?"'

Somewhat surprisingly, Graham rode with the punch, calculating perhaps that for all his defiance, Limpar on his current form had to be indulged. 'I have had a good chat with the boy and that's the end of the whole episode', he said. 'All it ever was right from the beginning was a medical situation. Some of the press built it up into more than it was.' It didn't need much building.

There were still more bitter words from discarded players, though that, in football, is always to be expected. Brian Marwood, who had given such balance to the team's left flank, found himself a non-person when he disagreed with Graham after the brawl with Norwich City. He was relegated to the reserves and eventually sold to Sheffield United in September 1990. 'I just hope he [Graham] doesn't create a monster of himself', said Marwood. 'If things went wrong he'd probably get more stick, simply because of the way he treats people.'

Another player who had success on Arsenal's left flank, Kevin Richardson, transferred shortly before Marwood, declared, 'The lads were great, so were the people working there, except him. George Graham has a string of nicknames at the club, some suited him better than others. His idea of discipline is too much for me. He was totally set in his ways. It was a personality clash between me and George. We just didn't like each other. . . . Graham was strict most of the time. And when he did try and be funny, like doing something daft in training, I found it embarrassing.'

To this Graham trenchantly responded, 'It's not merely disappointing when someone like Kevin Richardson throws names like The Ayatollah at me; it's absolutely amazing. He knows in his heart that Arsenal, through me, gave him success, excitement and achievement beyond his wildest dreams and probably beyond his basic ability.' Kevin had been picked up as a useful makeweight, stand-in, player by Everton when he was no longer wanted as a first team regular at Watford. 'His career was going nowhere, but he worked hard after I took him on as cover and I rewarded his industry by keeping faith with him and keeping him in the team most of the time.'

Charlie Nicholas' melodramatic cry that Graham had 'destroyed' him could be taken with a pinch of salt, as this gifted maverick was hardly a stranger to self destruction.

It was somewhat presumptuous of Tommy Docherty, hardly the most quiescent of managers, to warn Graham over the Limpar episode, 'If George carries on like this, his players will just stop playing for him. And when that happens, you start losing matches. Next thing you know, you'll be staring the sack in the face. It's the road George is going down, and he must be very careful. You can't rule by fear, and George should know better. You must have discipline, but it must be sensible discipline. You can frighten the young kids, but not seasoned professionals. . . . But maybe George is trying to be bigger than Arsenal football club and no manager or player is bigger than the club they work for.'

But the road Graham went down would lead to his second Championship.

Before then, however, there would be heartaches and natural shocks to suffer, notably concerning Manchester United. On 20 October 1989, at Old Trafford, I saw a skirmish which put the Norwich City farrago quite in the shade. It erupted in the first half, and I wrote, 'The trouble started when Limpar, Arsenal's Swedish international, and Winterburn together fouled Irwin. Then it was all flying boots and plunging bodies. Ince hauled Limpar off the field, McClair's were the boots that flew. Sealey [United's keeper] to do him justice tried to pacify the throng.

'Yellow cards were shown to Limpar and Winterburn where red cards might well have been flourished at several of those involved. We shall undoubtedly hear more of this.'

Indeed we did. As for the match, Arsenal somewhat fortuitously won it by the only goal. It came a couple of minutes from half time after the Gunners had largely been under pressure. Limpar scored it, which must have made Graham pleased that he hadn't dropped him. Until then, Limpar's clever if sporadic contributions had been just about all the Gunners offered. Now, taking a short pass from the previously obscure Paul Davis, he turned for a low left-footed unexceptional shot. Sealey, perhaps unsighted, fumbled badly and the ball wriggled out of his hands and over the line. He disputed it; referee and linesman confirmed it.

But that wasn't the end of this horrid affair. In the Corinthian traditions of his family, Chairman Peter Hill-Wood pre-empted any official sanctions by himself imposing fines not only on his errant players, but on Graham, too. 'The name of Arsenal has been sullied', Hill-Wood proclaimed. 'I am not proud of this. It must not happen again.' So Graham was fined £10,000, equivalent to two weeks of his salary, while Limpar, Rocastle, Winterburn, Thomas and Davis were fined £5,000 each, the money going to charity. 'Ultimate responsibility,' pursued Hill-Wood, 'for the behaviour and conduct of the team lies with the manager.'

When the Football Association disciplinary body met in November, it imposed a £50,000 fine and – more debatably – a two-point deduction on Arsenal, a one point deduction and the same £50,000 fine on Manchester United, who followed Arsenal's example in deciding not to appeal. George Graham observed, 'I believe points should be won and lost on the pitch.'

There was a major shock to come, though not in terms of violence, when Arsenal met Manchester United again, this time at Highbury in the League Cup; and were sensationally thrashed, 6–2; the heaviest defeat suffered at Highbury for almost 70 years. At the root of it was a scintillating, irresistible performance by the United outside-left, Lee Sharpe, who simply ran rings around a hapless Lee Dixon throughout the game. The odd thing being that at Old Trafford, Sharpe had given Dixon no such trouble.

In attempted mitigation, George Graham declared, 'We were too gung-ho', presumably meaning that when Arsenal found themselves 3–0 down, they threw caution to the winds and chased the game. Which hardly explained why they should have gone 3–0 down in the first place. Sharpe that evening was actually restored to the team, in place of the inside forward Neil Webb, and he would be involved in half his team's goals.

It was an evening which cruelly ridiculed Graham's often expressed faith in his defence. What defence? Dixon's positional play was abysmal, though he had been making goals in England's recent matches. Now, he gave Sharpe unforgiveable yards of space, which were duly exploited. The modern full-back, one reflected, tended to be neither fish nor fowl. As a defender, he was lacking. As a putative winger, he couldn't do what a natural winger does; as Sharpe on his occasion did so lethally.

What, I wondered in my column four days later, the Sunday when Liverpool then heading the League and pulling away were met, would Dixon now do against John Barnes? Arsenal in such circumstances would surely be happy to draw. But not a bit of it. Football being the sublimely perverse game that it is, the Gunners won in a canter.

In so doing, at 3–0, they owed much to the bizarre tactics of Kenny Dalglish, Liverpool's manager. For reasons that reason took no account of, he adopted a cringingly defensive crouch. He used two full-backs in his midfield. Three formidable international attackers, Peter Beardsley, up in the television gantry, Ronnie Rosenthal and Ray Houghton brought off the bench far too late to do damage, could surely have allowed their team to compete, even if David O'Leary, at odds with Graham since he refused to join a tour during the summer, returned to stiffen the defence.

Unbeaten till then in the League, Liverpool saw their lead at the top cut to three points which would have been just one had the Gunners not been fined those two. True, there was controversy over two of Arsenal's goals. Liverpool insisted that Paul Merson's opener, scored on 20 minutes, hadn't crossed the line, and that Limpar wasn't touched (he strongly disagreed) when Arsenal were awarded a 47th-minute penalty which Dixon, now attacking to his heart's content, duly put away. Alan Smith scored the third a couple of minutes from time.

But doom was waiting in the wings. On 19 December, at Southend Crown Court, Tony Adams was jailed for four months for drunken driving. The prospect, the probability, had hung over him, and by extension Arsenal, since the previous May, when, the morning after he had drunk heavily at a barbecue party in Rainham, Essex, he lost control of his Ford Sierra, sped at 70 miles an hour (112kph) across a main road, and ended up crashing, after 130 yards, into a garden wall, observed and arrested by a passing policewoman. Breathalysed, he was found to be three times over the legal limit.

George Graham, Pat Jennings and David O'Leary all gave evidence in Adams' favour. But he pleaded guilty and the judge, Frank Lockhart, said, 'It is incredible to think that you came out of that car alive, let alone unscathed. It was merciful that no one else was there.' Ken Friar, Arsenal's Secretary, who also spoke up for him, said that the club had already fined Adams £2,000. Controversially, it emerged that Arsenal would be paying his full salary while he was in Chelmsford jail. When Jan Molby, Liverpool's Danish international, had not long since been imprisoned – though he sped off in his car before he could be breathalysed – the club refused to pay him.

Friar announced, 'Our position now is that we will stand by our player. This has come as a very great surprise to everyone who knows Tony. He is a very level headed lad, which is one of the reasons George Graham awarded him the captaincy. Another is his resilient character.'

George Graham himself declared, 'Tony has been a colossus for Arsenal in the past and will be a colossus in the future.' Sadly and surprisingly, as Arsene Wenger would reflect when he arrived at Highbury in 1996, after yet another episode in Adams' chequered life, no one at Highbury seemed to realise that what Adams, in his alcoholism, so urgently needed was not eulogies, but help.

Many years later, Adams would complain that not only did Graham fail to help him, but that it was his fear of Graham, his inability to stand up to him, which started him drinking to excess. The explanation seemed debatable.

It was John Osborne who coined the phrase, 'As half educated as a football manager.' Tony Adams, like George Best, however much sympathy and tolerance he received from his club, never, till he found a Good Samaritan who introduced him to Alcoholics Anonymous, had the orientation that he so patently needed.

What seems so shocking in retrospect is not so much the squalor of Adams' sporadic episodes, but the fact that they occurred over so protracted a period. One in which he never came close to being cured, even if he was so readily forgiven.

In late February 1993, having gone to the races with friends, he fell down concrete steps at a West End club and suffered so severe a cut above his right eye that it required 29 stitches. The accident provoked sensational headlines, though Adams insisted, 'I have not done anything to be ashamed of. I've just had a few drinks, missed my footing and tumbled. It's the sort of injury I could get at any time in a football match.' Once more, George Graham showed tolerance. There were reports of 'a heart to heart telephone conversation' in which Adams was rebuked. 'He had an accident', said Graham. 'End of story.'

Not quite. The following October, it was reported that in the Pizza Hut restaurant in Hornchurch, Essex, where he and the then 20-year-old Arsenal right-winger, Ray Parlour, were part of a noisy group, Parlour, with a table knife, prised the pin out of a fire extinguisher and was encouraged by Adams to spray diners with it. They then, it was alleged, ran out of the restaurant laughing.

This was relatively mild by comparison with what was luridly and pruriently reported in late May the following year. Three Sunday tabloid reporters managed to insinuate themselves into a coach party of Adams and his friends, which set out on Cup Final day at an early hour, visiting various hostelries, initially in Clacton-on-Sea, eventually arriving at a public house called The Crown, in Billericay. There the scene, which also prominently included Ray Parlour, became increasingly Rabelaisian, with Adams himself lubriciously involved, so the tabloid reported. Yet why had things been allowed to go so far? Why so long after Adams' imprisonment, had he plainly had no help?

When it came, it came as late as 1996, and from a concerned mentor outside the club: Steve Jacobs, who had already been helping Paul Merson, not only with alcoholism but with his problems with drugs and compulsive gambling. He had persuaded Adams to join Alcoholics Anonymous; the news, indicatively, seemed to take both his fellow players and his temporary manager, Stewart Houston, who in fact had just resigned, wholly by surprise.

With this belated help, Adams managed to conquer his demons and, with exemplary altruism, to help others conquer theirs. 'He's done the hardest thing,' said Jacobs, that September, 'and admitted he's got an illness. Last week he didn't know what he was. This week he does. There is no cure. He's got to start a new life. He will have to learn to handle friends and people and he will know who is genuine. . . . He's been going to AA meetings for some time now, and he's happy for it to come out. The pressure will now be over for him and he just wants to try and get on with life.' This, in the very year when Adams had led the England team at Wembley to the semi-finals of the European Championship.

In 2001, he set up the Sporting Chance clinic, into which would in due course go half a million pounds of his own money. With three full-time staff, set in the Hampshire countryside, its mission was to help sports people with any kind of addiction.

After Adams' imprisonment, I wrote in mitigation:

'And if you're driving home tonight, and you've had too much to drink,' said Griff Rhys Jones, recently, at the end of a television show, 'you're probably a professional footballer.'

The breed, you see, is notorious. Tony Adams, though more condignly punished than most, is no more than the latest in a seemingly infinite list of players convicted of drunken driving. . . .

But though one does not want to shed tears for poor little rich boys, it is worth pointing out the predicament in which today's footballers find themselves. It is often lamented they have grown too far away from their remote predecessors who played before the maximum wage was abolished in 1961. Those footballers, we are reminded, earned what was little better than a good working-class wage, kept close to their roots, could be found at bus stops or in the pub, and retained close contacts with their fans.

This, however, was a matter of exigency, rather than choice. Footballers at that time greatly resented the way they were exploited.

They would have been only too happy to face the problems endured by the new generation, who earn, like Adams, £150,000 a year and more. [*Today, so much more!*]

But the poor little rich boys find themselves in limbo. They are earning upper-middle-class, middle-aged salaries when they are still young men. Their wealth can cut them off from their working-class origins, and even their families. Non-sportsmen who earn the same kind of money move in a different, bourgeois, more elderly world.

There is a massive void to be filled, and it tends to be filled by the hangers-on, the people Groucho Marx would have classified as 'better nouveau than never', shallow, flashy, jumped-up people, who flit from star to star. Adams is not a vicious young man, even if he seems, in recent months, to have been out of control. The V-sign he gave the Queens Park Rangers fans at Shepherds Bush recently, when Arsenal scored, suggests as much. 'He sees himself,' a more mature England defender told me last week, 'as a big-time Charlie.'

Before the 1990 World Cup Final, Maradona was involved in a squalid brawl at a training ground, after one of his brothers, driving his Ferrari, was stopped by police.

But Maradona is the world's best player. Should he set an example? Should Adams? Or should an example be made of them? We may be expecting too much.

Yet Adams or no Adams, Arsenal achieved an outstanding season, in which Graham's critics were made to look irrelevant. To lose but a single game on the way to another Championship was a remarkable feat, and it is surely arguable that even that one League game would not have been narrowly lost, as it was 2–1 at Chelsea, had not the Gunners been so ludicrously obliged to play not once but twice in FA Cup replays against Leeds United; ultimately with success. I saw that game in early February 1991, when a manifestly weary Arsenal team, without the commanding presence of David O'Leary at centre-half – and with Steve Bould dropping out at half time – lost what one called 'a depleted derby', with key players missing from both sides. Arsenal had gone unbeaten for the previous 23 League games.

The loss of Adams was compensated by the prowess of another centre-back in Andy Linighan who had providentially been bought for £1 million from Norwich City. Home-grown attackers in the rapid Paul

Merson and the well built striker Kevin Campbell made significant contributions.

A long, indeed wearying, FA Cup run came to an end in a semi-final staged at Wembley, against Spurs, for fear of what might happen in a smaller stadium, with the horrors of Hillsborough in mind. A superb right-footed free kick from Paul Gascoigne from 30 yards put Tottenham – then in deep financial trouble – ahead after only five minutes. Gary Lineker scored twice, sandwiching a goal by Alan Smith, and Spurs had reached a Final which would be disastrous for Gascoigne.

George Graham opined, 'There was nothing to choose between the sides after the first 20 minutes. That's where the match was won and lost. In fact we probably shaded it from that point, onwards, but the damage had been done by them. You can't give a highly motivated team a two goal start in Cup semi-finals because they're going to fight tooth and nail to protect it. It was a bitterly disappointing experience for my players; but the true test of their character is whether they can bounce back from these things.'

This they emphatically did. Nigel Winterburn, who didn't miss a game, admitted, 'We could easily have gone unbeaten in the League all the way to February for nothing. Nobody would have remembered us for coming second in the table and going out in the FA Cup semi-finals. Or at least they wouldn't have remembered us for the right reasons. If we'd blown the last few games, we'd never have lived it down. People would simply have thought we'd bottled it at Wembley and bottled it on the League run in, and we deserved better than that.'

Given the debacle against Manchester United in the League Cup, it seemed highly appropriate that the Gunners should celebrate their Championship – confirmed when Liverpool lost earlier that day – by comfortably beating United 3–1 at Highbury. There were joyous celebrations. Balls were kicked into the crowd, funny hats were donned, Anders Limpar, who had enjoyed a glorious season, whatever his early brush with Graham, juggled a football. He scored three of their half dozen goals when Coventry were thrashed 6–1 in the final home game.

Graham studiously eschewed the celebrations before the Manchester United game. 'I didn't think it was important for me to join in', he explained. 'The players are the ones who have done it. I can enjoy all the reflective glory because of their efforts, but they deserve all the credit and limelight. The fans pay their money every week to watch them play football, not to watch me in the dug out. I felt it was appropriate for me to stay in the background this time.'

The following season, 1991–92, was a strange anticlimax. Fourth position in the League, no disgrace but no triumph, alarming defeats in the FA Cup by little Wrexham, and in the European Cup, at home, by a Benfica team wiser in European ways; albeit after extra time.

Michael Thomas, disaffected, in waning form, was sold to Liverpool, where he promptly improved. And Graham turned the light of his countenance away from two favourites of the crowd, Anders Limpar and Paul Davis.

The new reality was beyond doubt Ian Wright, the centre-forward who arrived from Crystal Palace in September for £2.5 million. An extraordinary late developer he had not turned full professional, with Crystal Palace, till the age of 22, joining them from the local non League club, Greenwich Borough. In an FA Cup Final, he had terrorised with his electric pace and penetration a Manchester United defence which found him irresistible, Palace coming within a whisker of winning, though the game was drawn. For all Wright's coruscating gifts, it seemed legitimate to wonder why Graham should have bought a centre-forward when he already had such an array of them. Like Alan Smith, who to his frustration found himself reduced to Wright's artificer, expected now to flick the ball on for Wright, who knew just one *modus operandi*, to pursue at pace.

The Gunners also had the forceful young Kevin Campbell, not to mention Paul Merson, probably happier to function in the middle than on the wing. For a brief while Graham tried to field all three strikers, Wright, Smith and Campbell, but in due course Campbell would be exiled to the right wing, where he never looked content.

It took no time at all, however, for Wright to show his worth. Beginning with a midweek game at Leicester, the following Saturday, at Southampton, he scored a hat trick and went on to get no fewer than another 20 goals. It was surely arguable that had he been qualified to play against Benfica – he had been signed too late – and available to play against Fourth Division Wrexham, those two embarrassing results might well have been avoided. Exuberant, combative and ebullient, he would eventually score 184 goals for the club, thus overhauling Cliff Bastin's long-standing record.

To use this volatile fellow's undoubted gifts of ball control, thrust and acceleration, he had to have the ball in front of him, so he could race on to it. There is little doubt that the Wrexham defence would have found him very hard to hold, while Benfica, so much more sophisticated than an Arsenal team which had been all too long out of Europe – the five year ban on English clubs which followed the disaster of Heysel was surely a crude collective punishment – might have been less able to dictate a game which they eventually won in a canter.

Against FK Austria in their first European Cup round, Arsenal, with a long-ball bombardment, thrashed the Austrians 6–1 at Highbury, with four of the goals going to Alan Smith, though when it came to the return in Vienna, an unconvincing 1–1 draw was all they could do.

More impressive was the 1–1 draw in Lisbon against Benfica, managed by Sven Goran Eriksson, but the return game at Highbury would all too clearly show Arsenal's limitations. In Lisbon Paul Davis, in an unaccustomed role, marked Benfica's skilled Brazilian playmaker, Isaias. But at Highbury, there would be no subduing Isaias, who scored twice in his team's 3–1 win. The Gunners' goal was scored, surprisingly, by Colin Pates, a workaday central defender once with Chelsea, whom Graham had unexpectedly bought for £400,000 from Charlton, and who was playing only his 10th game in 18 months. Isaias' equalising reply was a 30-yard bullet.

New Year's Day 1992 brought a bad beginning, not only a 1–1 draw at home with Wimbledon but the sight of Nigel Winterburn, playing against his former club, three times going over to the East Stand to remonstrate with a Wimbledon fan who had been barracking him. How unlike the Arsenal of old.

Worse was to come that month; defeat at Wrexham, of the Fourth Division, in the third round of the FA Cup. There seemed no prospect of doom when Alan Smith gave Arsenal the lead just before half time. Nor did there seem any great danger for over 80 minutes of the second half, even though Wrexham were keeping the Gunners at bay. But on 82 minutes a fierce free kick by the 37-year-old Mickey Thomas, Wrexham's much travelled Welsh international winger, beat Seaman to make it 1–1. And almost at once, when Gordon Davies crossed from the right, Steve Watkin hooked the ball in for the winner. George Graham called it 'the lowest point of my career'.

The following season would be a strange switchback. Trouble over Limpar, trouble over Davis, a somewhat embarrassing recall of Martin

Keown, after his years at Everton, and Aston Villa, culminating dramatically with two Cup victories over Sheffield Wednesday at Wembley, one in the League Cup, the other in the FA Cup.

What seemed clear was that with the passing of time, Graham had succumbed to his natural pragmatism. It had been clear enough after the defeat at Highbury by a hugely more talented Benfica. After which Graham defiantly announced that though Benfica had been the better footballing team, he had no intention of changing the Gunners' more direct tactics, which he was sure would prevail in Europe in the end.

Davis certainly didn't think so, when he made his attack on Graham's methods in December 1991. 'I cannot play for a manager I no longer respect', he declared. 'My heart is still with Arsenal but no longer with George Graham. There's not a lot of creativity, and my game is based on that.' Somewhat surprisingly, knowing what short shrift Graham had given to other dissidents, Graham didn't accommodate Davis' demand for a transfer. But there was more trouble in store. Hardly to be assuaged by the £3,000 fine.

And now there was Limpar, another player reliant on skill and invention; in the new season, to the anger of Arsenal fans, kept on the bench. He would, indeed, become a *cause celèbre*. When on 3 October in a home game with Chelsea, Limpar was brought on a mere five minutes from the end, the crowd booed. And were substantially justified when Limpar promptly set up the winning goal. Graham stayed stubborn. Limpar began on the bench again in the next home game versus Everton. This time when he went on the field, it was to score an impressive goal himself, enabling the Gunners to win 2–0.

On 1 November, I wrote in *The People*:

> If there isn't room for such players as Limpar, the little Swedish international midfielder, what hope can there be of bringing skill, finesse and talent back into our game?
>
> To say that Graham's attitude to Limpar this season has been grudging would be kind in the extreme.
>
> His attitude was starkly displayed in the home match against Chelsea. Arsenal, after dominating play, found themselves only drawing 1–1, with five minutes left: and Chelsea were making the chances.
>
> It was at this moment that Graham belatedly threw Limpar into the fray. He had scarcely taken the field when he danced past two

opponents on the left, crossed, Chelsea's Frank Sinclair miskicked, and Ian Wright performed final execution.

Last weekend, against Everton, it happened again. Limpar came on as substitute, and this time he scored an elegant solo goal. Arsenal won 2–0.

A few days later, Graham gave a bizarre interview on television. Yes, he said, Limpar had it in him to become one of the best players in the Premier League. But he had to find consistency.

Doesn't it beg the question how, in the name of logic, does a player find consistency when he so seldom starts a game? At Derby, however, albeit it in merely the Coca Cola League Cup, Graham screwed up his courage, took a deep breath, closed his eyes, and put Limpar on from the first.

Quite a bold decision, not least because when Limpar comes up against Derby's Welsh international, Mark Pembridge, it's a case of Dracula meets the Wolf Man.

They've twice clashed painfully before. This time was no exception. But Limpar, eventually switched out of the middle to the left flank, cleverly set up Kevin Campbell for Arsenal's equaliser.

Yet Graham uses Limpar so sparingly in a team which, without him, is so clearly devoid of skill and surprise in midfield.

Graham has said, weeping crocodile tears, that while he's attracted to skilled football – and he was a most skilful player himself – realism rules in the English League.

Meaning, I assume, the kind of biff and bang football we see in match after Premier League match.

The fact is, however, that without the ingenuity and invention of a player such as Limpar, Arsenal have, time after time, game after game, been condemned to battering against opposing defences with the crudest of long ball tactics.

It's well known that Graham resents the way Limpar has often taken off, with contractual right to play for Sweden even in friendlies.

But if this is keeping Limpar out of the team which so badly needs him, then Graham is simply cutting off his nose to spite his face.

You only have to hear the Arsenal fans when Limpar ultimately comes on at Highbury to know what they think about it.

Down the ages, Arsenal have traditionally flourished and functioned around the creativity of a gifted schemer. Charlie Buchan, Alex James, Jimmy Logie, Jimmy Bloomfield, George Eastham, Liam Brady, Paul Davis.

Without one, they descend into the dross which is the common currency of the dreary Greed Is Good League. That Arsenal are now climbing the table has been less to do with their own merits than with the pathetic poverty of the League at large.

But Limpar, the little Swede whose father sought refuge from Hungary, has shown he can give them that extra edge which wins matches.

Pocket your prejudices, George and keep him in. From the beginning.

As for Paul Davis, he simply became a non-person, banished to the limbo of the reserves. So much so that in February, he phoned me at home and asked if he could come to see me. I invited him to tea, when he told me of his sheer frustration. In effect, Graham would neither play him nor sell him. Nor, he said, could he discover whether any bids had been made. Together, we worked out a careful strategy; a column in *The People* which might convince Graham rather than antagonise him. We knew all too well that George did not suffer defiance gladly. It was hardly the easiest of tasks.

The headline which *The People* put on the piece was 'Buy, Buy Davis. Invisible Man Paul Must be Rescued'. I wrote:

Paul Davis' situation at Arsenal is a real mystery. Why isn't George Graham using him? Why hasn't he gone anywhere else?

Arsenal, by general consent, not least among their frustrated fans, are a team without flair in midfield – except on those occasions when Anders Limpar plays, and then it's all done from the left wing.

Davis, a notable playmaker, seems to have become a non-person at Highbury, banished to the reserves where, I understand, he looks fully fit and fully competent.

Rumours that he is still not in shape, after eight weeks out for a calf strain, appear to have no basis. He has not asked for a transfer, but it is an open secret that his relations with manager Graham are about as friendly as were those of Michael Thomas before he was sold to Liverpool.

A sad end for the three gifted black players from South London, Davis, Thomas and David Rocastle, who made the wheels turn so well at Highbury not long ago.

Thomas had gone. Rocastle reluctantly went to Leeds last

summer, astonished to hear that the Gunners were prepared to let him go, and Davis cannot get a game.

So the club which, over the years, has boasted the likes of Alex James, Bryn Jones, Jimmy Logie, George Eastham and Charlie George, soldiers on with scufflers. Clone any one from three.

Clearly Davis has no future at Highbury. The face does not fit, even if the style should.

The sooner somebody comes in and buys him, the better for everybody. At 31, he should still have good years ahead of him.

Blessedly, I was wrong. Whether or not the article had anything to do with it, who can say, but Paul Davis was soon back in the Arsenal team at Norwich, and stayed there to take part in all three of their eventual Wembley finals with Wednesday.

Arsenal's League season was an oscillating one. A 3–0 win at Highbury over Coventry City in early November saw the Gunners briefly top of the League, but eight League games without a win and hope diminished.

Ian Wright's explosive temperament was hard to control. In December, he was lucky to escape unpunished when at Southampton he pushed a hand into the face of the opposing defender, Kenneth Monkou. A week later, in an ill-natured, 'travesty of a match', as I called it, won 1–0 against Spurs at White Hart Lane, with Limpar kept on the bench by the stubborn Graham, Wright threw a plain punch at Tottenham's David Howells; and got away with it again. At least, initially, since an FA panel later considered the evidence and suspended him for three games.

Two Scandinavians played for the Gunners in that game. Pal Lydersen, a mediocre right-back, making a costly mistake, John Jensen failing yet again to repeat the spectacular goal he had struck from long range in the European Cup Final in Sweden. 'Shoot, shoot!' the Arsenal fans at Highbury would implore him, but it would be an age before he did, and so scored. Later, both their transfers would mean trouble for Graham.

But by way of substantial consolation, there were two Cups to be won. Perhaps the hardest test on the way to the League Cup Final was, somewhat surprisingly, provided by Millwall. The Gunners couldn't beat them either home or away, and had Kevin Campbell to thank for having survived at all. At Highbury, Millwall were actually 1–0 ahead at half time, but Campbell came on as a late substitute to equalise. In the replay, it was again Campbell who equalised. So the game went to penalties, through which the Gunners scraped through.

Campbell it was again in the next round, scoring in both ties against Derby County, another of those 1–1 draws at The Baseball Ground, followed by a 2–1 victory at Highbury, Ian Wright scoring the first Arsenal goal. But little Scarborough gave Arsenal a run for their money at home, in the gathering fog, where only an untypical goal from Nigel Winterburn got the Gunners through.

More impressive was the 2–0 win at Highbury in the quarter-final against Nottingham Forest, both goals going to Ian Wright. Next came his former club, Crystal Palace, against whom he would demonstrate what the Italians call 'The Immutable Law of the Ex', whereby a former player always scored against his previous club. This Wright did both at Selhurst Park, albeit from a penalty, Arsenal winning 3–1, and again in the return at Highbury, where Palace were defeated, 2–0.

This put Arsenal into the Wembley final against Sheffield Wednesday. Short of fit players, Graham gambled, with success, on the fitness of Paul Davis, barely recovered from a hamstring injury, while deploying Stephen Morrow, a Northern Ireland international central defender, in central midfield. For Morrow, it would be a day of triumph and disaster.

Wednesday went ahead with an early goal by the resourceful USA captain, John Harkes, but Paul Merson's pace and enterprise would turn the tide for Arsenal. His equaliser came from a free kick, nodded down to him on the edge of the penalty box. Merson, with refined technique, struck the ball with the outside of his right foot, and it swerved tantalisingly away from the Wednesday keeper, Chris Woods, to land just inside the right hand post.

After 68 minutes, Merson burst clear on the left and crossed for Morrow to drive in his first ever goal for the Gunners. Alas, his jubilation would be short-lived. At the final whistle, with Arsenal still ahead 2–1, an exuberant Tony Adams hoisted Morrow up on his shoulders and dropped him, breaking his arm. A repentant Adams was so reluctant to climb the steps to the Royal Box to receive his medal that he had to be coerced to do so by Stewart Houston, at that time the assistant manager.

Against all odds, this game would prove a rehearsal for the final of the FA Cup itself. Arsenal's path to Wembley began on the notoriously

sloping pitch at Yeovil, where famous teams, notably Sunderland, had perished in the past. In the next round, Leeds United held the Gunners to a 2–2 draw at Highbury, Ray Parlour and Paul Merson scoring, which perhaps made Leeds favourites for the return at Elland Road. But the Gunners won there, then proceeded to beat Nottingham Forest 2–0 at Highbury, with a couple of goals from Ian Wright.

So to another North London derby of a semi-final against Spurs at Wembley, a match which might have been characterised as The Revenge of Tony Adams. In the previous, ill-tempered derby at White Hart Lane, the Tottenham full-back, Justin Edinburgh, had followed the perverse fashion among rival fans of calling Adams 'a donkey'. There seemed no basis in reality, given Adams' multiple accomplishments. On this occasion, Adams emphatically had the last word in a mediocre game, heading in Paul Merson's free kick from the far post for the only goal of the game.

The first of the two FA Cup Finals against Wednesday at Wembley also hardly rose above the mediocre. Arsenal had some excuse for this; the physical burdens placed on them had been excessive. This was their 58th game of the season, their 12th in six weeks, while Ian Wright bravely played with a broken toe. For all that it was he, after 21 minutes, who headed the Gunners into the lead.

But in a game in which Anders Limpar, his days at Highbury numbered, did not even sit on the bench, David Hirst equalised fo Wednesday after 68 minutes.

Luck may have smiled on the Gunners towards the end of the f period of extra time. When Mark Bright broke through on an ins right position, he plainly had the legs of Andy Linighan. He was a to return the ball to Hirst, in an evident goalscoring position, w hit Linighan's hand. Kerren Barrett the referee promptly gave kick but no yellow card, and Arsenal lived to fight anoth concluding the game without Ian Wright, obliged to leave the

By contrast with Wednesday, who moved Chris Waddle s belatedly out to the right wing for the second half and had lively form on the left, Arsenal kept Merson in the middle, t Davis had his constructive moments.

In the replay the following Thursday, there were torr Adams clashed with Hirst, Jensen with Waddle, but the was done when Bright's elbow broke Linighan's nose. C

of the third kind, you might say. For the winning goal would ultimately come towards the end of extra time, both teams predictably tiring, when both Linighan and Adams trotted upfield to the alarm of George Graham – shades of Leslie Compton in the semi-final against Chelsea in 1950 – to a corner by Paul Merson. Linighan, so often the butt of the Highbury crowd, soared above Bright to head the winner. Woods had stayed on his line.

Previously, on 33 minutes, Alan Smith's precise pass had launched Ian Wright to score his fourth goal in a Wembley Cup Final. Thirty-three minutes more, and Waddle's volley was deflected past David Seaman to force extra time, when at the last gasp, the Cup became Arsenal's.

In both these games, David O'Leary, for a notable last hurrah, came on as a substitute for Ian Wright. Now, after so many years of splendid service, he would retire.

O'Leary gone, the way in central defence was open for Martin Keown, Oxford born, who had joined the Gunners as a 12-year-old and had reportedly left for Aston Villa over the matter of a mere extra £50 a week. Domestically, 1993–94 would prove an unfruitful season, much of the Gunners' football being wearingly pedestrian. Fourth position in the League was once again no disgrace, but it was somewhat unusual to be knocked out of both League and FA Cups at home; 1–0 by Villa in the former, 3–1 after extra time, in a replay, by Bolton Wanderers in the latter.

In December, under a lurid headline – not my own! – in *The People*, 'Graham must sort out this midfield madness', I wrote:

> What will the New Year bring if Arsenal play as poorly as they have in two of their last three matches – all of which I have seen?
>
> The danger is that manager George Graham is allowing his resentment of Press criticism to blind him to the faults of his team. West Ham outplayed them at Upton Park but couldn't score. Newcastle's lack of height in defence plus their inability to support their strikers until too late allowed Arsenal to win a match which wasn't remotely as good as Graham thought it was.
>
> Then, last week, along came Aston Villa to give Arsenal a lesson in passing and tactics, knocking them out of the League Cup, which they held.
>
> After the match, unleashing another broadside at the Press, which apparently hadn't sufficiently appreciated Arsenal's win against Newcastle, Graham explained defeat on the grounds that too many

players were out of form. Shallow, self-deluding and potentially dangerous.

Arsenal lost that match chiefly because as in all three of those games, their central midfielders were so hopelessly pedestrian. Until, that is, Paul Davis (yes, we are singing the same old song) came on just 10 minutes from the end.

Graham said it would have been too much of a risk to bring Davis on earlier, in case someone else got injured. Then why not field him from the first? And why not bring him off the bench against Newcastle?

It's all very well endlessly relying on the pace, thrust and guts of Ian Wright, who nearly saved the game against Villa in the last minute, when his point blank shot was superbly blocked by Earl Barrett. But even Wright needs more to feed off than such central midfielders as Morrow and Jensen can give him.

Arsenal won't win the League. They could still win the FA Cup; the European Cup Winners' Cup? Not a hope if they don't do something about that midfield. I saw Torino beat Lazio in Rome two weeks ago. They have, in quick little Carbone, exactly the sort of player to embarrass Arsenal's big, heavy central defence. He himself has a big man beside him in the Italian Championship's leading scorer Silenzi. . . .

To his credit, Graham is a student of Arsenal's fascinating history. He should surely know that, traditionally, Arsenal have pivoted around a skilled playmaker in midfield. It's not too late for Graham to save Arsenal's season. If only he can take an objective look at himself and his team.

Things didn't look much better in January when the Gunners edged a dismal FA Cup tie at Millwall, of which I wrote:

Arsenal's fans, for their part, are enjoying a muted triumph. Their team, holders of the FA Cup, duly prevailed at Millwall, but in the dullest, scrappiest, most tedious way imaginable.

Graham didn't think so. He came out, smiling his familiar, satisfied smile, after it was all blessedly over, to tell us what a fine job Martin Keown had done in marking Millwall's Dutch midfielder, Etienne Verveer.

Hang on a minute. Isn't Keown an England centre-half, not a midfielder? And aren't Arsenal meant to be one of the most powerful, resplendent clubs in the country? And what could they be doing, going to the ground of a club a division lower, and worrying not about how they might play, but about stopping the other side?

Consolation would come substantially from the European Cup Winners' Cup. At the turn of the year, Odense and Standard Liege had been eliminated. To be held to a 1–1 draw at Highbury by the modest Danish team was ominous, but the Gunners won the return, beat Standard Liege at Highbury then dramatically thrashed them 7–0 in Belgium. When it came to Torino, Arsenal forced a goalless draw. At Highbury, they prevailed by a solitary goal, scored by the head of the ever enterprising Tony Adams.

Paris Saint Germain, unbeaten in 35 consecutive matches, were the opposition in the semi-finals. In Paris, fresh from a hat trick against Ipswich Town, on his way to a total of 23 goals, Ian Wright headed Arsenal into the lead from Paul Davis' free kick, though PSG would equalise. En route to Highbury for the return, the PSG manager, Portugal's Artur Jorge, told an astonished George Weah, his Liberian striker, and one of the world's best, that he wouldn't be playing. A goal by Kevin Campbell put Arsenal in the Final.

There, in Copenhagen, they would meet a highly talented Parma team, including Gianfranco Zola, Tino Asprilla, the Colombian *fantasista*, and the blond Swedish international, Tomas Brolin, all of whom would later play in England.

As for Arsenal, plagued by injuries, tiring from a recent burden of matches, the Final could scarcely have come at a more awkward time. Nigel Winterburn had been maltreated playing against Paris Saint Germain and was still not fully recovered. Still less was David Seaman, who had to play through pain. And Ian Wright, suspended, would not be there at all. However, cometh the hour, cometh the man. Wright's absence allowed Alan Smith to take centre stage, rather than be reduced to supporting cast, and how splendidly he responded! He was arguably the best player on the field, he'd score the only goal, and was just as impressive as he had been that night Arsenal won the Championship at Anfield. On the wing, the Gunners used the homegrown Ian Selley, from Chertsey, still not quite 20 years old.

To some extent, they rode their luck, their four in line defence, with Steve Bould outstanding, resisting the incursions of a dazzling Parma attack. The first half was full of made and missed chances, though it did bring Smith's 19th minute goal. The second half was unexpectedly more placid.

The Gunners should really have scored through Kevin Campbell, who missed clumsily after Paul Davis had so skilfully set him up. It was hard not to reflect that Ian Wright would have gobbled up the chance. And away went Parma to the other end, where Zola found Brolin whose shot cannoned off a post. When Asprilla cleverly served Zola, Seaman responded with a gloriously one handed save.

But then came Alan Smith's goal. Let him describe it: 'Lee Dixon threw it in to me. I took a touch and played it back to him and Lee kind of helped it forward, and from what I remember, it's just gone into their defence, and Minotti tried to kick it over his head. And I collected it and chested it down. Probably about three players were covering. I had to take it quickly. I had to take it quite high. I jumped and hit it with my right foot. Bucci, the goalkeeper, dived in front of the ball, and I couldn't see it then. Then he fell and I saw it; it was in the opposite corner, it had hit the inside of the right hand post and nestled in the other corner. It was an incredible feeling.'

Quite recently, Peter Hill-Wood, the Arsenal Chairman, had eulogised Graham as the greatest manager Arsenal had ever had, and suggested commemorating him with a statue, as Chapman had been famously cast in bronze, in that bust by Epstein.

But alas, this would prove to be George Graham's last hurrah.

Chapter 12

GOODBYE GEORGE

To say that season 1994–95 was a traumatic one for Arsenal would be to err on the side of the minimal. Its first cataclysmic shock, followed by a still greater one, came in November when it transpired that Paul Merson had problems with cocaine, alcohol and gambling. There had, indeed, been tempestuous moments in the outer suburbs of West London. Merson went swiftly into rehabilitation, was banned for a couple of months, and would reappear in the Gunners' ranks only in the following February. His pace, control, flair and thrust would, in the meantime, be substantially missed.

Much worse was quickly to follow, when George Graham, doomed for dismissal that same February, was accused of making large, surreptitious sums of money out of the transfer of two Scandinavian players, the full-back Pal Lydersen, a Norwegian, who'd seldom figure in the first team, and the little midfielder, John Jensen. The total sum, it would transpire, was no less than £425,000.

Yet it was almost exactly two years earlier that a book published in Norway by the investigating journalist, the diligent Henrik Madsen, alleged that Graham had made money out of the Jensen transfer. Then Fritz Ahlstrom, once a coach with Jensen's club Brondby, from whom the Gunners purchased Jensen, later a highly respected official of FIFA, alleged on Danish television that Hamburg, the Bundesliga club, which had transferred Jensen to Brondby, hadn't been paid the full 25 per cent of the fee due to them when Jensen joined Arsenal. Something, it transpired, of which Arsenal were quite unaware. In March 1994, when Madsen came to London Colney, interviewed Graham, and eventually asked him whether all this were true, an angry Graham responded, 'Me take money? Hey, you'd better be careful; that's a serious accusation', and threw him out, refusing him permission to interview Jensen.

In his book, *The Men from Brondby*, Madsen had emphasised the central figure in this and other transactions was the Norwegian agent, Rune Hauge. Changing television stations in Denmark, Madsen embarked on an investigative documentary into such practices which brought him and his camera to London Colney and to Graham. The following May, the documentary, which features in an interview with Hauge himself and showed Graham's seeming embarrassment, was shown on Danish television, but there were no repercussions in England or elsewhere.

By chance, however, whom should the Gunners be drawn against in the second round of the European Cup Winners' Cup, in which despite all their vicissitudes, they would reach the Final for the second successive season, but . . . Brondby. There, respective directors discussed the fact that – as Arsenal had confirmed at Hamburg's instigation in the spring of 1993 – they'd paid £1.75 million for Jensen, though Brondby had received £900,000. This they'd confirmed to FIFA when asked. 'FIFA's query,' wrote Mihir Bose in the *Sunday Times*, 'should have alerted the Arsenal board that something was amiss, but with Graham creating history by winning two cups, the talk at Highbury was of building a bust of Graham. Arsenal initiated no inquiries of their own.'

After the game in Brondby, however, the fat was in the fire, and now another Sunday newspaper detailed the facts revealed in *The Men from Brondby*. Hauge himself was investigated by the Norwegian authorities, prompting much to be revealed about his dealings. The Inland Revenue was made privy to some of this information, which prompted them to speak to Arsenal, in view of income tax that would be due. Arsenal questioned Graham and he, on the advice of his lawyer, paid the amount of money he had made out of the transfers of Jensen and

Lydersen to the club. It could hardly be said that he *repaid* it, since the money had not gone to Arsenal in the first place. As for the Inland Revenue, having collected their tax, they announced there would be no legal proceedings, something they usually tried to avoid.

On that same day in the *Sunday Times*, Joe Lovejoy, the Football Correspondent, wrote: 'According to Winther [Brondby's chairman] Arsenal knew something was amiss by 20 October. Why it took them more than four months, until 21 February, to sack Graham, is a mystery they are not prepared to clear up. Asked for his views, their vice chairman, David Dein, said, "I have no comment."

'The impression that they thought they could weather the storm and keep the most successful manager in their history, strengthened when, with the "bungs" inquiry in full spate, they allowed Graham to invest another £5.8 million in three new players – John Hartson, Chris Kiwomya and Glenn Helder.'

The Premier League appointed a three-man commission consisting of Steve Coppell, former England and Manchester United outside-right, by then a well established manager, with Crystal Palace, Robert Reid QC and the chief executive of the Premier League, Rick Parry. They interviewed not only Graham but also Hauge, both in London and in Norway. The consequence of their investigation was that 'In essence he [Hauge] acted as a middleman who appears to have identified an opportunity to take advantage of the differential in the market value of players in Scandinavia and England. It was never our job to determine guilt, but to establish facts. We have made progress.'

Sufficient for Arsenal, on 21 February 1995, to dismiss Graham without compensation. 'There is no evidence', said Peter Hill-Wood, 'to suggest that the Premier League will take any further action.' While Graham, himself, deplored what he called 'this kangaroo court judgement', and intimated he would be contesting his dismissal. 'I believe,' he added in his statement, 'that this matter should be fully investigated by the Football Association.' Alas for him, it would be.

By a supreme irony, on the very day that he was sacked, Arsenal defeated Nottingham Forest 1–0 at Highbury with a goal by Kiwomya, their first League victory for four months, at home. The crowd shouted its support for Graham.

Not till the following July did the FA committee convene, and then, bizarrely, it would be at the Hilton Hotel in Watford. Lawyers lined up on either side. Graham would lose. The disciplinary committee, under the aegis of Geoff Thompson, the FA Chairman, advised by a QC in Michael Brindle – Graham had his own QC – decided, after a three-day process, that Graham was indeed guilty of receiving the £425,000 from the Jensen and Lydersen deals. But not guilty of deliberately seeking to profit from them.

Peter Hill-Wood gave evidence at the inquiry. It seemed long, long ago that he and his board, in late December 1994, had pre-empted the decision by the Premier League Commission of Inquiry by announcing that Graham had their unanimous support. The inquiry decided to ban Graham from football for a year and to exact an estimated £50,000 from him, towards their own costs. Graham's legal costs were thought to be about £200,000 while he could lose some half a million pounds, through being unemployed until 30 June 1996. He threatened to appeal, but the threat would not be made good. Notionally, he could have gone all the way to the European court of human rights.

In his place, Arsenal appointed his coach Stewart Houston *pro tem*. At least the FA had fulfilled their duty. There had been a bewildering statement from David Davies, the Thursday after the Premier League trio had announced their findings, that the FA would take no action over Graham since, having been sacked, he was no longer under their jurisdiction! He was quickly overruled by Graham Kelly. In common with Joe Lovejoy and Mihir Bose, I was surprised at the inaction, rather than action, of Arsenal, after the Premier League's announcement. 'Their bizarre behaviour', I wrote in *The People*, 'should be heavily condemned. Explanations should be demanded from their directors.' But they never were.

Meanwhile, Houston was left to pick up the pieces of an increasingly unhappy season, salt rubbed in the wounds by the fact that Anders Limpar, allowed by Graham to move to Everton, was in such lively form.

The team sank to 12th position in the League and, though there was no shame in losing 1–0 at Liverpool in the quarter-finals of the League Cup, to lose 2–0 at home to Millwall in the third round of the FA Cup was catastrophic. Midfield and its sterility was the problem and even the return of Paul Merson, recovering form, after inevitably tentative beginnings, was no antidote to that. Nor, against Millwall, did the Arsenal defence distinguish itself, though at least Tony Adams, absent for weeks past, was able to return at last, albeit as a substitute.

Yet by way of contradictory consolation, the team made steady progress in the Cup Winners' Cup. Omonia of Cyprus were no great problem in the opening round. Brondby, the Danes, were eliminated in the next round, even though they forced a 2–2 draw at Highbury, the implications of the meeting in Denmark going, as we know, far beyond the match itself.

After the long winter break, Auxerre, managed by the wily veteran Guy Roux, who had brought them up from obscurity, were next. In the first leg, at Highbury, Auxerre held the Gunners to a 1–1 draw, but a spectacular goal from the blue by Wright won the return in France, 1–0. The Saturday before they were due to meet Sampdoria of Genoa, no mean opponents, the Gunners were encouraged by a 5–1 home win over Norwich City, big John Hartson, the Wales centre-forward, so powerful in the air and hard to dispossess on the ground, scoring twice. The elusive Dutchman, Helder, was on the left wing, but he was ineligible for European football.

The unlikely hero of the first leg against Sampdoria, at Highbury, was Steve Bould, scorer of two of the Gunners' goals in a 3–2 success. The first arrived when Walter Zenga, Samp's loquacious international keeper, could only block a shot by David Hillier, and Bould pounced on the loose ball. Bould's second was a leaping, near-post header from a corner by the commanding Swedish international Stephen Schwarz, a close season signing. In an exciting game, the Yugoslav Vladimir Jugovic on 59 minutes made the score 2–1. But when Merson's splendid long ball split the Sampdoria defence, Ian Wright went past two opponents, then flicked the ball past Zenga. Samp, however, playing the better football, scored again through Jugovic.

In Genoa, in the return, there would be abundant drama. Yet in the interim, Arsenal had gone down 3–1 at Queens Park Rangers, who thus completed the double over them. 'We looked tired from the start', admitted Houston. Only in the last minute did Adams head a goal in off the post. The score might have been still more embarrassing had David Seaman, despite an injured rib, not made a string of saves. He would do better still in Genoa.

Sampdoria had levelled the aggregate scores after just 13 minutes. Not until the 62nd did the Gunners equalise; it meant that Ian Wright technically at least had scored in each round. A corner by Merson, a typical header by Hartson, and the ball was deflected home via Wright.

Samp's quick response came when their free kick rebounded from the Arsenal wall, to be exploited by Claudio Bellucci.

In the very next minute, it was Bellucci again, after a characteristic run on the right by the tireless Attilio Lombardo and an accurate centre. So the Gunners were 3–1 behind, with six minutes to recover. After three of them, a free kick by Schwarz sped through the defensive wall and past Zenga. That made the overall score 5–5, necessitating extra time, when no more goals were scored. Now Seaman would rise, or dive, superbly to the occasion.

Lee Dixon took the first spot kick, for Arsenal, and scored. Seaman had then to face the renowned left foot of Sinisa Mihailovic. Moving smartly to his left, he saved. Alas, Eddie McGoldrick, who had come from Crystal Palace, shot over the bar. But there was Seaman, again, this time diving to his right to frustrate Jugovic. Hartson put in his penalty for Arsenal. Now the spot kicks were going home. Aspero for Samp, Adams for Arsenal. Sampdoria scored again, Paul Merson's kick was saved by Zenga. But when Seaman saved from Lombardo, Arsenal were in the Final; again.

The venue would be Paris, the opposition Zaragoza of Spain. There, the Gunners would lose to a freak goal; or a masterly long distance strike, according to which side of the argument you occupied. Having watched the game, my reaction was that 'Arsenal did fight their way to the second successive Cup Winners' Cup Final. But they simply hadn't the wit or the tactics to resist Zaragoza – who had been leaking away goals all season.'

Juan Esnaider, the volatile young Argentine striker, gave Zaragoza the lead at the Parc des Princes. John Hartson equalised, and extra time began to seem inevitable. There were just 25 seconds left when Nayim, a Moroccan-born playmaker, who had spent five somewhat unproductive years ironically enough at Tottenham, got the ball no less than 50 yards from goal. That he should decide to shoot was remarkable enough. That he should do so with such effect was phenomenal. Seaman, 10 yards out of his goal, surely forgivable enough in such circumstances, suddenly as the ball soared towards him realised the danger. Too late. In vain, he struggled to get back into goal. The ball inexorably flew over his head and landed in the net. Arsenal's Cup Winners' Cup run this time had ended in spectacular anticlimax.

In the close season, Stewart Houston left, joining Queens Park

Rangers, while Bruce Rioch moved from Bolton Wanderers to take charge of Arsenal. He had previously been in command at Millwall. Born in Aldershot, where his father, a Scottish sergeant major, was stationed, he was thus qualified for Scotland for whom, as an uncompromising left-half, he duly played, as he did for Derby County and Everton.

He quickly conducted two costly transfers, both from footballers playing in Italy, one of which would prove his finest legacy to Arsenal: in the shape of Dennis Bergkamp. The £7.5 million fee which brought him to Highbury from Internazionale of Milan was thought at the time by some to be excessive, and his early performances did not dispel such doubts. But it did not take him long to display his array of dazzling talents, and he would become one of the most spectacular and effective players in the club's history.

The other player was in fact an Englishman, David Platt, who came from that other leading Italian club, Sampdoria. Whereas Bergkamp's career had been a smooth one, beginning with the then most prominent Dutch club, Ajax, Platt had emerged from initial obscurity. A Lancastrian, he had begun with Manchester United, but when they discarded him as a youngster, he found himself in the much humbler surroundings of Crewe Alexandra. Crewe, however, under the shrewd managership of Dario Gradi, had the habit then of turning their younger players into future stars, flourishing with bigger clubs, and so it proved in the case of Platt, who moved successfully to Aston Villa, where he became an industrious and incisive inside-right; if one may be permitted to use the old nomenclature.

He did not really reach his apogee, however, until it came to the knockout stages of the 1990 World Cup, in Bologna. There, against Belgium, he won the game with a gloriously acrobatic goal from Paul Gascoigne's free kick. He emerged as a star of the tournament, and Bari brought him to southeast Italy.

There, he quickly mastered the Italian language, and did well enough to be brought northwest to Turin and Juventus; then Sampdoria. Arsenal paid £4.5 million for him, but he never quite reached the form he had shown in Italy.

Bergkamp took to Highbury from the start, finding it a more agreeable locale than the monumental San Siro stadium, which had never been the same since, in a fit of grandiosity, it had been furnished, or afflicted, with an extra tier. This had the effect of preventing the winds from getting at the ground. The result of this was that water would gather around the roots of the grass, making it come up in clumps, to the detriment and danger of those playing on it. So much so that when Fabio Capello was successfully managing Milan, he remarked that his team's most dangerous opponent was the pitch.

You might say that Bergkamp had two unhappy seasons with Inter, but, as he himself once told me, two happy seasons in Milan. The problem was that Inter insisted on playing him as an out and out striker, while his ideal position was just behind the front line. Strange to think that, years later, Arsene Wenger, in one of his few tactical aberrations, played a by then veteran and substantially slower Bergkamp all on his own up front in the 2005 FA Cup Final, in Cardiff, against Manchester United.

'For me,' said Bergkamp, 'Highbury was typically English. When I came into Highbury for the first time when I signed, I came onto the pitch. I saw an English stadium, typically close to the pitch. It wasn't what we knew in Europe. A small stadium, quite an old stadium, of course, and a fantastic pitch. That was probably my first impression. At Highbury you had the combination of a fantastic pitch and the really great atmosphere of the stadium, which for me, as a foreigner, was always a fantastic experience.'

To his abundant natural talents, Bergkamp allied a devoted perfectionism. An hour or so after his teammates had abandoned the training pitch, there he was, practising his free kicks. 'However hard you work,' remarked Paul Merson, 'you can't work as hard as Dennis.'

His sleight of foot could be bewildering in its speed and dexterity; as evidenced by a goal he scored at Newcastle, when he conjured a ball around bewildered defenders, before putting it into the net. But there were times when, surprisingly, he could show the cloven hoof. Thus, in the 1998 World Cup in France, he displayed what one might call both sides of the coin. In each case, it might be said that Bergkamp's action was crucial to the outcome. In Toulouse, in the second round, Bergkamp's dreadful foul on Yugoslavia's Sinisa Mihailovic – not, admittedly, the gentlest of players himself – forced Mihailovic off the field after 78 minutes. Somehow Bergkamp got away with this, perhaps because the referee could not believe so elegant a player could have committed so gross an offence.

But in the ensuing quarter-final in Marseille, against Argentina, Bergkamp would score one of his most breathtaking goals. Controlling almost casually a long, diagonal pass from Frank De Boer, he used the sole of his foot to take the ball away from the formidable centre-back Ayala, then deploying the same right foot to beat the keeper, Roa. The fee Arsenal paid Inter for his transfer was the largest yet for the Gunners, but however huge it seemed at the time, it would ultimately seem a bargain.

Overall, after the traumatic departure of Graham, this might be seen as a season of retrenchment, even of convalescence. The League position was a reasonable fifth, though in the FA Cup, the Gunners went out at once in a replay at Sheffield United. They did better in the League Cup, which the club still, then, took seriously, defeating in turn Hartlepool, Barnsley, Sheffield Wednesday and Newcastle United, while defeat in the semi-finals by Aston Villa, after a couple of drawn games, came only on away goals.

Things doubtless would have gone better for Rioch and his team, had it not been for a plethora of injuries; to Tony Adams, David Platt, Ray Parlour and Steve Bould. In the absence of Adams, Martin Keown showed resilient form. In a spell of 13 games, the defence let in just seven goals. The very last League game, at Highbury, saw the Gunners come from a goal down against Bolton, with eight minutes to go, Platt and Bergkamp giving them a 2–1 victory which took them into the following season's UEFA Cup. It was something of a vindication for Platt, who had been criticised for lying too deep. Somewhat surprising, since this was precisely what he had complained about when playing for Juventus under the tactical aegis of Giovanni Trapattoni. 'That's what I bought them for!' exulted Rioch after this success, but he would not survive the close season.

His 3–5–2 tactics had been moderately successful, with Bergkamp, if not prolific, scoring some important goals. Not least that which defeated Manchester United 1–0 at Highbury in November 1996. Yet there is little doubt that when they sold their two players to the Gunners, both Inter and Sampdoria felt that they had got the best of the bargain and they probably had a case. Inter's, however, was a somewhat paradoxical one. Misusing Bergkamp as they did, they would certainly never have got the best out of him. Platt, however, had with the passing of time, arguably lost the edge of his game, whose forte had been to burst through strongly to strike from midfield.

That Ian Wright, in February 1996, should ask for a transfer was emblematic of the fact that Rioch had persisted in trying to make him abandon his natural game: to accelerate after the ball played over the defence. A great deal more sophisticated about the game than he was usually given credit for, Wright knew that holding the ball up and playing it to the encroaching midfield would never be his way.

True, in April, after scoring twice at Highbury in a victory over Leeds, he declared that he would like to spend, at 32, the rest of his career at Highbury. 'My main concern is to be in there and scoring goals,' he said. 'Arsenal is the main thing in my life just now.' To which Rioch added, 'Why should it be a surprise that we sit here together? We are always talking about the game together below stairs, because it is my job to get results for the club, and Ian's job to score the goals. That doesn't change.' Indeed it didn't, but Ian's way of scoring goals was surely well enough known to be unchallenged.

It was the influential economic historian J. Schumpeter, author of *Capitalism, Socialism and Democracy*, who once wrote, 'The true hero of capitalism is the entrepreneur.' By that token, David Dein might well be accounted a hero, at least in the annals of the Arsenal club. Rising, like so many entrepreneurs, not least the Russian oligarchs of recent times, from relatively modest origins (though not remotely as humble as those of Chelsea's Roman Abramovich) it was he who, becoming the motive force and the largest shareholder in the Gunners for some years, brought to the club the victorious manager, Arsene Wenger. That Dein should finally be forced out of the very club to which he had rendered such incomparable service was at once ironic and yet in some sense all of a piece with the frequent fate of entrepreneurs. They can burn and blaze like comets, and like comets they can suddenly come swooping down to earth.

Not that Dein, in his entrepreneurial life outside Highbury, did not have his intermittent crises, did not at times seem almost on the brink of disaster. The son of East European Jewish immigrants, who moved across London from Forest Gate, after his father had made money out of being a tobacco salesman, to a house in Alyth Gardens, North Finchley, Dein was born in 1943. His road was very familiar to me, since my own family lived in the next road up, Haslemere Gardens, from 1937 to 1951. Not that Dein and I ever met.

In due course, he worked for the family in that long lane called

Shepherd's Bush Market. Arnie, a fruit-stall worker there, recalled Dein 'flogging cheap dented cans of beans or soup or something and they had no labels.' Dein's enterprising mother, however, transformed the family fortunes when she shrewdly saw a market in their customary food for West Indian immigrants, and went out personally to import it.

Dein himself won a place at Leeds University but, impatient to become a businessman, walked out before he had completed it. He was 22, and he rapidly grew rich. From childhood, however, he had been a fervent Arsenal fan, and however much money he eventually made out of the club – not only through his shares, but also from a reported £550,000 a year he received from it when Vice Chairman – his commitment to the club was never in doubt.

In 1963, he bought, from the Arsenal Chairman Peter Hill-Wood, scion of the family which had largely guided Arsenal since the 1920s, 1,161 unissued shares at a cost of £290,250; being at that time 16.6 per cent of the total. This to the amusement of Hill-Wood who declared, 'Some rich men like to buy fast cars, yachts or racehorses. But David is more interested in Arsenal. I'm delighted that he is, but I still think he's crazy. To all intents and purposes, it's dead money.'

Not for so long. By 1998, it was estimated that Dein's shares, which by then made him the major shareholder, were worth not far short of £35 million. He had become, in Chekhovian terms, the Lopakhin of the Arsenal. Though, unlike Lopakhin, he did not expel the aristocrats whom he had supplanted. Yet in 1983, the very year in which he bought those shares from Arsenal, one in which he is reported to have made £283,000 from his London and overseas commodities company, he is said to have gone into what has been described as a 'questionable' and ill omened deal with a 'controversial' commodities dealer named Rajendra Sethia of the Esal Commodities Company. An organisation which, after Sethia had decamped from England, turned out to have accumulated £200 million of debts, of which the hapless creditors recouped merely 4p in the pound.

Dein's attempts to recover from Esal's bank, the Punjab National, £13 million failed both in the High Court in 1992, and a year later in the Court of Appeal. In January 1995, the *Mail on Sunday* reported that London and Overseas Sugar had 'massive debts'.

Dein meanwhile had increased his Arsenal shareholding to 42 per cent but he was now obliged to come to an arrangement with the diamond and property millionaire, Danny Fiszman, himself an Arsenal supporter from an early age, who bought 7,000 shares from Dein and had a reportedly joint interest in 3,000 others. It was Fiszman who would increasingly supersede Dein as the real power at Highbury, and a board of directors which, for so many years, had been an oasis of tranquillity, became increasingly internecine.

Where this left Peter Hill-Wood, now that he had sold his shares, was inevitably on the margins. This was surely to be regretted, however sentimentally, by all those who over the many years had seen Arsenal and the Hill-Woods's the epitome of *noblesse oblige*. Hill-Wood, in fact, did not sell the vast majority of his own shares to Dein until the club was about to become a public limited company midway through 1991. There were 7,000 issued shares, Hill-Wood had about 1,100 of them, of which he sold Dein a thousand. To be fair, he did well out of the deal, allegedly receiving some £350,000.

Yet in the new century, it was distressing to find him grandiosely dismissing the American sports franchise owning billionaire Stan Kroenke, as not the sort of person Arsenal wanted to do business with, only to be obliged not long afterwards to come to Canossa – where the Holy Roman Emperor begged mercy from the Pope – or at least to fly to America, asking Kroenke to join the board. Kroenke by the summer of 2009 would be the main shareholder, just short of 29 per cent which would oblige him to bid for full control.

As for Dein, it might be said that all is darkest before the dawn. The dawn being his colossal coup in bringing Arsene Wenger to Arsenal. In the latter stages of season 1995–96, Dein's relations with Bruce Rioch were in tatters. Early in March, Rioch, declaring that Dein had suggested signing several French stars, Zinedine Zidane among them – said that he didn't want any of them, inveighing, 'David Dein doesn't speak for me, he will never speak for me.' But since, as Mao Tse Tung had it, power comes out of the barrel of a gun and Dein, metaphorically at least, held the gun, Rioch was surely dicing with death.

There was more trouble in August, after Arsenal had lost in Scotland to both Rangers and Celtic and were giving an abysmal account of themselves in a mini-tournament in Florence, losing in turn to Fiorentina and Benfica. Outraged Arsenal supporters stood before the 'Tribune of Honour' abusing Dein, singing, 'We love Arsenal, you don't! Where's our Arsenal gone?' and, 'Dein out! Dein must go!' How fortunate for them that he didn't. It was reported that he was asked to leave the *tribuna* to talk to them, but that he disappeared. Who could blame him?

Rioch, meanwhile, was in explosive mood again. 'It's obvious,' he declared, 'we need two or three new faces. They have to come in. Some of our play was very poor, and I am very disappointed. A club with the credibility and reputation of Arsenal have to play the top teams in Europe and we've tested ourselves against the cream during our pre season. But we have lost.'

He had, in fact, as we know, bought a player destined to be one of the most influential in the club's history in Holland's Dennis Bergkamp.

By the time Peter Hill-Wood went off on holiday, contracts to renew Rioch's role had still not been signed. It was suggested that he demanded sole approval over transfer policy, but since the George Graham affair, Arsenal, explicably, had changed their *modus operandi*, making the board ultimately responsible. So it was that Arsenal dispensed with Rioch and, at the initiative of Dein, brought in his friend Arsene Wenger.

The persisting insularity of the English game and its chroniclers was all too plainly exposed when Wenger was widely described as 'unknown'. Unknown only to those so parochial that they had no awareness of football beyond the Channel. Wenger, though he arrived from Grampus 8 in Japan, had previously had many years in charge of Monaco in the French League, during which he had won the national championship. He would now proceed to revolutionise Arsenal, in time becoming the most successful manager since Herbert Chapman. And if it was not he who innovated the Gunners' success, he would maintain it over a far longer period than any of his predecessors.

Chapter 13

WENGER ARRIVES

IT WOULD TAKE SOME TIME FOR THE SMOKE TO CLEAR BEFORE Wenger arrived at Highbury – and London Colney – in September 1996. In August, soon after the upheavals at Florence, Dein had to endure a stormy meeting of the Arsenal shareholders. Some, including one of the chief dissidents, Alan Esparza, were incensed that even though Grampus 8 had announced that Wenger would be leaving them for Arsenal, no official confirmation had come out of Highbury; while Wenger himself wouldn't arrive until September. Peter Hill-Wood insisted that there was a legal agreement that he couldn't name the new manager 'until the time is right'.

There was also sharp criticism of the amount the club had paid for Dennis Bergkamp, and discomfort over the admission that it was Wenger who had recommended the acquisition of the two French midfielders, Patrick Vieira and Remi Garde; deals which were concluded within a couple of days of Rioch's defenestration. Had the disenchanted fans only known then what an immense contribution Patrick Vieira would make to the team, they would surely have masked their batteries.

As for the transfer of Bergkamp, some of them insisted that Dein could have had Bergkamp for £2 million less than the Gunners paid, to which he angrily replied, 'You are questioning my integrity.' He was, he insisted, never offered Bergkamp at a price of £5.5 million. But here too Dein surely had the last laugh, given the outstanding service the club would have from the Dutchman. The dissidents were in no way assuaged, Esparza insisting, 'The meeting was a joke, just like the club at the moment.' But the joke would emphatically be on the dissidents.

Particularly on those loud mouthed, misguided supporters who so mindlessly railed against what would turn out to be so felicitous. Alan Esparza, the voice of the so-called Independent Arsenal Supporters Association inveighed, 'I just hope the reports about Wenger are wrong because he wouldn't be able to attract players to the club as [Johan] Cruyff would. If they are true, there is going to be trouble and David Dein is going to bear the brunt of it.'

Such sentiments, born surely out of ignorance of the realities, were contradicted by those better placed to know; notably two English international players who had played under Wenger at Monaco and were well aware of his qualities. Glenn Hoddle, surely one of the most gifted English footballers of his generation, recently made manager of the England team itself, and Mark Hateley an England, Milan and Portsmouth centre-forward. Hoddle enthused: 'I would not be where I am today if it were not for him. Working for Arsene in Monaco stimulated me to go into management. Wherever he has gone, he has been a major success.' Hateley observed, 'He will try to introduce his Continental ideas at Arsenal. He'll know everything about the club and the players because that's the kind of guy he is.'

Wenger himself declared, a year earlier, 'Your country is the place to be. The English League now is as good as the Italian League was a year or two ago. So many top foreign players are in your country, raising the standards.'

Wenger, certainly, was a *rara avis* among English club managers; a living antithesis of John Osborne's sour words, 'As half educated as a football manager.' By extreme contrast, the multi-lingual Wenger was very highly educated indeed. Born in Strasbourg on 22 October 1949, he, like many another prominent manager, not least at Arsenal – Knighton, Chapman, Allison – was no great player. He began as an amateur defender with local Mutzig, Mulhouse and Vauban. He had a brief spell as a professional but played only three games in Strasbourg's 1978–79 Championship winning season. . . . 1983 saw him become player-coach with Cannes, the club which would eventually launch Patrick Vieira. The following year saw him coaching Nancy, but the team was relegated to the Second Division.

By 1987, however, he had done enough to convince Monaco to make him their manager. He would spend seven impressive years there, making a scintillating start by winning the French Championship immediately. Twice during his years at Monaco he was asked to manage the French national team, but twice he turned it down, believing that the time was not ripe. In 1989, he won the French Cup with Monaco and the following season, took them to the Final of the now much mourned European Cup Winners' Cup.

In season 1993–94, he could have gone to the Bundesliga with Werder Bremen or even Bayern Munich, but he steadfastly remained at Monaco; who duly sacked him when the club finished only ninth in the French League that season. In his Monaco years, he nurtured the explosive raw talent of the Liberian George Weah, later to become top player in the world, and Thierry Henry; whom he would save from frustration at Juventus, at a cost of £10 million, and turn him from a right-winger into one of the game's best centre-forwards.

Wenger, who gained a degree in economics in his native Alsace, brought a refreshing and stimulating modernity to Arsenal and their training grounds at London Colney; which in time he would replace with more grandiose facilities, nearby. Not that his inception at Highbury was an easy one. Contractual problems meant he could not leave Grampus till September, which meant that he had no influence on Arsenal's pre-season training, though at least he had been instrumental in the signing of Vieira. Moreover, he had to deal with a vicious and totally spurious campaign, a thing of rumour and malign chants by supporters of rival clubs, accusing him of sexual deviance.

There were fears that he might not be able to arrive until January, to find the club in confusion, but in fact he was on board in time to sit on the bench in Cologne beside Pat Rice, in temporary charge after the resignation of the equally transient Stewart Houston. Rice, a resilient full-back for Arsenal and Northern Ireland, would in fact be confirmed as Wenger's second in command, to remain there successfully for many years to come.

In the UEFA Cup, for which they had narrowly qualified, the Gunners had already lost 3–2 at home to Borussia Mönchengladbach, inspired by a dazzling performance by Stefan Effenberg, the stormy petrel of German football, playing unusually upfront rather than in central midfield, and tearing an abysmal Arsenal defence to shreds; though the team wasn't helped by an injury which forced Dennis Bergkamp off.

Tony Adams' dominant presence in defence was clearly missed. In Cologne, where the return took place rather than in Borussia's home city, he reappeared, though clearly not yet fully match fit. The major disappointment of the evening, when Borussia repeated their 3–2 success, Effenberg again the star, first in midfield, then up front, was the form of Patrick Vieira, clearly off the pace. Before long, however, he would become the motor of midfield, putting behind himself the previous season's frustration at Milan. Having signed him from Cannes, the Italians were expected to send him out on loan. Instead, they kept him but didn't use him.

On the bench, wearing a bright red top, Wenger celebrated as enthusiastically as Rice, when Arsenal scored. Though he may have wished, as many supporters did, that the Gunners rather than Chelsea had brought the formidable Gianluca Vialli from Italy, when they had the chance.

Wenger lost no time in introducing radical new methods at London Colney. Plyometrics was one of them. 'The idea', explained Wenger, 'is to increase the explosive strength of the muscles. It makes the players stronger, more powerful, more agile. It involves all kinds of jumping, one leg, two legs, long jump, high jump. The coaching of it must be handled with a fine touch because it can damage the muscles.

'But I know what I want to do. I try to think about my training routines and I've used this system wherever I've worked. I try to get as near the game as possible in terms of intensity. I try to work the players in match conditions. I have worked for sixteen years in football and I have explored all the ways of improving the condition of the players. I have worked with experts like nutritionists and psychiatrists. You learn and after a while you choose what you can apply to footballers.'

Diet was a priority. Japan's was the best he had known: boiled vegetables, fish and rice, no fat, red meat, eggs or sugar. Hence, no fat people. Pre-match meals at Arsenal would no longer be a matter of steak and toast. The emphasis would be on fish and chicken.

English players, he had found, were 'more generous' than those in

France, 'they give more in competition and are ready to fight to win. But the basic education of young players in France is better.'

How odd and ironic in retrospect, however, that, a few months after taking charge at Arsenal, he should declare, 'There is a danger the foreign players will soon outnumber the English players because the financial situation is against the Englishmen. There is a real danger for the future of English football at the top end. It will have to suffer if this continues. Why? Because every manager in the Premiership will tell you that if he has to buy a continental player or an English player, the salary is the same, the ability might be the same, but one transfer fee is high, the other might be nothing.'

Yet Wenger himself in due course would pay £10 million for Thierry Henry, a massive sum for his compatriot, Sylvain Wiltord, while before long, the Bosman decision would mean that British players, too, could leave their clubs for nothing when their contracts ended. And the day would come when Arsenal teams would often consist of 11 foreign players, sometimes with five more on the bench.

If Patrick Vieira's start was unimpressive, it would not take long for him to show himself as a propulsive force, with Dennis Bergkamp, his fellow foreigner, one of the two, contrasting inspirations of a rapidly improving team. Vieira did well enough on his first appearance for the Gunners, as a substitute against Sheffield Wednesday. But if he had been ineffective in Cologne, he looked still less impressive a few days later in a laborious home win against a Sunderland team reduced by expulsions to nine men. The tide would turn. Emphatically. Still only 20 years old, tall, powerful and rangy, the very essence of what used to be called the attacking wing half, he could win the ball then drive forward with formidable impetus and speed. His one major fault, it would transpire, lay in his impetuosity, his penchant for collecting a plethora of red cards. Once, when he came off the field at West Ham, spitting in the face of an opponent.

Not that you would suspect such excesses when meeting him: a young man of modesty and charm. Born in Senegal, his mother had brought him to France when he was seven and his brother eight. Each morning, she would get up at 4.30 to go to work at the Cuisines Generales in Versailles.

His first club was Tours, his second Cannes. Equable and self-effacing to a degree, when he set up a goal against the formidable Paris

Saint Germain, he simply observed, when lauded, 'There's nothing to say. Me, I listen to the advice of the veterans. They teach me to stay humble and modest. I don't want my head to swell.'

His temperament served him well when Milan bought him then kept him on ice for a season. 'It was an experience I wanted very much,' he told me. 'If it was to be done again, I'd do it again.' No intimation, then, of times to come, when a stand off summer after summer occurred between Vieira, who wanted to seek pastures new, and a club that was desperate to keep him but finally and surprisingly were quite willing to let him go.

Even in his first season, there were signs that Wenger, most unexpectedly, had something of an Achilles heel when it came to discipline on the field. True, things did improve after the Gunners had reached an alarming total of 72 red cards. As early in his regime as January 1997, I found myself writing in the *New York Post*:

> Arsene Wenger is a sophisticated, professional figure, but his Arsenal players are few of these things.
>
> I was therefore moved, after the Gunners' recent Cup tie against Sunderland, to ask Wenger whether he would be working on his players' discipline, given that he would be without strikers Ian Wright and John Hartson due for suspension for the replay at Roker Park?
>
> To this, Wenger gave a full if somewhat ambiguous answer. 'You can have it two ways,' he said. 'To improve the behaviour of the referees or to improve our behaviour. We must have cards when we deserve to be suspended.'
>
> No fewer than four Arsenal players have in fact been recently suspended all after being sent off. Tony Adams was dismissed after running into the Newcastle centre-forward Alan Shearer, who himself admitted that the decision was a hard one. Steve Bould went off for fouls in defence. Wenger would like to make an exception in these two cases. 'I don't want the players to change because a defender is a defender.'
>
> But then Wright got himself sent off in the silliest of ways, which still led Wenger to defend him. Wright is invaluable to Arsenal with his supreme opportunism, his lightning reactions. He is also, for those of us who know him personally, a shrewd and original analyst of the game. But every now and then something snaps.
>
> In that fatal game at Nottingham Forest, he had already run full

pelt deliberately into his own teammate Paul Merson, who'd displeased him. Subsequently, fouled by Forest's Croatian stopper, Jerkan – against whom a free kick was duly given – Wright ran some twenty yards before crashing into his back.

The linesman convinced the referee that the contact was a spiteful one, and Wright was sent off. Wenger insisted that the contact was trivial and that Jerkan had exaggerated his fall, which he unquestionably had. But why in the first place should a player of Wright's quality want to take such a chance?

Hartson went off on New Year's Day at Highbury when, having been painfully fouled by Middlesbrough's veteran player-coach and ex-England captain Bryan Robson, he did not get justice from the referee. And although referee Mike Rea was a feeble performer on this occasion, it was suicidal of Hartson to explode with a torrent of abuse. Off he went.

'What should be punished the most,' said Wenger, 'is what goes against the spirit of the game and not only the player who speaks to the referee. Of course they don't have to do it.' By which I hope he meant that he *shouldn't* do it. But special pleading is not enough. It's not an easy problem for a French intellectual to solve, but Arsene must try.

So one discerned a strange ambiguity, an ambivalence, perhaps, in Wenger's approach to the game. Urbane, objective, highly educated, innovative, he would seem strangely reluctant to condemn his players, not least Vieira, when they showed the cloven hoof. There was even, here, a resemblance to a very different, less sophisticated figure in George Graham, who somehow never seemed to see any incident of detriment to his team – 'I was just coming up; I was just going down!' So much so that Wenger himself eventually made a joke of his propensity, and one was tempted to suggest that his favourite half-back line would be The Three Wise Monkeys.

Wenger's impact at Arsenal was both swift and impressively positive. He brought in a resourceful team from abroad. Boro Primorat, who had worked with him at Grampus 8, became the first-team coach. As a player, he had won 38 caps for Yugoslavia as a centre-half. Two French dieticians, Dr Yann Rougier and his adjunct, Herve Castel, were engaged. Liam Brady, that hero of the midfield, was brought back to Arsenal after 16 years, to preside over the club's Academy. Where, for all his and his fellow coaches' efforts, it would sometimes seem harder for a young Englishman to break into the first team than, in Biblical language, a camel to pass through the eye of a needle.

Vieira was soon doing all or more than Wenger could ask of him. Under his impulse, the team climbed swiftly up the League. Not a single home match would be lost until Manchester United beat the Gunners 2–1 in February. Against Leeds United shortly before Christmas, Vieira, already dear to a crowd which would chorus, 'He comes from Senegal! He plays for Arsenal!' showed what a force he could be, with a 40-yard run past a bemused defence. Ending unselfishly with a pass rolled to his right-back, Lee Dixon, who duly and easily scored.

Four weeks later, on the eve of a 3–1 victory over the eternal north London foe, Tottenham Hotspur, Wenger spoke with fluent clarity of Vieira; and his own approach to the game. 'What is great here in England is that the crowd loves him because he does the right things at the right moment, not because he is beautiful to watch. I have seen many players who look wonderful outside of the game but when you see them play they are a disaster. They exasperate you because they don't do the right thing at the right moment. Beauty for me is efficiency. It's not just making nice movements.

'I think we should have enough players here already to be creative. For me, being creative is scoring goals. When you have the best attack in England, you cannot say you are not creative. I was lucky to find Ian Wright scoring goals and at the top of his confidence.

'When you have one player making the play with his strong points, working on his weak points at 33 could just destroy him. You can only be successful if you concentrate on your strong points. Nobody can be perfect. If you have one strong point in life you are already lucky. Why try to destroy it? Just play with it.'

He praised

the technical qualities of the defenders. English defenders had a reputation just for kicking the ball. You should come to training and see that our five defenders are technically good. Tony Adams and the other ones are able to play. They last so long because they have the quality. If they had only physique they couldn't last.

We have an experienced team. Some people say we have an old team. Their minds are really young because they are ready to fight against everybody every three days to win games. For me, being a professional isn't just playing once a week, and playing well from time to time, it's trying to be at your best every time. For this you need a strong mentality.

When you have players like I have who have been doing it for ten years, that means there is something special inside them which makes them want to win. What I like on the field is the best way to win. When you argue with the referee, you are not concentrating on the game. You lose one or two seconds and every second can be important. But sometimes you have to accept some things of players because it's their way of being better in the next action and getting out their frustrations. Ian Wright needs sometimes to say something – I don't know what he says – maybe just to be better for the next action.

In another context, he would praise Wright for his remarkable achievement of having broken through into professionalism 'at the age of 23'.

In February, in a remarkable and even ruthless coup, the precocious 17-year-old striker, Nicolas Anelka, arrived from an infuriated Paris Saint Germain; for nothing. The lack of fee was because, under the rules then prevailing in European football, Anelka was too young to be a professional. He had already made an impact, in more than one way, at PSG, not only for his exceptional abilities – pace, flair, control, penetration – but for his headstrong behaviour. Though PSG at the time had two experienced French international strikers, Anelka became incensed when he wasn't in the team; something which certainly propelled him towards London. Arsenal in due course would throw PSG a patronising, ex gratia, £500,000, eventually selling Anelka to Real Madrid for some £23 million.

He would make a delayed debut in the last League match of the season as a substitute against Newcastle United, who won 1–0, at Highbury. The fact that he was an inveterate *enfant terrible* was compounded by the fact that he brought with him as his agents his two belligerent brothers, always it seemed ready to incite him.

Arsenal would eventually come a satisfactorily improved third in the League, having at one stage looked as if they might even win it. Successive home defeats within a few February days by Manchester United and, more surprisingly, Wimbledon, killed effectively what hopes they had.

The unexpected aspect of their 1–0 loss to Wimbledon was that the winning goal should be scored with a ferocious right-footed volley by, of all people, Vinnie Jones, a true dog of war, notorious for the way he had grabbed the genitals of Paul Gascoigne in a game against Newcastle United. Joe Kinnear, then manager of a Wimbledon team, famous or infamous for its long-ball tactics, said that Jones 'does it week in week out in training'.

For all its reputation as a Route One team, the fact is that Wimbledon possessed, in the Norwegian playmaker Oyvind Leonhardsen, the very kind of motivator the Gunners had featured for so long but which now they lacked. Not that Leonhardsen was on the field for very long; an opponent's studs ripped open his calf.

Ian Wright did hit the post in the first half, but then faded away. Arousing speculation that this might be the aftermath of his bitter confrontation in the United match with the giant, blond keeper Peter Schmeichel, enraged by Wright's dangerous late challenge.

As for the FA Cup, the Gunners surprisingly went out 1–0 at home in the fourth round to Leeds, the team they had beaten so comprehensively in the League, a few months earlier.

The one major blemish on the season was the fact that the Gunners came bottom of the so-called Fair Play table. The cloven hoof? The Achilles Heel? Choose what metaphor you wish, but there was much, much more of it to come.

Wenger himself, at a subsequent Parisian seminar for international coaches, spoke frankly and revealingly about his early, somewhat tenuous, experiences at Highbury. Not least of all his first game in charge at Blackburn, when his players were plainly taken aback on the morning of the game when he took them into the ballroom of their hotel for a gentle session of aerobics. 'Frankly,' he admitted, 'I think the players found some of my methods ridiculous, but they did as they were told because they were curious.'

> Initially, the players laughed at some of my methods. This went on for some time after my arrival, but eventually they started to realise it was having a positive effect on their health, their performance and the team's results. When I arrived in England, I wasn't exactly welcomed with open arms and I had to overcome a great deal of resistance, especially off the pitch. That's when I really appreciated

the fact that I had been in Japan, because I was prepared for a certain amount of scepticism and scorn psychologically. In Japan, I had been through many testing moments, and looking back, if I had gone to England directly from Monaco, I don't think I would have survived. But because I spent those two years in the Far East, I became much stronger and developed a much thicker skin.

In a way it made me much more motivated so I was able to cope with all the problems I encountered when I arrived in England and came under attack from people who called me Arsene Who.

Pat Rice (made assistant manager after Stewart Houston walked out) helped me such a lot. I would not have lasted without him. A good assistant is vital and Pat was probably born in a red shirt with white sleeves. But you have to be your own man in football so I decided upon two principles concerning the management of the team. First of all I resolved to remain true to myself so that the players could accept me as I was. I was determined not to play any games or charades with them and I would not behave as a coach might normally behave.

At Blackburn . . . we were winning 1–0 at half time and during the break I didn't say anything to them for about six minutes. The English players in particular were looking at me and thinking 'Why isn't he saying anything to us?' because I wasn't living up to their expectations. They thought the manager or coach needs to shout at you, or motivate you by ranting and raving, so they would go back out on the pitch with his words still ringing in their heads. But I decided I would remain true to myself. Like every other coach, I have my qualities and my faults, but I did not want to keep up a pretence that I couldn't keep up.

So I didn't act as they expected me to, and that probably made them think about the way they went about their jobs. They cannot have been too disturbed, because we won, 2–0. Yet even today, if you talk to the players at Arsenal, they are quite surprised by my behaviour because they do not understand my culture.

The second policy decision I took was to create a new cultural identity for the team. I didn't say anything to anyone about this, not even the chairman, but I wanted to reconstruct the club, to give it a new image.

That was always going to be more difficult. In Japan, a lot was expected of me because I came from a country with a strong foot-balling heritage, but in England I was greeted in rather a cold way because the English did not have a tradition of employing foreign coaches.

At the end of my first season I decided to change the side because it had been much the same for ten years; seven players had been in the team the whole time. Obviously I wanted to keep the soul of the club because Arsenal have a strong tradition and a strong club spirit, so I set myself a limit that I was going to keep five English players in the side if possible.

But as we know, in time he wouldn't find it remotely possible.

Just before the season began Wenger, who had already been criticised for his unconvincing defence of errant players, duly and characteristically defended them. 'We are not a dirty side,' he insisted, 'but a fair side. This game is about physical contact. I want positive aggression. If you're too soft, you don't win many games.'

'Quite apart from the puzzle of what constitutes negative aggression,' I wrote in *The Times*, 'two questions are raised by this odd statement. First, does Wenger still not see how much harm his team's parlous record did to their chances? The suspension of such key players as Ian Wright and Dennis Bergkamp deprived Arsenal of their contribution in games they might otherwise have won.

'Second, is there reason to think Wenger is over compensating? The last thing with which one would associate so donnish, even philosophical, a figure is "physical" football. Of course this is a contact sport, but Wenger had never been associated with the kind of team that plays like the Argentinians thirty years ago. This season, Wenger must stop making excuses and simply see that these things do not happen.' Which proved easier said than done.

For all his insistence that he did not want to pay large fees and didn't want to import too many foreign players, Wenger in the close season of 1997 spent lavishly; on players from abroad. Two of them would make important contributions to the team. Marc Overmars, the ambidextrous Dutch winger, bought for £7 million, had tormented England in a Wembley international, and had recovered after a long absence from severe injury. From Monaco, where Wenger had coached him, came Emmanuel Petit and Gilles Grimandi. Grimandi was a scrappy, sometimes abrasive, little midfield player, but Petit would emerge as an exuberant force in midfield. Tall, blond, muscular and formidably left-footed, he was said by Wenger to be able to play in a variety of positions.

Left-back, however, was hardly one of them. When I saw him operating there in a pre-season friendly at Leyton Orient, he was constantly out of position. But he would not stay there for long, before moving into the middle of midfield. He and Grimandi between them cost £5 million. The Portuguese Luis Boa Morte, who would never quite fulfil his promise at Highbury, a left-winger with strength and pace, cost £1.5 million. Unexpectedly, the young Matthew Upson, a promising centre-back who had played just one game for Luton Town, came for no less than a million pounds. Often injured, he would never establish himself at Highbury, though it would be surprising to see Wenger let him go to Birmingham City – and subsequent England caps – while hanging on to the plainly unconvincing French centre-back, Pascal Cygan, for whom he paid £2.1 million. It is with something of a shudder that one remembers Cygan heading with unerring power into his own net at the Clock End, in a European Cup match.

It was Grimandi who made a spectacular if, ultimately, a somewhat illusory start, coming exuberantly out of defence to score two out of six Arsenal goals at Norwich. Ian Wright, almost 34, still in hot pursuit of Cliff Bastin's aggregate goal record of 178, was fined £15,000 in early July by the FA, for his disciplinary record. Even in this Norwich game, he was involved in a contretemps with an opponent, Scott. Wenger, he related happily, 'virtually said that to me, that your place will be there for as long as you're fit enough to claim it, and you can't be fairer than that.'

No more Paul Merson. That gifted forward, that erratic fellow, had been sold to Middlesbrough, much to the regret of Dennis Bergkamp who, in parenthesis, had also lamented the going of Bruce Rioch who was, after all, the manager who had signed him. 'He was one of the players who could decide a game', he said of Merson. 'He's got a lot of skill. Sometimes decisions are made and I don't know by who.' He could, one imagines, have offered an educated guess. Overall, however, this would be a triumphant first full season for Wenger, who would win the Premier League and win it in style. His transfer policy would be abundantly justified.

But with Arsenal back in Europe again, albeit in the UEFA rather than the European Cup, they had to contend with Bergkamp's refusal to fly. It was believed that this had its origins in his experience during the 1994 World Cup Finals in America. The Dutch team was about to board a plane, when a fatuous Dutch journalist, asked to open his bag, announced that there was a bomb in it. Boarding was instantly aborted, the journalist lost his job; and Bergkamp was reportedly traumatised. It meant that when Arsenal played in Europe, Bergkamp would go only overland by car, provided the journey was not too long and onerous.

Salonika, where Arsenal met Paok in the first leg of the first round, was a city too far. Arsenal played without him and, thus deprived of his incisive partnership up front with Wright, were beaten. Bergkamp did score in the return at Highbury, but the match was drawn 1–1 and the Gunners were out.

It was, said Emmanuel Petit, the presence of Ian Wright – not Wenger, his former mentor? – which attracted him to Arsenal, and they quickly seemed to have established a kind of mutual admiration society. Yet Petit, in a farcical episode, had so nearly joined not Arsenal but Tottenham. Arriving originally at White Hart Lane, he asked them for some English currency and promptly took a cab to Highbury; and signed for Arsenal! 'I'm desolated,' he bewailed. 'I didn't know about the rivalry between them.' Wright eulogised him. 'What I've seen of Manny, he's a real top class player, got a lovely left foot. I really look forward to playing with him.'

Overmars, recovered at last from his long travail with an injured knee, already had a profitable understanding with his compatriot, Bergkamp. Like Bergkamp, he had excelled with Ajax of Amsterdam but, unlike Bergkamp, he was not a product of that club's famous youth scheme, having joined them as an 18-year-old from the Willem II club. He had, he said, decided eight months ago that he wanted to leave Ajax and ideally join Arsenal. 'I was telling myself it would be my last year. Arsenal are a very big club in England and I followed them the last few years.'

It was without the decisive influence of Bergkamp, suspended as were and would be so many Arsenal players, no matter the elaborate excuses Wenger continued to make for them, that the Gunners in early November lost their first League game. Lost it by a wide 3–0 margin at Derby, who had been their nemesis in the past. It was a day on which Jim Smith, alias 'Bald Eagle', celebrated his resourceful 25 years as a club manager.

Derby themselves, another polyglot team, had several key players missing, but the long-legged black Costa Rica striker, Paulo Wanchope, was emphatically there to trouble an Arsenal defence, penetrating with two goals a defence which simply hadn't got the pace to keep up with him. Brushing aside the suggestion that Bergkamp's absence had been crucial to Arsenal's debacle, Wenger said it was a 'collective' matter. And he was grudging in his opinion of Wanchope. 'He has the potential to be a player', Wenger said. And Wanchope was still showing that unusual potential as late as 2002, when he played for his country in South Korea's World Cup, against Brazil.

'You look at the senior players in Arsenal's side,' remarked Jim Smith, 'and you could see they were very nervous whenever they got the ball.' Embarrassingly true. 'Arsenal's heavy mob,' I wrote, 'burdened by the weight of years, tends to look good until actually put under pressure.' True, Wanchope's first goal was deflected past David Seaman off Steve Bould's heel, but to score it, Wanchope had run half the length of the field unchallenged. At least Wenger honestly admitted, 'After we were exposed to the speed of Derby on counter attacks, we could not cope with that.' It was an unusually subdued day for Ian Wright and beside him, up front, making his first League start, the 18-year-old Nicolas Anelka was no better.

Yet the following weekend at Highbury, Arsenal and their 'old men' were good enough to beat Manchester United 3–2, Anelka being one of the scorers. His was the opening goal, Patrick Vieira made is 2–0, United recovered to level the score, but a header from David Platt decided the game. All this without Bergkamp, the jewel in Arsenal's crown, suspended for three matches after collecting five yellow cards. Of him, Arsene Wenger enthused, 'He has this feeling always to know where his position is a threat to the opponent. Sometimes he's in front, sometimes he's between the lines, sometimes he's in midfield.' It was a victory which left the Gunners in strong contention for the title.

Yet things, at home, would fall strangely apart in the next two Highbury matches, a 1–0 defeat by Liverpool, a still more alarming 3–1 loss to Blackburn. Both games, significantly, were played without the full dynamic presence of the injured Patrick Vieira, and even a 2–1 Boxing Day success against modest Leicester City, with Vieira, only a substitute against Blackburn, back in midfield, found the Gunners fully 12 points behind Manchester United, reduced to sixth in the Premier League.

Form, in the New Year, was somewhat erratic. It took the Gunners two games to dispose, in the FA Cup, of humble Port Vale, who had the temerity and audacity to hold the Gunners to a goalless draw at Highbury, succumbing in the return game only on penalties, after extra time. There would be another 0–0 draw at Highbury in the fifth round against Crystal Palace, who were beaten in the replay at Selhurst Park. Gradually, as the smoke began to clear and results continued to improve, the chimerical double of League and Cup, achieved in 1971, looked an increasing possibility.

All this, despite the slump in late 1997, when the lack and loss of Paul Merson, now emerged from his manifold problems and doing bright things for Middlesbrough, looked a mistaken decision, the more so as Ian Wright, despite overhauling Cliff Bastin's scoring record in September with a hat trick against Bolton – 'The crowd sucked the goals in!' he joked – was firing blanks. Could it be, one wondered, that his visits to a psychologist for so-called 'anger management' had blunted the edge of his game?

I impugned at the time Wenger's transfer policy suggesting that even Emmanuel Petit, however powerful, lacked the finesse of the ideal midfield player. And had Wenger, given the lack of thrust up front, been too quick to get rid of John Hartson? The big Welsh international had begun, after an uneasy start, to run into form at West Ham. But Wenger would have the last emphatic laugh. Yet where was the midfield general to succeed in the tradition of Alex James? Paul Davis had been the last of the Mohicans and there were times when the absence showed. Not least against brave Port Vale.

A three-match sequence against West Ham United, who had been beaten at Upton Park in early January in the League Cup, featured three draws; the first at Upton Park, 0–0 in the League, the next two in the sixth round of the FA Cup; the replay at West Ham in fact being won only on penalties. Hartson played in the League game but was suspended for the subsequent Cup match, Bergkamp missed the League game but played in the Cup. After the initial goalless draw at Upton Park, Wenger somewhat resignedly said that one point wasn't enough for a challenge in the Premier League, but it might help to gain second place. 'We have to put the ball on the ground more and create more movement with the ball', he admitted. 'We will try.' They were still 11 points behind Manchester United.

The gap, when they went to Old Trafford on 14 March, had narrowed to nine points; and Arsenal won. Marc Overmars scored the game's only goal, racing on to a headed pass from Anelka and shooting through the legs of Peter Schmeichel. The race was suddenly and unexpectedly open. United's hopes were further diminished by the fact that injury would rule Schmeichel out for weeks. It was plain, too, that they missed the inspiration given them by the virtuoso, if sporadically violent, Frenchman, Eric Cantona. He of the kung fu kick and the strange allusion to sardines.

As for Wenger, he, too, had to put up with a missing goalkeeper, the commanding Seaman missing for numerous matches, replaced, not always solidly, by the young Austrian keeper, Alex Manninger. There was also the continuing problem of suspensions, not least of the irreplaceable Bergkamp, with Wenger forever citing mitigating circumstances. Thus, when at the end of the Cup game against West Ham at Highbury, Vieira appeared to mount a double assault on West Ham's John Moncur – himself once a victim of Cantona – Wenger with no apparent sense of irony asserted that though Vieira may have tried to punch and kick Moncur, he had missed each time! In the return tie against West Ham, Vieira swung a gratuitous kick at Ian Pearce, the home centre-back.

Yet with or without Bergkamp, and with Vieira somehow largely surviving, Arsenal embarked on an imperious run of 10 successive League victories. A mercurial little Liberian centre-forward, Christopher Wreh, he too from the Monaco club, added thrust to the attack when called on, not least in a dire overall performance at Wimbledon where Arsenal won 1–0. They won by the same score at Highbury against Sheffield Wednesday, when Bergkamp, available then and remarkable, scored the early goal. While, in the FA Cup, Wolves were defeated in the semi-final, meaning that for the third time, Arsenal would play Newcastle United in the Wembley Final.

In early May, at Highbury, they made sure of the Premier League by thrashing Everton 4–0; even without Bergkamp. Overmars, Bergkamp's compatriot, maintained his ebullient form, a trial to any opposing full-back. Of him, Wenger had said, how delighted he was that Overmars had metamorphosed from the Dutch type of winger, making space for the midfield players, to one who was constantly in the game. 'It took him some time to adjust to that,' said Wenger, 'because physically it is much more demanding.' But with memories of how, in a World Cup eliminator at Wembley, Overmars, on the Dutch right flank had utterly eluded the fast Des Walker, who brought him down, enabling Holland to score from the penalty, it was plain that Overmars, even then, was doing much more than just creating space.

Overmars would score twice in that game and, to the delight of the crowd, Tony Adams, in the final minute, roared out of defence on to a through pass by Steve Bould, and drove home the fourth. Arsenal, coming from so far behind, were champions. Perhaps the fact that they had so dramatically overhauled Manchester United may have given Wenger extra satisfaction, since he had had his exchanges with his United equivalent, Alex Ferguson, especially after Wenger had dismissed a piece of special pleading by Ferguson when he'd wanted the season truncated a year earlier, to accommodate United's fixture list.

In the past, Ferguson had successfully played mind games with Kevin Keegan, when Keegan, managing a Newcastle team, at one time a dozen points ahead of Manchester United, had risen to the bait, lost his equilibrium and had the mortification of seeing Manchester United win the League. Just, you might say, as Arsenal now made up a 12-point gap against United.

It wasn't only suspension which ruled Bergkamp out of Arsenal matches. He had missed the last three of them with a hamstring injury and was desperate to be wholly fit in time to play in the Final. 'I am hopeful but I will not let the team down,' he declared. 'I will not say I am fit if I am not. I could not do that. . . . the FA Cup is something special. I used to watch it back in Holland. . . . to play in one would be a dream. Wembley is a fantastic place and it has such a great atmosphere, and I want to be part of it.' Alas, he would not be fit; but Arsenal beat Newcastle without him.

After the defeat of Everton had clinched the Premier League, Wenger had said, 'This is my greatest ever achievement as a manager. I am surprised but delighted that we have won the title so soon, but this team can get better.' After his team had completed his triumphant double, he observed, 'The Championship was our main aim, but it would have been terrible to have lost at Wembley when we really wanted the FA Cup.'

Even without Bergkamp, they got it, denying The Magpies a third success against them at Wembley. Two of the players Wenger had so shrewdly acquired in the close season contrived the first goal. When Emmanuel Petit chipped the ball forward, Overmars, exploiting his electric speed, raced through a powerless Newcastle defence and shot home between the legs of Newcastle's Irish international keeper, Shay Given.

There were always fears that Newcastle, especially given the formidable presence of Alan Shearer at centre-forward, might hit back. And indeed, in the first half, David Seaman was called on to save from the elusive Temuri Ketsbaia. In the second half, an error by Martin Keown allowed Shearer to break clear, and it seemed odds on he would score, but luck now favoured the Gunners as it hadn't in their two previous Finals against Newcastle. Shearer duly shot, Seaman was beaten, but the ball rebounded from the post.

Another five minutes, and it was Nicolas Anelka, destined to score for club and country at Wembley, who raced through on to a pass from Ray Parlour, driving the ball into the corner of the goal. In his first full season, Arsene Wenger had done the double.

Now, he would make two more significant transfers, and let the veteran Ian Wright, all-time top scorer of Arsenal, move, like John Hartson before him, to West Ham. The gifted striker who arrived was the talented, nonchalant, long-legged, endlessly elusive, Nigerian international, Nwankwo Kanu. His very presence a major tribute to the skills of an American surgeon, who had operated with success on a damaged aorta in his heart. On his day, Nwankwo was capable of picking his path through a bevy of defenders, when there seemed no possible way past them. He'd be introduced, chiefly as a substitute, in the New Year.

The other major signing was that of the 21-year-old Swedish international Fredrik Ljungberg, from Halmstad. A right-footed midfielder, of energy and drive, he would figure largely on the left flank.

Games in the European Cup, for which Arsenal as Champions had automatically qualified, would be played not at Highbury but at Wembley, the Arsenal Stadium, being converted after the Taylor Report and the horrific disaster of Hillsborough, into an all-seater ground, with a capacity of just above 38,000. To play at Wembley made good commercial sense, yet the team never seemed happy there and Wenger would later say that he thought it had been a mistake. One argument adduced, however, that the team suffered from the fact that the Wembley pitch was bigger than Highbury's, seemed without real merit. Not least since it was sometimes accompanied by the assertion that in his time at Highbury, George Graham had had the pitch reduced in size. This he strongly denied to me, pointing out that in his opinion, a smaller pitch would help rather than hinder a technically good team, since there was so much less space in which to operate.

Be that as it may, Arsenal certainly made a bright beginning at Wembley, trouncing Manchester United there 3–0 in the Charity Shield, as they would again by the same score at Highbury in September with goals by Tony Adams, Anelka and Ljungberg, who came on as substitute for the young Frenchman. United's defence was bewilderingly porous, with their big, Dutch centre-back Jaap Stam sadly at sea; though he would improve. Tony Adams headed in a free kick with superabundant space and time, Anelka had raced through the middle for the second without challenge, and Ljungberg scored on his debut within six minutes of taking the field.

As for Arsenal, Wembley would turn out to be an ill-omened ground. Their European quest began with a disappointing 1–1 draw in Lens, a match they should have won. Panathinaikos, who had lost the 1971 European Cup Final there to Ajax, were the first visitors to Wembley; crowds of 73,000, rather than the mere and meagre 38,000 at Highbury, would attend; but they would see little to enthral them; at least from the displaced hosts. The Greek champions had actually beaten Dynamo Kiev, managed by the supremely modern and scientific Valeri Lobanovsky, but at Wembley they were merely pedestrian.

Yet Arsenal found it very hard to score against them, even with Anelka, who would flourish with France against Russia in Moscow, partnering Bergkamp. Indeed, it was Panathinaikos who shocked the Gunners by scoring first, and Arsenal had to thank their centre-backs, Tony Adams and Martin Keown, for the two headed goals which gave them such a narrow win.

Now Dynamo Kiev, who had themselves failed to beat Lens, besides going down in Greece, arrived at Highbury with a much admired attacking partnership of Andrei Shevchenko, the Ukrainian international centre-forward, fast, elusive, powerful and a fine finisher, and little Sergei Rebrov, a Belarus international who complemented him perfectly. Arsenal, without both their muscular Frenchmen, Patrick Vieira and Emmanuel Petit, were seriously weakened in midfield, where young Stephen Hughes and an anonymous Frenchman in Remi Garde, were simply overwhelmed. Ljungberg would have been a welcome reinforcement, but he was not eligible to play.

Had Wenger failed in the summer to buy sufficient reinforcements? The question had been and would be raised. Ironically, despite Dynamo's large superiority throughout most of the game, the Gunners went ahead with a splendid goal by Dennis Bergkamp. Dynamo duly equalised late on, and had a perfectly good goal disallowed for a non-existent offside, but the fact remained that for all Lobanovsky's multi-faceted regime, something had gone missing. Essentially the deadly finishing which, a season earlier, had characterised their destruction of Barcelona.

In Kiev, however, they were too good for an Arsenal team which, despite the presence of Petit and Vieira, was seriously below strength, and went down 3–1. Now it was essential to beat Lens, the surprise of the group, at Wembley. Though they had lost four of the players who had enabled them so unexpectedly to win the French Championship the previous season, Lens had risen superlatively above themselves. Where the Gunners had lost in Kiev, they had drawn. 'One must be humble to play for Lens', said their goalkeeper, Guillaume Warmuz. Their manager, Daniel Leclerc, was running a restaurant on a part-time basis when he was appointed to a managership previously held by Gerard Houllier, endearingly committed to a policy of attack.

And it worked. They actually defeated Arsenal – again a much-weakened Arsenal, deprived of Petit, Vieira and Bergkamp – 1–0; on their merits. It was an Arsenal team which never really came to life and which disgraced itself late in the game. First, Ray Parlour, who may well have been provoked, reacted by kicking his opponent in the back and was promptly sent off. When Lee Dixon heavily and gratuitously ran into the Lens striker, Tony Vairelles, it was the Frenchman, ludicrously, who would be sent off, though Dixon would later be suspended on television evidence.

So Arsenal were out of the money, yet they had the slight consolation of an extraordinary victory in Athens against Panathinaikos with what was largely a team composed of young reserves. A similar team at Highbury had lost 5–0 to the full Chelsea team in the League Cup. The only first teamers in the side in Athens were David Seaman, Steve Bould and Nicolas Anelka. Who, no doubt goaded by his brothers, had lamented that the two Dutch players, Dennis Bergkamp and Marc Overmars, were deliberately starving him of the ball.

Yet the young Gunners won, for what it was worth, in a canter, creating chance after chance. Teenagers such as Paolo Vernazza, a local boy and David Grindin, from France, rose above themselves. Anelka was outstanding. Three–one was the winning score.

During the ill-starred European series, Wenger had much to say about bad luck and indeed he had a strong point, in terms of so many crucial injuries to key players. But it was Arsenal, rather than Dynamo Kiev, who were lucky that night at Wembley, when Wenger insisted that the move which finally brought Rebrov's equaliser should never have developed, since the Gunners should have had a throw in. And if he might well have had a point in claiming that Lens' winning goal at Wembley should have been ruled offside, there was no doubt that on the night, Lens were palpably the better team. Accusations that he defended the indiscipline of his players in public but failed to deal with it in private were of some substance.

The victory in Athens was the more astonishing for the fact that far from it being a dead rubber for Panathinaikos, as it was for Arsenal, the Greeks still had a chance of reaching the next round. So Wenger was amply vindicated and critics like myself, who had insisted that to field such a side was the dire equivalent of fielding weak teams in the English League, an indictable offence, were amply refuted.

There was reason though to feel that being put out of European competition at so relatively early a stage released Arsenal's energies for domestic competition; and at least Bergkamp didn't have to fly to any fixtures there. In the Premier League and the FA Cup alike, the joust with Manchester United continued almost to the wire in both competitions.

Anelka, supremely effective against England at Wembley, continued to be endlessly dissident and resentful. He even complained of unfair treatment in the Press, whereby one handsome Arsenal win without him was duly emphasised in his disfavour, whereas a crushing 6–1 success at Middlesbrough where he was emphatically present passed without him receiving his due. Things just couldn't last, and off he would go at the end of the season for that £23 million to Real Madrid, where he was just as rebellious and intransigent, whatever his great gifts.

The New Year arrival of Kanu, a bold and successful gamble by Wenger, when Inter decided to let him go, gave further alternatives to the attack. A superb ball player, utterly calm and confident, Kanu could conjure or set up goals out of nowhere. But it was his unfamiliarity with a current convention, rather than an established law, of the game which provoked a curious controversy when in February Arsenal met Sheffield United at Highbury in the fifth round of the FA Cup, having previously beaten Preston and Wolves away.

The score in the second half was 1–1 when with Arsenal, largely on top, The Blades put the ball into touch to enable the United player Lee Morris, who was brought down by Gilles Grimandi in the box, to have treatment. Peter Jones, the referee, refused a penalty but Morris lay prone, needing treatment. When play resumed, Ray Parlour threw the ball towards a United player, such being the practice of the time. But Kanu, who'd been on the field only eight minutes as a substitute, clearly knew nothing of this.

So, to the shock and amazement of the United players, he trundled the ball down the right wing, finally crossing, for Overmars to knock it into the net. At this, to the outrage of the United players and their manager, Steve Bruce, Peter Jones signalled a goal, whereby the Gunners won 2–1. After the game, Arsene Wenger generously suggested that the game should be replayed. David Davies, then holding the fort over the weekend at Lancaster Gate, the FA headquarters, took it upon himself, as a senior executive, to decree that the game indeed should be replayed. Cheers all round for such manifestations of the Corinthian spirit, but with no regard to the hapless referee, who, in fact, had given the only legal, as opposed to moral, decision possible. For the custom of returning the ball in such circumstances to the team which had put it out, though more honoured in the observance than the breach, had no basis in the Laws of the Game. So poor Peter Jones was humiliated, Arsenal duly won the replay by the same 2–1 score, and things went on however anomalously from there. Kanu, who had cost £3.5 million, again came on as a substitute, though it was the two Dutchmen who scored the goals. But he'd win the Cup tie against Derby.

Having lost 3–1 at Villa Park in mid-December, the Gunners embarked on a coruscating spell of 19 unbeaten games. Kanu's sixth-round goal at Highbury against Derby came in the very last minute of the game. Could the double be done again?

Alas, defeat at Leeds in the League to a goal scored by Jimmy Floyd Hasselbaink, after an error by Nelsen Vivas, the Argentine left-back substituting Nigel Winterburn, put a spoke in the wheel, and when Manchester United were met at Old Trafford, the 1–1 draw was of little help to the Gunners, who'd eventually lose the League by a single point.

Manchester United would be played in the FA Cup semi-final, too; and the tie would go to a replay. Again, Vivas was a culprit, getting himself sent off in the first of the games, at Villa Park. The Gunners, however, held out for a goalless draw. In the replay, David Beckham scored for United, Dennis Bergkamp for the Gunners, United's Roy Keane was the one this time to be sent off; and Arsenal arguably threw the game away. A missed penalty in the final minute, and an untypically careless pass across field by Patrick Vieira, snapped up by Ryan Giggs, who set off on a glorious solo run to score the winner.

Before the first semi-final, Bergkamp spoke cogently about his career, and one tried with some difficulty to reconcile the polished, adroit, inventive attacker with the player who from time to time flared up into violence. Not least when, playing for the Gunners, he once kicked an opponent at Sunderland and elbowed another at West Ham. According to one Dutch journalist, this Jekyll and Hyde persona had much to do with Bergkamp's high regard for that inspired centre-forward, Marco Van Basten, who could always, in the vernacular, look after himself, but in a manner which happened on the blind side of referees. Bergkamp, whatever happened in the 1998 World Cup, wasn't always so subtle.

'I felt privileged that I played with Van Basten in Holland', Bergkamp said. 'You can learn a lot playing next to him. Role model may be a big word, but he was one of the players I looked up to, even when I was playing beside him.' But Johan Cruyff, who managed him at Ajax, was a still greater idol. 'For all that he knows and teaches, it's a blessing from Heaven for the youngsters to have him as manager. He let us do things on the field that other managers, because of the pressure, would never have allowed. He didn't care about what journalists, directors and the public said. He did what he thought was right. More than that, he has the formidable merit of going against the current. When everyone else worked on reinforcing the defence, Johan went for taking risks and for spectacular football.'

Chapter 14

WENGER'S
FOREIGN LEGION

Before Arsenal's potentially decisive league match at Old Trafford, I wrote in the *Sunday Times*:

> Nothing has succeeded for Arsenal like failure in Europe. Again spared the punishing demands of a European Cup campaign, they may well win the Premiership, but claims that they are a better side than Manchester United cannot be taken seriously. For a United team that has finally broken through in Europe, comparisons with Matt Busby's European Cup exploits are valid. But Arsenal have yet to get to European first base.
>
> It must be a sobering thought for Arsenal's manager, Arsene Wenger, that Dennis Bergkamp's fear of flying will again restrict his contribution to Europe next season.
>
> Though I have banged this drum before, Arsenal's abandonment of their great tradition of creative inside forwards – Charlie Buchan, Alex James, Jimmy Logie, Liam Brady, Paul Davis – is in itself regretrable but, more persuasively, removes much of their capacity for the unexpected. Today, Arsenal have two powerful French

international midfielders in Emmanuel Petit and Patrick Vieira, each talented, athletic, capable of driving their team on and dominating the opposition. Each seems to me, in the old terminology, essentially an attacking wing-half.

Petit, admittedly, constantly hits long, left-footed balls forward, and by the sheer law of averages, some of them will become through balls, or catch a defence on the turn. But we saw in the recent match against Derby County how Arsenal's present team can run on to the rocks of defensive opponents.

At the highest level of football, sheer surprise is invaluable. Bergkamp can supply it but the burden of scheming and scoring is vast. An Eyal Berkovic (the Israeli international) might make a difference. Indeed, with some sixty matches in daunting prospect, next season, should Arsenal survive in Europe, Wenger will have to reinforce his squad.

To give him his due, his expensive gamble in buying Kanu has proved supremely successful. I confess to being among the doubters when the lanky Nigerian arrived at Highbury. In the event, he has given Arsenal new options and dimensions in attack, himself the very essence of surprise. It was puzzling that George Graham should have damned his defence for the goal Kanu scored at Tottenham – a marvellous flick over his head to deceive Luke Young, the young Spurs centre-back, followed by an irresistible drive.

But there is still a lack of depth in Arsenal's squad; the likes of Grimandi, Garde, Vivas and Boa Morte are really supporting cast. Injury will always rule out key players and on top of that, there is Arsenal's abysmal disciplinary record. Vieira, Petit and Bergkamp have each been sent off more than once, depriving Arsenal of their essential presence. The volatile behaviour of Arsenal's players on the field is so strangely at odds with Wenger's own, professional, detached demeanour. Until he can get to grips with the problem it will continue to threaten the team's success.

It also remains to be seen whether Arsenal can even keep Petit, whose recent diatribes may have more substance than those of the perpetual malcontent Nicolas Anelka, a striker of great potential and seemingly infinite grievance. . . .

Wenger knows as well as anybody that his present back four is a triumph of willpower over seniority, but how long can it last? Matthew Upson, who came so young and expensively from Luton Town, shows promise, but reinforcement is surely mandatory.

Where are the graduates of Liam Brady's no-expense spared youth scheme? We have seen little homegrown talent convincing enough to give the likes of Lee Dixon and Nigel Winterburn reason to pause, in hope rather than expectation, before the team sheet which has listed their names for a decade.

Unless Brady starts giving Wenger the kind of young talent that has been a cornerstone of Alex Ferguson's success at Old Trafford, reinforcements will continue to cost money. And when it comes to transfer market funds Arsenal are inevitably worried by the fact that their admirable stadium can now hold only 38,000. . . .

Nothing, of course, creates demand more than a winning team and Wenger knows that, title or no title, the foundations at Highbury are not so secure as might be imagined.

Arsenal, however, would boldly take the bit between their teeth and build their splendid new 60,000 capacity stadium and build it, remarkably, within a stone's throw of the Arsenal Stadium itself.

How ironic it seems, a full decade later, to read Wenger's eulogy of Tony Adams, late in the 1998–99 season. 'I am sure Tony will manage Arsenal one day. I have discussed the future with him and want him to go on playing for as long as possible. Captains and winners like him do not come around very often. But when he decides it is all over as a player, the natural thing would be for him to become manager of Arsenal.' But when Adams did retire, Wenger was emphatically still manager of Arsenal. As for Adams, he did become, with no great success, manager of Wycombe Wanderers then, later, manager of Portsmouth. There he was given a wretched hand to play, two of his key players just being sold, and those players he had committing abysmal errors, leading to his abrupt demise. It was bruited that he had 'lost the dressing room'. Pompey's erratic goalkeeper, David James, was especially critical. But there was surely a case for believing that the dressing room had lost Adams.

Arsenal, it should be said, were not universally beloved around this era. Least of all in France, where their aggressive policy of snapping up juvenile talent, a policy they'd also pursue in Spain, was much resented. Certainly by Paris Saint Germain, who had lost Anelka, though, in good time, they would even get him back, and by the very President of the French League, Noel Le Graet. Incensed by Arsenal's seizing of the 15-year-old striker, Jérémie Aliadière, a member of the French national academy, and rated the best of his age group. Still a schoolboy, he was signed to a contract for no less than seven years, worth £1.4 million.

How any club could be so sure of so young a player's future as to give him so long a contract was surely debatable. And in fact Aliadière, for all his undoubted talent, would never really break through at Arsenal, being lent to various clubs, finally settling down with Middlesbrough; for whom, in the old Italian fashion of 'the immutable law of the ex', he scored in 2008 a decisive goal against the Gunners. 'He is a schoolboy,' declared Le Graet, 'coached through our national system who has gone to the highest bidder. Parents and teachers have got to ask questions about the auction of a lad of 15.'

Aliadière's father defended the deal, but Le Graet inveighed, 'This is shameful. There are boundaries to correct behaviour and they have been passed with Wenger. Let's get things straight. There is no doubt that Wenger has someone on his payroll hanging around our main football school in the Clairefontaine.'

Wenger replied, 'My plan is to assemble about 15 youngsters of high quality who will take two or three years to be part of the professional group. We are working towards tomorrow's team and Jérémie is part of that plan.' The Gunners in fact did have an expert scout combing the Continent, just as, all those years ago, they had shrewd scouts in Wales and Ireland. The policy would reach its apotheosis when Cesc Fabregas as a 16-year-old was spirited away from Barcelona, to become perhaps the outstanding Arsenal player of his time.

Before the new 1999–2000 season opened, controversy was in the air. A young right-back called Jason Crowe, hardly destined to pull up trees after his sale to Portsmouth, lamented that he wasn't given a chance, even when Lee Dixon, the long-serving incumbent, was absent. Wenger preferred to give the role to one of his French recruits in Gilles Grimandi or Remi Garde, though neither of these was a full-back by profession. The most unkindest cut of all came when Wenger decided to spend £1.8 million on the Dynamo Kiev and Ukraine right-back, Oleg alias 'The Horse' Luzhny, who had impressed when playing against the Gunners in the European Cup. In the event, Luznhy would never show such form at Highbury, but for Crowe, it was clear evidence that he had no future with the Gunners.

'If there was an English manager at Arsenal,' said Crowe, 'a lot more of the players who have come through the ranks would have played.'

But Crowe's case was far less persuasive than that of the promising young midfielder, Stephen Hughes, who agreed to go on loan for three months to Fulham, then a division lower down. And Hughes, who would never quite fulfil that promise away from Highbury, was at that point the only recent British product of the Arsenal youth scheme – which once produced so much British talent – to have made any impact.

But as Geordie Armstrong, such a prominent exemplar of it himself, and by this time in charge of the club's reserves, put it, 'If my generation of young players had been playing now, a lot of us might not have got a chance. There is so much more competition for places and so much more pressure on managers for success. They are not going to take a chance on young players unless they are exceptional. . . . If we had an exceptional teenager, I'm sure Arsene Wenger would play him. But because of the competition I can see more young players being unemployed than there used to be.'

Now, I wrote, 'Millions are being spent, but to what effect' on the youth programme. Liam Brady was in charge, on a long term deal, Don Howe came back to the club as the head youth coach. Brady, for his part, said that he had some fine young prospects to come through but didn't want to name them since it would hardly be in their interest.

Meanwhile, Wenger, that summer, spent lavishly on foreign stars, his greatest coup being the £10 million acquisition of Thierry Henry, his former protégé at Monaco, from Juventus. That figure was hardly negligible, though indeed it would be by comparison with the grotesque amount of money thrown around in years to come. Henry had emerged as an outside-right, as such figuring occasionally in the French team which won the 1998 World Cup, though never as a first choice.

He had become unsettled at Monaco, together with his friend and fellow star turn, in attack, David Trezeguet. Between them, they gave a very hard time to the hapless Jean Tigana, once such a star himself, when he managed Monaco, sometimes provocatively reading newspapers, while he attempted to give a team talk. An infuriated club President had no alternative but to sell them both, yet Henry found it difficult to settle in Turin and was happy to rejoin Wenger in London; where his old mentor promptly converted him to centre-forward with prolific results.

Tall, strong, electrically fast, a superb ball player, even if heading was never his forte, Henry would excel at Highbury; beating the aggregate goal-scoring record of Ian Wright. His forays to the left flank would prove especially effective. And he developed an almost mystical affinity with the Arsenal Stadium. 'There's something about the whole stadium when you're there, something happens to me. It just happens when I leave the car park to go to the dressing room past the Clock End, and you turn right in front of the benches. When I walk, it's just strange, I feel like I remember some games that I played, some stuff that I did. Some good moments, some bad moments, it's difficult to describe. You have no one in the stadium, but I can still hear some stuff in my head. I know it's not the most modern stadium ever, but there's something you can't describe, you need to play, it's always something special about Highbury.'

Later, he would pay great tribute to his manager. 'Wenger', he said, 'has revolutionised the club and its structures. I am happy with my life in London and love Arsenal. Most of all, I am happy working with Arsene Wenger. I owe him so much.'

To give that intransigent *enfant terrible*, Nicolas Anelka, his due before he left, criss-crossing with Henry, he paid similar tribute to Wenger and what he had learned with him. Having refused to turn up for the ceremony at which his Young Player of the Year trophy was to be presented, he declared that his problem was not with the club but with the Press, hence his defiant absence.

Two other summer signings were of the notable Croatian opportunist Davor Suker, and of the fluently adventurous Brazilian left-back Silvinho, who appeared to be qualified, under the rules then in force, by Portuguese citizenship. He would continue to play with brio until well into the following season, when confusion about his exact national status led to an abrupt departure for Spain, where he went on to play resourcefully for a decade to come.

Waiting in the wings was a young left-back who did indeed seem to vindicate Arsenal's youth system; Ashley Cole, an exuberant overlapper who would play many years for England, though later, in the colours of Chelsea, after an embittered departure over his hyperbolic claims for more money.

In the Charity Shield, the Gunners duly beat Manchester United again, but when United came to Highbury for Arsenal's second home League match of the season, there was no Petit to oppose Roy Keane, who scored twice to give United a 2–1 win, Arsenal's first home League defeat for 20 months. Petit indeed would be missing, injured, for many weeks to come.

Once again, the Gunners played their home European Cup ties at Wembley and again, with decidedly mixed results. Opening in Florence, with Dennis Bergkamp present – he had made the long journey by car – they held Fiorentina to a goalless draw. Then to Wembley, where they beat AIK of Sweden 3–1, with Bergkamp in majestic form. Holding Barcelona to a draw in the Nou Camp was a more than satisfactory performance especially after going in a careless goal down at the break. The word was that Tony Adams then effectively shouted the odds in the dressing room and the team revived to draw 1–1.

But at Wembley the wheels came off, and although it's true that Barcelona went ahead with a cynically acquired penalty, Arsenal's ageing back four simply hadn't the pace to keep up with such as the flying Dutchman, Patrick Kluivert. That opening goal came when Philippe Cocu flung himself theatrically across Tony Adams' outstretched leg and gained the dubious spot kick; which was converted. When Barça scored their third goal in a 4–2 victory, it was because Lee Dixon played the ball straight across his own goal, but that was because he was trying in vain to cope with Kluivert's electric speed. Barça indeed could well have had a couple of other goals.

So Fiorentina had to be beaten at Wembley for Arsenal to stay afloat, and the omens looked good. Indeed they would have won in Florence had Nwankwo Kanu not missed a penalty. Fiorentina at that moment looked a team in trouble; they came to Wembley in what seemed a state of disarray, floundering in Serie A, their veteran manager, Giovanni Trapattoni, anything but optimistic. Yet at Wembley, they won, thanks to a goal achieved through the dynamism of their prolific Argentine centre-forward Gabriel 'Bati-Gol' Batistuta, his powerful burst and ferocious shot from the right exploiting the failings of Arsenal's elderly defence.

The tortuous dispositions of UEFA and their cups meant that the Gunners were not wholly out of Europe. Bizarrely, teams knocked out of the European Cup could rise from the dead and take part in the UEFA Cup; a tournament already well under way. So Arsenal would go all the way to a torrid Final in Copenhagen, notable for the appalling violence of the warring fans.

Meanwhile, Arsenal had to contend with the six-match ban imposed on Patrick Vieira, for spitting in the face of West Ham's Neil Ruddock when he was expelled from the field at Upton Park. Vieira had already been in conflict late in August when Manchester United came to Highbury, having headbutted his embattled rival, Roy Keane. He wasn't booked, and Wenger strongly defended him. 'Patrick did not provoke the incident,' he insisted, 'and it is important for me to protect him from his aggressors. I always feel he is the target for the other teams to pull down and he gets no real protection. He suffered some bad tackles early on Sunday and everyone was after him. . . . It happens so often with Patrick. Other teams try to get him in trouble. They know how important he is. Obviously they are not going to try to get rid of bad players.'

But in the same month, a year ahead, Wenger would have his own disciplinary problems, which in due course – though after several months – he would properly and belatedly surmount. Thereby exposing the inconsistencies of FA disciplinary policy.

Arsenal would make an early, surprising exit from the FA Cup against Leicester City, whom they'd easily beaten 3–0 in the League. In the fourth round, they were held to a draw first at Highbury then at Filbert Street without a goal being scored. Leicester won on penalties after extra time.

For the second of three consecutive seasons, Arsenal would take a more than respectable second place in the Premier League, drawing 1–1 at Old Trafford but then surprisingly and expensively losing away to modest Bradford City, such unlikely and transient a presence in the senior league. A 1–0 home defeat by Liverpool made the Premier League still more chimerical, Patrick Vieira remarking, 'We have to improve or we could end up with nothing.'

They did, in the event, end up in the UEFA Cup Final, making strong progress en route. Two French teams were conquered, Nantes initially being brushed aside 3–0 at Highbury, with both Vieira and Petit in central midfield and Nigel Winterburn adventurously scoring the second goal. In the semi-final, Arsenal would meet a Lens team radically different from the one which had won at Wembley in that torrid affair.

The second of Arsenal's opponents were the Spaniards of Deportivo La Coruna, and the 5–1 score somewhat exaggerated the difference between the teams. Lee Dixon, with a header, and Thierry Henry had scored before half time but the whole profile of the game would change when Deportivo's inspiration, the costly Brazilian, Djalminha, was sent off soon after scoring from a penalty after clashing with Grimandi. The punishment seemed debatable, but Deportivo proceeded to fall apart, Arsenal adding three more goals, two of them by Thierry Henry. But the *pièce de resistance* was a goal by Kanu, to rival the one he had so remarkably scored at Chelsea in a 3–2 victory, picking his way from the left past man after man. Now, he casually dummied the Deportivo keeper, Jacques Songo, trotting on to find the empty net.

Arsenal lost 2–1 in Coruna, but sailed through on aggregate to meet Werder Bremen in the fifth round. Werder Bremen were beaten 2–0 at Highbury without excessive hardship, and in the return in Germany. Ray Parlour excelled himself. In irresistible form, he scored three times and Arsenal won 4–2, the only disappointment being the contentious expulsion of Thierry Henry, who thus missed the first leg at Highbury of the semi-final versus Lens.

Early in the French season, the much changed Lens team seemed in crisis, but a new manager had steadied the ship and they'd knocked out strong Spanish opposition in Atletico Madrid and Celta Vigo. Lacking the pace of Henry, the Gunners still squeezed through 1–0 at Highbury, with a goal by Dennis Bergkamp, scored after just a couple of minutes following a fine through ball from Emmanuel Petit. Henry and Adams were back for the return which the Gunners won 2–1. This put them in the Copenhagen Final against the Turks of Galatasaray.

Not that the return leg in Lens had been any kind of cakewalk. Late in the second half with the score at 1–1, despite the Gunners' dominance, a lucky rebound found Pascal Nouma, who'd already headed the equaliser against a culpable defence, all alone in front of goal. He could only shoot past the post to David Seaman's relief. 'If that had gone in,' admitted Lee Dixon, 'it would have been the Alamo.'

Henry, with a glorious spin and shot, scored for Arsenal. Overmars, when belatedly brought on for Ljungberg, no true left-winger, made a substantial difference. David Seaman proclaimed, 'The spirit is really good and the lads are settled down now. What's happening is, we're getting a pattern here.'

Before the ill-omened Final in Denmark, there were already fears that violence might ensue, as it so disastrously did. This because of the aftermath of the brutal and gratuitous stabbing to death of two harm-less, middle-aged Leeds United fans before the first leg of the semi-final, in Istanbul. Galatasaray did their best to keep the thugs away, by raising the price of match tickets sold to a whopping $250 each, but it proved an inadequate palliative. Ironically, both Galatasaray and Arsenal had reached the Final only after their elimination from the senior European Champions League.

And before the Final, in Cockney parlance, it 'went off'. The fear that English hooligans unconnected with the Gunners might run riot proved all too fully born out. There was vicious fighting in the centre of Copenhagen before the match, in which Arsenal failed to find a rhythm. Martin Keown missed their clearest chance when he shot over the bar in the second half, and the game dragged on to extra time and penalties. Of these, Suker and Vieira both hit the woodwork, and the last word went to a former Spurs player (shades of Paris and Nayim!), who scored the decisive penalty. It was exploited by the Romanian international, Gheorghe Popescu. So the season ended without a trophy.

The summer of 2000 saw significant buying and selling. Both Emmanuel Petit, somewhat reluctantly, it seemed, and Marc Overmars were transferred to Barcelona. Robert Pires, the French international winger, came from Marseilles, where he had been increasingly unhappy. He would provide skill and flair on either flank, but, arguably, his most telling contribution would come in Arsenal's famously unbeaten League season, when his histrionic dive in the penalty box, at the Clock End, gained the Gunners a fallacious penalty against Portsmouth, enabling them to save an early season game which they would otherwise have lost.

Lauren, a versatile Cameroon international, adept at right-back or in midfield, arrived from Mallorca. Late in August came the formidable French international striker, Sylvain Wiltord, from Bordeaux, for £13 million. In the New Year, the Brazilian international midfielder Edu would finally come from the Corinthians of Sao Paolo, having the previous July been turned back by immigration officials at Heathrow airport for producing a false Portuguese passport. On his second attempt to enter England, his passport proved perfectly valid, making one wonder why he hadn't produced it in the first place. But he would make minimal appearances in what remained of the season.

In August, after a 1–0 defeat at Sunderland, Arsene Wenger was involved in a disciplinary fiasco which took many months to be finally and properly resolved in his favour. Wenger was accused of having run down the tunnel and laid hands on the fourth official, one Paul Taylor. In October, an FA disciplinary committee which, in the words of *The Times* correspondent, had made him the victim and 'gone mad', suspended him from the dug out for 12 matches, and fined him £100,000. It seemed not without significance that this arcane verdict was emitted just when England were due to play a World Cup qualifier against Finland, and Press and public attention might be thought likely to be elsewhere. 'It is as if I killed somebody', said an outraged Wenger, who immediately appealed.

He and Arsenal had to wait until the following February before that appeal, a two-day affair, took place. In the meantime, it had been known since the previous December that Paul Taylor was hardly an immaculate official, it having emerged that in October 2000, he had made obscene remarks to a Notts County player, Sean Farrell, while refereeing a match at Meadow Lane; thus potentially undermining his evidence against Wenger. Who, it appeared, had done no more than place a hand on Taylor while trying to end a confrontation between Thierry Henry and a Sunderland player, Darren Williams. 'I just wanted to avoid any violence after the game,' explained Wenger, 'and sometimes you get yourself involved in a situation you shouldn't do.'

Grudgingly, refusing to dismiss the absurd accusations entirely, the FA committee commuted Wenger's sentence to a reprimand and a fine the tenth of the one originally imposed. It still seemed an unjust punishment, but perhaps it was inevitable the FA couldn't bear to concede that they'd been so utterly wrong.

That Wenger, who as he pointed out had never been suspended throughout his career till then, should be suspended at all was bewildering. That Vieira, sent off at Sunderland somewhat contro-versially, would subsequently be sent off again soon afterwards at home to Liverpool – beaten for the first time in six years – and thus suspended for five matches, was by then hardly astonishing. Yet even without his powerful presence, and with Petit now in Barcelona, the Gunners embarked on an unbeaten run of a dozen games. And Vieira himself, just before his enforced departure scored twice at Highbury, in a roller coaster 5–3 win against Charlton.

The *pièce de resistance* was a 1–0 win at home against the old enemy, Manchester United. Henry, who had scored a remarkable 26 goals the previous season – and modestly doubted he would do as much again – was the scorer of the coruscating winner: flicking the ball up, spinning, then curling his volley past the keeper, Fabien Barthez. Henry himself, however, was restrained: 'We've got an important result against a big team, but you can't just base a whole season on beating Manchester United.' How right he was. By mid-January, the Gunners were 13 points behind United and this time, they weren't destined to make up the distance. Indeed, a 6–1 beating at Old Trafford would make very sure of that.

In the European Cup, or Champions League so called, the Gunners now abandoned Wembley, to play their home games at Highbury. They began their group games in Prague where they prevailed with a spectacular goal by Silvinho whose Portuguese status, alas, would ultimately prove less impregnable than Edu's. Next, at home, came Shakhtar Donetsk, from Ukraine. A defence lacking the still resilient Tony Adams let through two goals in just three minutes. Wiltord, arriving soon after the second of them, made it 1–2 and in the second half, the unlikely saviour and scorer was centre-back Martin Keown, with two goals, to make it 3–2.

The next visitors were Lazio who had spent huge sums of money during the summer on reinforcements. Somewhat surprisingly, however, the Gunners had less trouble with them than with Shakhtar, not least thanks to the return of Tony Adams. Bergkamp, in majestic form, created a goal in each half for Freddie Ljungberg. In Rome, the Gunners forced a 1–1 draw, Pires scoring his first goal for the club, where he was soon very happy.

Interviewing Pires some years later – despite his several seasons in London, it had to be, to the amusement of Thierry Henry, in French – he told me: 'I was very, very surprised to see the supporters so close to the pitch. I found this fantastic because, you know, before coming to Highbury, Thierry Henry, Patrick Vieira and Emmanuel Petit had told me, Robert, you'll see at Highbury, when you play here, you are going to explode. And it's there every time I go out on the field. It's always a gift. I never thought beforehand of a "quarter" like Highbury. That I would find a stadium in the middle of all those houses, those apartments.

'When I look at Olympique Marseille, it's always the same circus, and the players' daily life is always as difficult. Arsenal is the opposite of that ambience. It's enough to see the relaxed atmosphere which exists at the London Colney training ground. All you see there are people from the club, it's super functional. You arrive knowing for sure that you are going to work calmly. That goes with the philosophy of Arsene Wenger. When their club goes through a bad patch, the fans show their support with a lot of energy. At Highbury, if you are behind at half time, the crowd applauds you the moment play resumes.'

Well, not always, as Pires himself would find in mid-January when, held to a 1–1 draw at home by Chelsea, in which he himself had scored, the Gunners at the end were booed off the field. They were hardly helped by Seaman's extended absence through injury, Alex Manninger, though he would enjoy a long European career, never giving full confidence, least of all on the crosses. While the Latvian centre-back, Igor Stepanovs, was hardly one of Wenger's successful acquisitions, too often to be found badly wanting, not least in the late February rout at Old Trafford.

Almost as hard to understand was Wenger's persistence with the ever abrasive Gilles Grimandi. When Arsenal, in the second phase of the European Cup, were held to a 2–2 draw at Highbury by Bayern Munich, after going a couple of goals ahead, Grimandi, in the words of a reporter, 'appeared to jab an elbow at the excellent Jens Jeremies, then fell like some child's Christmas toy. . . . Grimandi epitomises the ill-discipline which permeates this otherwise talented squad.'

Mid-January, even before the debacle at Old Trafford, found Wenger lamenting, 'It will be very difficult for us to catch them [Manchester United] because the months of November and December were catastrophic for us. The danger is that the gap can get wider than the eighteen points from last season. Our pride must not let that happen. I am already embarrassed by the gap.'

Results in that period were, in fact, haphazard. Thus, Newcastle United were thrashed 5–0 at Highbury with a domestic hat trick, this time, by Ray Parlour, but at Anfield, Liverpool brushed the Gunners aside, 4–0. On Boxing Day, Leicester City were thrashed 6–1 at Highbury with a hat trick, this time, by Thierry Henry. The most spectacular of those goals, however, went to Tony Adams, running half the length of the field before scoring.

In the European Cup, Arsenal had already qualified from their group when they travelled to Donetsk, where Shakhtar beat them 3–0, but the wound was not mortal. Visits to the old Soviet Union continued to be ill-starred since, in the first of their second stage matches, they went down in Moscow 4–1 to Spartak. In early December, the formidable Bayern Munich team came to Highbury, including that old nemesis of the Gunners, Stefan Effenberg, who would again be a doughty opponent.

There were others up front for Bayern in the shape of the elusive Brazilian, Giovane Elder and the insidious Hasan Salihamidzic, ably supplied from midfield by the experienced German international, Mehmet Scholl. Two excellent goals by Kanu and Henry seemed to have given Arsenal a solid cushion but, as the game wore on, so Bayern began to exploit the failings of an Arsenal defence in which Luzhny stood in for Keown. Athough Ashley Cole, still only 19, and thus bringing down sharply the average age of the back four, had a resilient game, after which he said, though admitting he had tired in the latter phases, 'With four games to go, it's not the end.' A sentiment with which Uli Hoeness, once a star turn in the Bayern attack, but now the general manager, concurred: 'Even with one point, Arsenal have a good chance.' But the longer the game went on, the more the Gunners, in the words of the same official, 'lost their equilibrium', and even Wenger – who disclosed before the game that he would have managed Bayern had Monaco only been disposed to release him – had strong words with the fourth official. It ended 2–2.

With January came the FA Cup which, for Arsenal, would so nearly, had the luck been with them, become a Cup of consolation. Carlisle United were beaten 1–0 away in the third round, Queens Park Rangers 4–0 at Loftus Road in the fourth, with David Seaman, blessedly back at last, keeping goal against his former club. Then came Chelsea, who, banishing memories of the pedestrian draw in the League, were beaten 3–1 at Highbury, all three goals going to the French strikers, a penalty for Thierry Henry, two for Sylvain Wiltord, who'd already justified Wenger's confidence that he would 'come good' in time with a formidable show at Loftus Road.

Three days after the FA Cup victory over Chelsea, Lyon came to Highbury, in the European Cup. In neither case could the Gunners call on their first choice centre-backs, Adams and Keown, in each case Luzhny was pressed into service alongside makeshift partners. In such circumstances, a 1–1 home draw with a talented Lyon team was perhaps as much as could be expected. Bergkamp scored for Arsenal and, somewhat ironically, the Brazilian Edmilson – on whom Wenger had passed after Edu's passport fiasco, got the goal for Lyon.

Disaster followed four days later at Old Trafford, where the defence, now with Luzhny and Stepanovs struggling in the centre, was simply overwhelmed. 'Everything went wrong with us today', admitted Wenger, who accused his defence of playing like a youth team. But surely there were extenuating circumstances. And indeed, the Gunners quickly recovered by beating, at Highbury, 1–0, a Spartak Moscow team plainly still to recover from its long winter break. It had previously lost 3–0 to Bayern Munich. Henry's vital goal arrived eight minutes from the end.

At home to Blackburn in the sixth round of the FA Cup, Arsenal cruised through 3–0 despite using Henry and Vieira only as substitutes. Tony Adams scored another of his goals. So to the return with Bayern in Munich. It was lost to a single goal by the ever insidious Elber. At full time there were still another four minutes to play in the Moscow match between Spartak and Lyon. The score was 1–1 and Lyon needed a win to pip Arsenal at the post. They didn't get it and the Gunners were through to the quarter-finals. 'It was like ninety minutes for me', said a relieved Wenger.

The quarter-finals would be against Spain's resilient Valencia, who had rebuilt to impressive purpose after parting with three of their leading players. But they still could boast the clever little inside-forward, if one might use the term, Pablo Amar and his Argentine compatriot, that formidable centre-back Ayala; however susceptible he might be in World Cup finals to Michael Owen. The centre-forward was John Carew, the giant, black Norwegian international, who, a full eight years later, would still be playing successfully with Aston Villa.

At Highbury, Valencia had the better of the first half, and led 1–0 at the break. In the second half, however, the Gunners brought Wiltord on for Ljungberg and scored twice within as many minutes, through Henry and Parlour. Chances were missed.

Once again, the opponents in the FA Cup semi-final would be the local rivals, Spurs, though this time the match would be played not at Wembley, but far away from North London at Old Trafford. The tall, versatile Irishman, Gary Docherty, gave Tottenham the lead, but subsequently Spurs lost their dominating centre-back, Sol Campbell – destined so soon to make a bitterly contentious move to Highbury – and Arsenal, increasingly in command, equalised in the 33rd minute when Patrick Vieira broke through, and scored the winner in the second half.

The return European quarter-final in Valencia largely saw the Gunners with their backs to the wall. For 75 minutes they held out for the draw which would take them through, but then Carew soared above Tony Adams to head the winner, and so Valencia came through on their away goal.

The FA Cup Final would be at Cardiff, while work on refurbishing Wembley made the gestation of an elephant seem a trivial affair. Liverpool would be the opposition, as they had been in the past. Would things have been different had Arsenal been awarded the penalty they should have had after a mere seven minutes? When Thierry Henry went clear, he coolly eluded the Liverpool keeper, Sander Westerveld, and shot. On the line, standing beside the post, it seemed plain that Liverpool's Swiss international defender, Stephan Henchoz, blocked the ball with his arm. The referee may have been unsighted, the linesman had a perfectly clear view, but saw nothing wrong. So Liverpool survived until the 72nd minute, when at last Freddie Ljungberg scored.

Alas, it wasn't enough. Too quick for the ageing legs of the Arsenal defence, the elusive young Michael Owen scored twice to take the Cup to Liverpool. First, exploiting a free kick by Gary McAllister, he beat David Seaman for the equaliser. Some five minutes later, the 88th, he skipped away from Lee Dixon and Tony Adams to score the winner.

There were still a couple of League games to be played. A draw at Newcastle consolidated second place, but the final game was lost at Southampton, prompting me to ask Arsene Wenger whether he had any plans to bring back Emmanuel Petit, so manifestly missed all season, to Highbury. The response was evasive. Petit, as it transpired, didn't return.

Owen's winning goals in Cardiff showed how badly Arsenal needed stiffening in central defence, where the heroes were understandably tired. So it was that, to the outrage of Tottenham Hotspur and their vitriolic supporters, Wenger persuaded the Spurs and England centre-back Sol Campbell to traverse the few miles from White Hart Lane to Highbury in the summer of 2001. To add insult to injury, the existence of the Bosman rule meant that he came for nothing. Tottenham's ultras hanged his effigy. Over seven years later, enough rancour remained for them to abuse him viciously when he was playing for Portsmouth against Spurs at Fratton Park; as a result of which a number of the miscreants, photographed by the police, were arrested.

'This team has huge potential,' Wenger had said, at the end of the previous season, 'but we need some extra quality to take us that step further. I know who I want, and we have enough time to sort it all out.' Campbell would go a long way towards doing that, but by bleak contrast, Francis Jeffers, who cost £9 million more than the dominating Campbell, proved to be one of Wenger's least inspired acquisitions. What was widely known at the time of his arrival from Everton was that Jeffers, a young striker of undoubted promise, was wretchedly prone to injury. True, a proportion of the fee depended on the number of appearances. But as these were a mere half dozen in that season, after which he returned for a time to Goodison on loan, he was hardly a bargain.

There were two other, major signings in the shape of the Dutch international left sided midfielder, Giovanni Van Bronckhorst, and, from Ipswich Town a young goalkeeper with what seemed a bright future in Richard Wright. In the event, he'd prove disappointingly fallible. Perhaps the worst place to err was at White Hart Lane in the classic North London derby, where Wright let through an embarrassing goal and Arsenal drew a match they should have won. But Campbell, in resplendent form, was quite unworried by the abuse of fans who so recently had been his fervent admirers. His dominant presence had much to do with the fact that the Premier League would be regained.

Not for the last time, Wenger had to deal in the summer with the unsettled Patrick Vieira, something which would become a close season theme. Signed from Milan for £3.5 million, Vieira by now was said to be worth 10 times that, and certainly the merits were in some measure Arsenal's.

Vieira's ambition was reportedly to win the European Cup and to become European Footballer of the Year, ambitions he felt he was unlikely to achieve at Arsenal, where major stars from abroad had not been bought. Wenger himself acknowledged that until the Gunners moved into their new stadium, they couldn't generate the money from a Highbury reduced to its 38,000 capacity which the likes of Old Trafford, now hugely enlarged, could command.

'It is not a question of going into conflict', Wenger said. 'But I have responsibilities to the club and Patrick has duties. The irresponsible thing would be to say to him, okay, leave and we will take the money. Whatever feelings you might have for an individual, the overall interest is more important; that of other players, the club and its fans. For that reason, the law must be respected. It is pointless to imagine what might happen if he left. He is irreplaceable.' How strange and remarkable to think that when Vieira did leave, a player so much younger, so much smaller and less physically powerful in Cesc Fabregas would justify all Wenger's hopes for him, and make a waning Vieira no more than a memory.

'This,' said Wenger, 'is an affair that has affected the supporters deep down. . . . Patrick is more than a player. He is somebody who symbolises the link between the team and the fans.' As evidenced, in fact, by the long familiar adulatory choruses of, 'He comes from Senegal, he plays for Arsenal.'

Wenger pursued, 'He is the umbilical cord and that is why the fans are suffering today. Letting him go would be a sign of lack of ambition. . . . Arsenal are not ready to separate themselves from a player like him. . . . I do not see why we should let the best go. It shows he is not wasting his time with us. He has gone up a level in every one of his last four seasons. So, on a sporting front, I do not think it is in his best interests to leave Arsenal.' Vieira stayed: *pour le moment*.

A League season which would end so victoriously had an uneven beginning, the defence much missing the presence, for a number of matches, of Sol Campbell himself and David Seaman, who, after the disappointment of Wright, was successfully understudied by the homegrown keeper, Stuart Taylor. But an extraordinary 4–2 home defeat by Charlton Athletic, who hadn't won at Highbury for 46 years – Wright in goal, no Campbell – evoked memories of the previous season's roller coaster game in which the Gunners had prevailed, 5–3. This after a run of eight unbeaten League games.

In their European Cup group, the Gunners made an uneasy start. They lost in Mallorca to a team which was hardly one of Spain's finest. The only goal came from a penalty conceded by Ashley Cole, who was sent off. Next, the Germans of Schalke 04 came to Highbury, and went down narrowly, 3–2. When Ljungberg and Henry gave the Gunners a 2–0 lead within a couple of minutes of the first half, it seemed all would be plain sailing. Just before the break, Schalke reduced it to 2–1, just after it, Henry made it 3–1 from a penalty. But Schalke scored again through their incisive Belgian international striker, Emile M'Penza, and the score would then remain at 3–2. The Gunners' group form continued to be inconsistent. In Athens, they went down 1–0 to Panathinaikos, then beat them 2–1 at Highbury, thanks to a couple of goals from Thierry Henry, but hardly with any ease. But when Mallorca came to Highbury, they were beaten 3–1 – Pires, Bergkamp and Henry – before Arsenal lost in Gelsenkirchen to Schalke. But they qualified for the next stage.

In this, they made an ill-starred beginning, losing 2–0 away to Deportivo La Coruna, a team looking very different from the one which had gone down at Highbury, 5–1, in 2000. But in late November and early December, things looked up. Manchester United, now the traditional rivals, had in fact been beaten earlier in November 4–0 at Highbury in the League Cup, but it wasn't the real thing. By then, major clubs no longer deigned to put out their first teams in an increasingly marginalised tournament. Arsenal did deploy Sylvain Wiltord, who scored a hat trick, and Kanu, who got the other, up front, but the team was full of secondary players. And when United came to Highbury for the League game, Wiltord was not among those present.

It was a memorably successful debut in goal for Stuart Taylor. Though the Gunners made the early running, it was United who went ahead, through Paul Scholes. Three minutes after half time, however, Ljungberg lobbed over the head of United's famously eccentric French keeper, Fabien Barthez, who seemed to be unsettled by the goal. To the joy of the crowd, he began to take strange risks, which, in the closing minutes, his fellow Frenchman Thierry Henry duly exploited, his two goals giving the Gunners an important 3–1 win.

Now Juventus arrived at Highbury with a glittering side, in the European Cup. Marcello Lippi, Juve's celebrated manager, destined to win the 2006 World Cup, expressed the view that Arsenal, in the first 10 minutes, were *intimorito*, intimidated. Seemingly a favourite word of his, since I write this soon after, in February 2009, he brought his Italian team to the Emirates Stadium, where it lost 2–0 to Brazil, asserting that the *azzurri* had at first been *intimoriti*. In fact Juventus, in those early stages, looked as if they would take the Gunners apart, especially with Alessandro Del Piero, a major star, playing havoc with the right flank of the Arsenal defence.

Yet oddly enough, it was the shaky form of Juve's much admired international keeper, Gianluigi Buffon, rather than the form of the tyro Taylor, which tipped the balance. Taylor cost Arsenal nothing, Buffon cost Juve the record fee for a keeper of £32 million. But it was Buffon who dropped a shot by Vieira which he should have held, enabling Ljungberg to knock the ball into the net. Thereafter, the electric pace and insidious free kicks of Henry, Ljungberg's opportunism, Vieira's dynamism, the sublime dexterity of Dennis Bergkamp, combined in Arsenal's finest display of that season.

Henry was far too quick and clever for his compatriot, Lillian Thuram. Bergkamp was at his most inspirational. The cool skill with which he set up Ljungberg for his second goal was incredible. Confronted by a posse of defenders, he calmly kept the ball where a lesser player would have lost it, and took 11 touches before Ljungberg arrived to score with great finesse. Thierry Henry, with a 25-yard drive, scored the Gunners' other goal.

Yet in a season which was crowned with another triumphant domestic double, the Gunners would find the European Cup, or whatever it now called itself, no more than a frustrating anticlimax.

Domestically, there was one strange hiccough at Highbury when a week before Christmas, though Pires put Arsenal ahead at home to Newcastle United, the Magpies proceeded to score three times and win. Bergkamp came on only as a substitute that day, but he and the Gunners would have their 2–0 revenge at St James' Park, the following March, when Bergkamp, that consummate artist, scored a goal worthy of comparison with the one he had scored against Argentina, four years earlier.

Receiving the ball with his back to goal, from Pires, he somehow contrived to send the ball spinning past one side of his marker, meeting it on the other, and shooting home. Only one week after that, the Gunners found themselves back at St James' Park in the FA Cup sixth round, though they had to be content with a 1–1 draw. In the return at Highbury, however, they came through comfortably enough, 3–0, Pires, Campbell and Bergkamp the scorers. Alas, Pires was so badly hurt that he was forced to miss the rest of the season. Arsenal, nevertheless, were unbeaten in their last 21 Premier League matches.

In Europe, things went less well, though the resumption of the tournament began brightly enough with a 1–1 draw away to Bayer

Leverkusen, followed by a 4–1 victory over them at Highbury, in which Bergkamp, back after injury, simply excelled. While Vieira quite overplayed his celebrated midfield opponent, Michael Ballack, Bergkamp contributed another of his spectacular goals, Arsenal's fourth, on 83 minutes. Once again, he controlled the ball with his back to goal, this time turning sharply to lob over Butt, the keeper, from 20 yards. But Deportivo La Coruna maintained their Indian sign over the Gunners, arriving at Highbury two weeks later, for another 2–0 success.

Meanwhile, steady progress was made in the FA Cup. Watford were beaten 4–2 at Highbury in the third round, then came Liverpool: with whom Arsenal, hard on the heels of defeat by Newcastle, had enjoyed a 2–1 success at Anfield, though reduced to 10 men. Liverpool drew the return League game at Highbury, but the Gunners beat them 1–0 in the Cup, through Bergkamp's goal. Meanwhile, things looked up defensively when David Seaman was, at last, able to return in late February.

The FA Cup semi-final was played at Old Trafford against Middlesbrough; a hard-earned win, secured only through a Boro own goal. The Final would be an all-London affair, albeit at Cardiff, against Chelsea. Seaman would be between the Arsenal posts, a disappointment for Richard Wright who, regaining form, had played in all the other Cup ties.

Meanwhile, who should be opposing Arsenal in central midfield but Emmanuel Petit, back to London from Barcelona. He, indeed, it was who started the 57th minute movement which ended with David Seaman leaping to turn over a shot from Eidur Gudjohnsen. Twice previously in the 17th minute Seaman had been obliged to save, first a left-footer from Graeme Le Saux which he lost then retrieved, then when he went full length to a drive from Frank Lampard, snapping up a careless free kick by Patrick Vieira. A second, second-half, error by Vieira brought Seaman into action again to thwart Jimmy Floyd Hasselbaink. This, just one minute after Chelsea's Carlo Cudicini had got one hand in full flight to a shot by Thierry Henry.

In a match which didn't ignite for a while, the Gunners ultimately went ahead on the break in what you might call traditional fashion, when Tony Adams, back since March and crowning his Arsenal career, began a move, finding Wiltord. He in turn found Ray Parlour some 40 yards out. Advancing another 15, Parlour let fly a ferocious drive which sped past Cudicini. Twenty minutes remained and the Gunners scored again when Ljungberg netted a memorable solo goal, picking up a ball on the left, avoiding Chelsea's dominating centre-back, John Terry, and swerving his shot past Cudicini.

That was half the double, but the League was still to be won and it duly was. It was especially satisfying to make sure of it by winning at Old Trafford against Manchester United, with a second half goal by Wiltord, after Barthez had blocked a shot by Ljungberg. The success was celebrated at Highbury in the final game, when a team including several reserves, but with Henry and Bergkamp getting three goals up front between them, had a 4–3 win over Everton. The other goal went, some kind of consolation, to the unlucky Jeffers. Two more proud feathers in Arsene Wenger's cap.

He did, however, give hostages to fortune when, on the eve of 2002–03, he declared that the Gunners might go through it unbeaten. In the event they didn't, though they would accomplish the feat the season after; albeit with the assistance of that gratuitous Portsmouth penalty. New faces arrived, notably that of the Brazilian midfield stalwart and World Cup winner, Gilberto Silva. Kolo Toure, the Ivory Coast international defender, was another recruit, as was, somewhat more controversially, for £2.1 million, the 6 foot 5 inch (1.95m) stopper Pascal Cygan, from Lille, to whom Wenger would subsequently cleave through thick and, more often, alas, thin. Tony Adams had gone at last, but Sol Campbell and Martin Keown were still formidably there.

In the curtain raiser at Cardiff, now called the Community Shield for some reason, Gilberto Silva it was who got the only goal of the match against Liverpool. Just as he would, in a mere 22 seconds, score what was then the fastest goal in the history of the Champions League in Eindhoven against PSV, in the Gunners' second group game.

Their first at Highbury, with Bergkamp in buoyant form, was a 2–0 home win against Borussia Dortmund, Bergkamp himself getting the first goal. In the League, Sylvain Wiltord scored half a dozen goals in as many games, and the unbeaten sequence was extended to 24 games. Only to come down with a crash at Everton. No shame, really, to succumbing to a spectacular goal from the precocious teenager, Wayne Rooney.

Three days later came another disappointment, this time at home. Auxerre, guided by the wily Guy Roux, who had built up the French club from humble beginnings, came to London and won 2–1. An Arsenal team which stuttered and struggled so palpably missed the inventive presence of Dennis Bergkamp. All very well for Wenger to blame the reaction to the Goodison defeat and the alleged weariness: the Gunners looked disjointed and unimaginative, Guy Roux himself admitted he had eventually been surprised by the long ball tactics of a team which he had associated with a far more sophisticated approach, in its passing. Against Borussia, Bergkamp had reigned supreme and had inspired a fine performance by Freddie Ljungberg, on the left. Compare and contrast with Ljungberg's dull display against Auxerre, when he constantly wandered from the left flank to scant effect. Thierry Henry, who often made dynamic use of that space, this time scarcely used it. In fact, his two best runs were made on the right.

Was the exhaustion of Henry and his compatriots, Wiltord and Vieira, in the legs or in the mind? One way and another, Arsenal survived into the next European stage; this despite losing in Dortmund and being held 0–0 at Highbury by PSV Eindhoven, a match in which Bergkamp came on only as a substitute for Henry while Jeffers, who started the game, was substituted by Wiltord. Cygan had now become the centre-back preferred, but he would never inspire great confidence.

Things looked up, however, in November, with three Premier League wins in a row, and an inspiriting 3–1 European victory in the first game of the second stage against Roma in the Stadio Olimpico where Thierry Henry, in devastating form, scored all three goals in the 3–1 success. But in the next European game before the winter break, there was another frustrating goalless draw at Highbury, this time against an all too familiar foe in Valencia.

The New Year saw Arsenal fall just short in the League, but striding to a second consecutive victory in the FA Cup. Jeffers, in parenthesis, showed in a number of appearances that, with a little better luck, he might indeed have justified the fee Wenger paid for him. In February, coming on, as he several times did, as a substitute against Fulham at Highbury, he inspired a very hard-earned victory, 2–1.

Manchester United, perennial rivals, would be met three times. In the League, United beat the Gunners 2–0 in an important game at Old Trafford, in December. But in the fifth round of the Cup, again at Old Trafford, Edu and Wiltord scored the goals in a 2–0 victory. But when United came to Highbury for the return League match, one which was essential for the Gunners to win, they drew 2–2, both goals by Henry, Arsenal reduced when Sol Campbell was expelled.

Arsenal, in those days, still had a hoodoo over Chelsea, which Chelsea themselves enjoyed for years over Spurs, though Chelsea managed to draw 2–2 at Highbury in the FA Cup sixth round where Jeffers scored Arsenal's first. But the Gunners won comfortably 3–1 at Stamford Bridge. So, back to Old Trafford but this time for the semi-final against a vigorous young Sheffield United team whose luck would be atrocious. For the only goal came when their midfielder, Michael Tonge, was heavily obstructed and felled not by an Arsenal opponent but . . . by a clumsy referee, in the shape of Graham Poll, later famous in a World Cup tournament for his 'Three Card Trick'. There was thus no redress for The Blades as Arsenal swept upfield to score. A narrow victory, preserved only by a glorious save by David Seaman.

In the Champions League, soon blessedly to abandon the redundant second mini league stage of its competition, Arsenal met Ajax at Highbury, days after their Cup victory at Old Trafford. On the eve of the game, Wenger disclosed that he could have become the Arsenal manager a year before he actually did. 'I nearly came to Arsenal when they sacked George Graham in 1995,' he said. 'I met the board, but at that stage it was still regarded as a very conservative sort of club, very conscious of its history and traditions. So they appointed Bruce Rioch instead. Even when they approached me a second time the following year and I said that I would take the job, I knew there would be resistance. After all, there was no history of success for foreign coaches when I arrived.'

He was already, he said, in love with English football; ever since the first game he saw between Liverpool and Manchester United. 'I could feel straight away that football had been created here. There was a different quality of passion and the way the supporters lived the match was distinct from anywhere else in Europe.'

But now, when it came again to Europe, anticlimax was in store. When after a mere five minutes Bergkamp sent Sylvain Wiltord away to score, all seemed set fair. Twelve minutes later, however, the Dutch international midfielder Nigel De Jong, destined in time to join Manchester City from Hamburg, equalised, and so the score stayed.

It was legitimate to expect victory in the next European game at home to Roma, so clearly and comfortably beaten at the Olimpico, but, yet again, the Gunners found it hard to defeat foreign opposition at home. Despite the fact that the ever volatile Francesco Totti, a Roman himself and his team's talisman in attack, was sent off, Arsenal could only draw 1–1. It was thus essential that they did not lose at Valencia, their Spanish nemesis, but lose they did, 2–1, and out of the tournament again they went.

The FA Cup was consolation. Once more, the Final was in Cardiff, the opposition a moderate Southampton team. Ten goals in their last two League games, half a dozen of them at home against Southampton themselves at Highbury – a hat trick for the turbulent but talented young right-winger, Jermaine Pennant – meant they took second place in the League. They would get only one goal at Cardiff, on 38 minutes, but it was enough to win. Parlour to Henry, Henry to Bergkamp, he in turn to Ljungberg, whose shot bounced off the Southampton centre-back, Lundevkam, to Robert Pires, who scored from close range. A fitting last Arsenal game for David Seaman, who observed, 'We were so determined to win the game today after our disappointment in the League and we knew we would be under pressure until the last minute from Southampton. It may not have been a great Final, but we are lifting the trophy and that's all that matters.'

Sol Campbell, serving a four match suspension after his elbowing of Manchester United's Ole Gunnar Solskjaer at Highbury, missed the Cup Final, as did Patrick Vieira, and Campbell to Wenger's ire was in trouble again at Wembley in the August Community Shield game; once more against United. Djemba-Djemba, the United midfielder, caught him with a high boot on the thigh, Campbell kicked back at him. An infuriated Wenger insisted that Campbell was within his rights and that Djemba-Djemba's challenge was 'obscene'. All too predictably, Alex Ferguson saw it the other way around. 'He's just trying to save Campbell. There's always an excuse at Arsenal.' Wenger, for his part, agreed that Campbell should not have reacted, but said that he had been unable to walk for two days.

All this, however, was as nothing to the tumultuous sequel when the following month the teams met in the League at Old Trafford. No goals, but infinite commotion. Six Arsenal players were charged by the FA. When United's high scoring Dutch centre-forward, Ruud Van Nistelrooy – Wenger's *bête noire* – missed a penalty, Martin Keown jeered in his face and later struck him on the back of the head. Wenger, in fierce defensive mood, still more so than he had been after the Community Shield match, lashed furiously about him. He impugned the FA, the media, Sky Television, offered an apology of a sort, but hardly seemed repentant.

Van Nistelrooy, he inveighed, had brought things on himself with his behaviour during the Old Trafford Cup tie the previous February. 'There is a history between Lauren and Van Nistelrooy from the Cup game and I will give you the tape of what he did to Keown, what he did to Ljungberg.' He demanded, 'Do you really think Martin Keown doesn't realise what happened? He knows he shouldn't have done it.' He would, he insisted, demand personal hearings for all six of his players who had been impugned.

They included the big German international keeper, Jens Lehmann, who had joined the Gunners during the summer, a player no stranger to controversy, a player with a very low boiling point, known in the Bundesliga for his outbursts. Arsenal's board, meanwhile, took three days to emit a brief and guarded statement. But when push came to shove in October, the Arsenal board left Wenger high and dry, pleading guilty to nine charges, evidently fearful of the consequences if they fought the case.

At least Arsenal, on this occasion, escaped defeat and were able to move on to what would prove their unbeaten League season. Yet in their previous home match against Portsmouth, they were surely fortunate to dodge defeat. It was a game which I reported. Pompey, on a roasting afternoon, had deservedly gone into the lead with an expert header from Teddy Sheringham. After 38 minutes, however, Arsenal obtained their highly debatable penalty. Robert Pires, advancing on goal, was challenged by the Pompey defender Dejan Stefanovic, and fell dramatically. The referee, Alan Wiley, gave a penalty. To add insult to injury, he enabled Thierry Henry to take it twice before he scored. It seemed a dubious decision.

Harry Redknapp, Pompey's ever-voluble manager, was in no doubt about it. 'We were in control and playing very well. Then the referee gets a very important penalty decision wrong. It was never a penalty. Pires trod on Dejan Stefanovic's foot and threw himself down. I turned to my Chairman and said, "Pires will get a yellow card for that for diving," but the referee gave a penalty. It was a terrible, terrible decision. And I've seen so many this season. I thought up to that stage we were far the better team. We went one up, deservedly so, and it brought them back into the game. It's happening every week. I know refs don't do it on purpose but terrible, terrible penalty decisions are turning too many matches.'

Between those games, Arsenal had what might be described as another of their European *nuits blanches* against an Inter team which had certainly not been pulling up trees in Italy, yet cruised through 3–0 against a Gunners side which, on paper at least, looked strong and talented. Patrick Vieira played in that game, but suspension hung over him. Yet Wenger surely had a point when he'd assert that Vieira was more sinned against than sinning. Certainly at Old Trafford he was the victim of perverse refereeing, sent off for a phantom foul on Van Nistelrooy, which was at the root of what happened so explosively later in the game. But in due course the Gunners would take spectacular revenge on Inter.

The Euro-domestic dichotomy continued. Without Vieira, Campbell and Ljungberg, the Gunners still managed to draw with Lokomotiv Moscow 0–0. Back again in Eastern Europe, however, they went down 2–1 to Dynamo Kiev. Meanwhile in England, game after League game was won. Liverpool were beaten at fortress Anfield ('This Is Anfield' were the minatory words inscribed above the exit from the match tunnel), Leeds thrashed at Elland Road. In between these games, Chelsea, still striving in vain to beat Arsenal, went down 2–1 at Highbury, with Edu and Dennis Bergkamp – still not making the long European trips – scoring.

Late January saw the arrival of one more of Wenger's shrewd acquisitions; the 20-year-old José Antonio Reyes, from Seville. An accomplished, swift and versatile striker, he would settle eventually on the left wing. The fans took to him quickly, with choruses of 'José Antonio, José Antonio!' to the tune of '*La Donna è mobile*'. Yet he never really settled in London and would, in time, return to Spain.

Playing for Arsenal's virtual reserve team in the semi-final of the League Cup at Middlesbrough, he contrived to put through his own goal. More significantly, however, in mid-February he equalised against Chelsea at Highbury, in the fifth round of the FA Cup, darting in from the right wing, rather than the left, to score with a spectacular 25-yard shot. Seven minutes later, he scored again and when he eventually was substituted, it was to an ovation. Six days later the Gunners beat

Chelsea by the same 2–1 score in the League at Stamford Bridge. All five February League games were won and victory at Wolverhampton established a new club record of 24 unbeaten games.

Meanwhile progress had been made in that tantalising mirage, the European Champions Cup (or League if you prefer it). Notably and sensationally at San Siro in November where Inter, 3–0 winners at Highbury, were dramatically beaten 5–1. A triumph which followed the defeat at Highbury of Dynamo Kiev, thanks to a goal headed by of all people Ashley Cole near the final whistle.

At San Siro, the extraordinary success was made the more remarkable by the fact that neither Patrick Vieira nor Dennis Bergkamp, for whom it was another country too far, was playing. By way of compensation, however, Nwankwo Kanu made a somewhat rare appearance. The first half hardly suggested the deluge of goals which followed in the second. Thierry Henry scored for the Gunners, Christian Vieri, Inter's centre-forward, equalised with a shot which deflected in off Sol Campbell. Four minutes after the break, Ljungberg gave Arsenal a 2–1 lead and Inter seemed demoralised.

The last five minutes saw them sensationally fall apart, with the Gunners scoring no fewer than three times. Henry and Edu took the lead to 4–1, and the final nail in Inter's coffin was struck home by young Jérémie Aliadière, now 20, on this occasion seeming to justify all the hopes put in him, perhaps burdensomely, when he came as a teenager. He broke through with splendid pace and control to make the final score 5–1. No English team had beaten Inter at San Siro since season 1960–61, in the shape of Birmingham City. A 2–0 home win over Lokomotiv Moscow, Pires and Ljungberg scoring, put them into the next phase, the following February. Celta Vigo were beaten in both ties.

Heartening news came when it emerged that Arsenal had the money in place at last to build their vast, spectacular new stadium, nearby at Ashburton Grove, on the site of a gigantic council rubbish tip. This, to the disappointment and the eventual estrangement of David Dein, who was variously reported as having preferred the venue to have been at Kings Cross, or even Wembley. The chief power at Highbury by then, however, and for years to come, was the wealthy diamond magnate, Danny Fiszman, to whom Dein had sold so many of his shares. That the new stadium in its grandeur should be so close to the old one seemed an astonishing development. And it would go up with exemplary speed.

In the FA Cup, the Gunners demolished Leeds United 4–1 at Elland Road, and Middlesbrough by the same score, at Highbury. In the sixth round, they demolished Portsmouth 5–1 at Fratton Park and 'even the ranks of Tuscany could scarce forebear to cheer'; the home supporters applauded Vieira, Henry and Ljungberg when substituted. But things skidded to a halt in the semi-final at Villa Park soon after United, the Gunners' only pursuers in the League, had forced a 1–1 draw at Highbury. Now, in the Cup, they prevailed with the one goal of the match, scored by Paul Scholes.

The quarter-finals of the European Cup saw Arsenal drawn in an all-London tie against Chelsea, whom they had already beaten three times that season. Not this time, however. Chelsea, for so long frustrated by the Gunners, now held them at Stamford Bridge and beat them at Highbury. Would things have been different were it not for an impetuous blunder by Jens Lehmann at Chelsea? Rushing pell mell and quite superfluously out of the penalty box, to his right, he kicked the ball against Chelsea's Icelandic attacker, Eidur Gudjohnsen, who, with the keeper stranded, put it into the empty net. In the second leg at Highbury, Pires having equalised at The Bridge, the odds were on Arsenal, who deployed Reyes up front beside Henry. And a minute from half time, they combined to give the Gunners the lead. But in the second half, Reyes' point-blank header would not prove enough. Chelsea reshuffled, putting on the clever Danish right-winger, Jesper Gronkjaer, equalising through Frank Lampard. Three minutes from time, the unlikely scorer of Chelsea's winner was their overlapping left-back Wayne Bridge, who shot from the edge of the box.

In the Premier League, the unbeaten run continued, with Thierry Henry increasingly prolific; a hat trick at home to Liverpool, four more goals there against Leeds. Once again the title was clinched at White Hart Lane, but this time rather less dramatically. The Gunners went 2–0 up against Spurs who hit back to make it a 2–2 draw, but the one point was enough. A 2–1 win at home to Leicester completed this extraordinary unbeaten League season, whatever the European disappointment.

In the summer of 2004, Martin Keown and Ray Parlour left Highbury. There were two notable arrivals. Robin Van Persie came with the reputation of being both talented and turbulent; he had reportedly been involved in heated incidents, not always his own fault, in his native Holland. But the arrival of a tall, strong, quick player with clever control and a fierce left foot was always going to be of benefit, and Van Persie would become a force in the team for years to come. If, in his first season, there was a shamefully violent incident, it would be one in which he himself was the innocent victim.

After the final whistle of the winning FA Cup semi-final against Blackburn Rovers in Cardiff, when he had just scored the second of his goals, within four minutes, he was painfully and disgracefully charged in the back by Blackburn's Andy Todd.

The other new face was that of the busy French midfielder Matthieu Flamini, who would steadily grow more influential until Wenger reluctantly lost him to Milan on what might be called a Bosman free, in the summer of 2008.

The Community Shield match at Wembley to open the new 2004–05 season saw Manchester United encouragingly beaten 3–1; but two months later at Old Trafford it would be another, dismal story. Now the splendidly precocious Spanish teenager, Cesc Fabregas, whipped away from an outraged Barcelona, was staking his place in the team, a player of technical accomplishment; speedy, intelligent and progressive, one of the most exciting talents to grace Highbury for many years.

In the Champions League, the Gunners came through the first stage somewhat ingloriously. Only an own goal by the big Brazilian centre-back, Alex, gave them a laborious win at home to PSV Eindhoven, after which they could only draw 1–1 against Rosenberg in Norway. Equally disappointing were draws in Athens and at Highbury against familiar foes in Panathinaikos. But when in mid-October the Gunners had outplayed Aston Villa at home, winning 3–1, their former centre-half David O'Leary, now Villa's manager, was lavish in his praise: 'It's the best team that has been at Highbury for me. They've got a wonderful team to go into a wonderful new stadium. They're big, they're strong, they're quick, they're fit. Everything about them is good to watch.'

But hardly when it came soon afterwards to Old Trafford, defeat in the Gunners' fatal 49th match after the long, unbeaten run; one more of those United–Arsenal affairs which degenerated into violence and chaos. Certainly the Gunners had cause to be aggrieved, not least by the flaccid refereeing of Mike Riley. He gave no protection to José Antonio Reyes from the rough treatment he got from the United right-back, Gary Neville, and he awarded United the highly contentious penalty which arguably transformed the game, on 72 minutes. Ruud Van Nistelrooy, still a red rag to Wenger's bull, converted the kick, given after Wayne Rooney sprawled over Sol Campbell's leg. Previously the Dutch striker had been guilty of a dreadful foul on Ashley Cole, which brought him a three-match suspension.

Arsenal, by general opinion, had looked the better team, but they fell away in the last minutes, and Rooney, served by Scholes and Alan Smith, scored United's second goal. The Gunners – shades of what happened to Kevin Keegan's ill-fated Newcastle – were 11 points ahead, but all too quickly, that lead melted away and once again, United would leave them runners-up.

The game may have been over, but not the ill-feeling and aggression. In the tunnel, United's manager, Alex Ferguson, had soup and pizza thrown over his suit though he generously made little of it. He and Wenger, ever the best of enemies, duly exchanged broadsides. Wenger accused, 'Riley decided the game, like we know he can do at Old Trafford. We were robbed. We got the usual penalty awarded against us, whenever we come to Manchester we come to Manchester United and they're in difficulty.' To which Ferguson rejoined, 'If you're brought down in the penalty box it's a penalty kick; I think. The guy has obviously got a mental problem with Ruud Van Nistelrooy, for some reason. It's always Ruud Van Nistelrooy.'

'I can assure you that I have no mental problem with Van Nistelrooy', retorted Wenger. He would add,

> I love football. I respect Manchester United and the referees. So I don't have any malicious ideas before games. But Manchester United did not play with the spirit I like football to be played in. I cannot agree, despite the result, with the way they approached the game. We didn't play well but I didn't think there was anything in our approach which was wrong, or immoral. That is what I stand for.
>
> The spirit of the game was not right from the first minute. I cannot accept that when Reyes gets kicked off the pitch, the referee accepts it. Arsenal have shown restraint and I simply don't know if we were not committed enough to go above United's physical intimidation. At half time, we thought Reyes would not be able to run out any more, as well as Ashley Cole, who will miss an entire week's training.

I am not responsible for the way United approach the game. I am here to answer for our behaviour and our attitude. . . .

I don't know about food throwing. I did not see if something was thrown. You will have to ask someone else, because I don't know. The whole story is invented; nothing happened after the game at all. . . . why should I know what happened to Ferguson's shirt? Ferguson should know and he should say so. . . .

The way the game was turned, you feel robbed. You cannot say you feel happy because the referee made a genuine and honest mistake. I did say Riley decided the game from nowhere like he can do at United. But when he has given eight penalties in eight games you cannot say it is unusual.

In December, Wenger was fined £15,000 and severely censured by the FA for his tirade. He was predictably unrepentant. Nor did he show up at the tribunal. 'Was it an expensive sentence?' he demanded. 'No. I said what I had to say and nothing has changed. I knew it would cost some money. It is down to the FA to spend the money now. I take my responsibilities seriously after the game and I say what I feel I want to say. If you cheat with the rules I cannot find another word. In England it's a word you cannot say. I don't know why.'

One's old doubts about the lack of invention in midfield had still not been assuaged. So much depended on the skills and subtleties of Dennis Bergkamp, yet he was also expected to score goals. On those rare occasions when he was off form – or, in the case of distant European venues, simply absent – the wheels could fail to turn. As indeed happened in the home draw with Panathinaikos, when, with Bergkamp below par, the Gunners laboured to a draw. And Cygan scored a spectacular own goal at the Clock End.

Subsequently, Arsenal scraped a draw in Eindhoven against PSV, but ended buoyantly at Highbury by thrashing Rosenberg, who had held them in Norway, 5–1. One of the goals was scored by the exuberant 17-year-old Fabregas, though Wenger expressed fears of playing him too often. So the second stage had been reached, though it would not be survived. Yet the omens were not good. The embarrassing memory of Cygan's devastatingly headed own goal lingered, while Lehmann's sometimes erratic goalkeeping was another concern. He had let through a plainly avoidable goal in Athens. Meanwhile, late in the year, another keeper, Manuel Almunia, had arrived from Spain.

Initially, he looked somewhat suspect on the crosses but he would improve and eventually establish himself as first choice.

Progress was made in the FA Cup, but not without difficulty. Indeed, when Stoke City came to Highbury in the third round, it looked, for an alarming while, that the Gunners might lose their first FA Cup tie at Highbury for eight years. A goal behind, Arsenal eventually saved the day through scores by Reyes and Van Persie. Two more home draws followed, a comfortable 2–0 victory over Wolves, followed by an anything but comfortable draw with the habitual Cup opponents, Sheffield United. It was a fractious game in which Bergkamp's expulsion reduced the Gunners to 10 men. Pires, however, put Arsenal ahead, only for the young Swiss centre-back, Philippe Senderos, to handle in the box, enabling The Blades to equalise from the resulting penalty.

Nor could Arsenal win the replay at Bramall Lane, after extra time. The match went to penalties and this time Almunia, adept 'on the line', was the saviour in every sense, keeping out two of the spot kicks, enabling Arsenal to survive. In the sixth round, the Gunners won at Bolton 1–0 through Ljungberg's third minute goal, while in the semi-final, played at Cardiff, Van Persie's goals were decisive, despite inspired goalkeeping by Blackburn's big American keeper, Brad Friedel. Van Persie certainly deserved better than to end the game flat on the turf after Todd's spiteful assault.

As for the European Champions League, the mirage tantalisingly remained, though who could have foretold the defensive ineptitude which so untypically betrayed the Gunners in Munich, against a rampant Bayern? Even the usually reliable Toure, so successfully converted to centre-back, blundered wretchedly on one of the three goals by a Bayern team which had, until then, scarcely looked a match for the tremendous teams of the 1970s. Though Wenger, putting the best face on the rout, declared, 'We lost to one of the best teams that we have played in the last few years in Bayern.'

Arsenal, having gone down 3–1 in Munich, managed to win the return at Highbury 1–0 with a superb goal by Thierry Henry, but out they still went. Questions were raised. Should £13 million Sylvain Wiltord, however, dissident, have been allowed to leave gratis for Lyon, where he was frequently scoring goals? What of Reyes, in poor form in the second leg game, who'd been duped by a Spanish journalist over the phone to say that he would willingly go back to Spain?

It was, however, hardly Wenger's fault if the essential Dennis Bergkamp had lost form. Nor that he lacked the injured Sol Campbell for so important a tie. Nor that Patrick Vieira, himself no longer such a dominant force, should summer by summer play brinkmanship over a possible move to Real Madrid. And it was known that Vieira and Lauren had had heated words on the team coach after the disappointing earlier draw at Rosenberg, while Ashley Cole was greedily set on joining Chelsea, scorning his £55,000 weekly wage.

'During Wenger's eight years at Highbury,' I wrote in the *Sunday Times*, 'Arsenal have achieved great things domestically. But Europe is the litmus test and they have failed it so often that there is a danger of their being seen now as just a big fish in a small pond.'

In the FA Cup Final in Cardiff, against Manchester United, they may ultimately have won, but there was nothing big about their success. Mysteriously, after two League defeats by United, Wenger seemed to have decided that discretion was the better part of valour. Even so, to deploy a now ageing, one-paced, Dennis Bergkamp in unsplendid isolation up front was inexplicable. True, Henry and Campbell were both missing, injured, but by way of compensation, Philippe Senderos had an exceptional game in central defence. This was as well, given that the full-backs Lauren and Cole were having a tricky time against Wayne Rooney and Cristiano Ronaldo.

Jens Lehmann, in resilient form this time, repelled a shot from Wayne Rooney with his feet, Rooney hit the post, Ljungberg resourcefully headed out a point-blank header by Van Nistelrooy, Arsenal's nemesis, from under the bar. Not till the last minutes of normal time was Roy Carroll, the United keeper, obliged to make a notable flying save, from a free kick by Robin Van Persie, who surprisingly in the circumstances wasn't brought on until the 86th minute. And there was still time for Lehmann to frustrate Paul Scholes' shot on the turn from just a few yards out.

So, perhaps according to Arsenal's cautious strategy, it came to penalties. Van Nistelrooy put away the first spot kick for United, Lauren replied for Arsenal. But when Paul Scholes, usually so reliable, took the next penalty for United, Lehmann, surpassing himself, dived down to his right, to save. So at 4–4 it came down to Patrick Vieira, soon at last to be on his way, though not to Real Madrid but Juventus, to take the decisive penalty. He duly scored and the Cup, however ingloriously, was Arsenal's.

Now in the new 2005–06 season Arsenal finally faced life without Vieira; he had gone to Turin and Juventus. How could he be replaced, and by whom? Standing in the August sunshine on the famously sloping Barnet Underhill pitch, after a pre-season friendly, Wenger seemed amiably unworried. It was suggested to him that Matthieu Flamini, who in fact could play impressively at left-back, though a right-footed midfielder, or the 17-year-old *wünderkind* Cesc Fabregas might be the answer. He conceded they could be in the running, though had they, you wondered, the weight, in every sense?

'Don't forget,' Wenger told us, 'when Patrick Vieira arrived, nobody knew him and he made his mark.' Indeed he did, but he might well have been expected to, having cost £10 million from Milan, even if they'd made little use of him after signing him from Cannes. Wenger pursued, 'When a player like that leaves he can be replaced not necessarily by somebody who has a big name but someone who wants to make a name.' How emphatically right he turned out to be, though one wonders if even he at the time was thinking that Fabregas could so coruscatingly fill the breach; in so different a way. On show that day at Barnet was a talented new winger in Alexander Hleb, a Belarus international signed from VFB Stuttgart. 'Hleb,' I wrote, 'looks a quick-witted, versatile fellow with clever feet.'

This, of course, would be the last season that the Gunners played at Highbury where they'd been established since 1913, rising from obscurity to years of innovation and dominance. An ambitious jamboree was planned for the last game of the season, then it would be goodbye to a stadium famed not merely for the achievements of the team but for the aesthetic splendour of the West and East stands, so far ahead of their time when they were built and still a cynosure. But with Manchester United ever expanding Old Trafford, without being forced to move from their site, and eventually reaching a colossal capacity of 75,000, it was imperative and inevitable that Arsenal should move. And this they did with remarkable speed, initiative and architectural adventure. There were those who regretted the new stadium would be commercially called The Emirates, after its airline sponsors, but the colossal expense inevitably demanded a sponsor.

Looking back to 1913, it was decided that the team for this last season wear the deeper red jerseys worn by the then still Woolwich Arsenal team which began in the new stadium. A 52-metre (170 feet) mural was painted on the walls of Arsenal Station; which of course had so been named at the behest of Herbert Chapman. 'It's wonderful,' said Thierry Henry, 'that the Arsenal community has come together to depict Highbury's history and express in this way what the Arsenal Stadium means to them.' In due time, the stands would be converted into flats.

The season, by contrast with those of the recent past, was domestically arid, but rewarding in Europe. Chelsea, with Roman Abramovich's Russian oligarch billions behind them, left the Gunners standing in the League, in which they finished fourth, while Bolton, almost literally, bundled them out of the FA Cup in the fourth round. Nor did the Gunners make a specially auspicious start in Europe. Faced by the modest Swiss of Thun, at Highbury, the score was 1–1 until injury time, when Dennis Bergkamp came to the rescue with a goal arguably better than Arsenal's performance itself.

Things would improve. Sparta were beaten 2–0 in Prague and the second of the goals Thierry Henry scored that evening broke Ian Wright's aggregate scoring record for the Gunners. Shortly before Arsenal comfortably beat Sparta 3–0 in the Highbury return, Wenger locked horns with Chelsea's flamboyant and often provocative manager, Jose Mourinho. It did at least make a change from the bitter words which had flown between Wenger and Alex Ferguson the previous season.

Mourinho had been provoked when Wenger suggested, after poor results by Chelsea against Everton and Charlton, that 'a little bit of the belief' had left Chelsea, who, at that stage, were 14 points ahead of the Gunners in the League; making Wenger's periodic insistence that Chelsea could still be caught seem a form of wish fulfilment. Mourinho's response, however, was excessive though not untypical. 'I think he is one of these people who is a voyeur. He likes to watch other people. There are some guys who, when they are at home, they have a big telescope to see what happens in other families.' Wenger was predictably incensed. Less predictable was his odd tirade at the Press Conference which followed the win against Sparta, when asked about his relations with Mourinho.

His response was to tell us that he was tired of reporters hiding behind newspaper headlines for which they claimed no responsibility. He was contemplating 'action'. He seemed incensed at having been reported as having called Mourinho stupid, which seemed a mild enough response to being called a voyeur. What Wenger actually had said was that with success, some people became stupid and said stupid things. To whom could he conceivably, and quite justifiably, have been referring but Mourinho? A strange episode.

To rub salt in the wound, Chelsea came to Highbury in December and won 2–0, thus spoiling Arsenal's previous 100 per cent record. The only other team to beat them at home was also in a London derby, West Ham United on 1 February; largely because Sol Campbell, evidently suffering a nervous crisis, and having ineptly and untypically given away first half goals, simply walked out of the stadium, let alone off the field, at half time.

In Europe, things looked up in the spring. Real Madrid, in the first knock-out round of the competition, seemed in prospect a daunting obstacle, but the Gunners surmounted it in style. At the Bernabeu, they were worth far more than the 1–0 win given them by Thierry Henry's brisk opportunism. Emmanuel Eboue, the tough, attacking right-back who had joined them in mid season from Belgium's Beveren – born like Kolo Toure and another centre-back in Johan Djourou in Abigi-Abidjan, on the Ivory Coast – was in lively form. Still to come, though he wouldn't play in Europe, was the giant centre-forward Emmanuel Adebayor, bought from Monaco; his 10 goals had dramatically propelled little Togo into the finals of the 2006 World Cup. Philippe Senderos, who sometimes rose to the great occasion but sometimes – especially when faced by Chelsea's Didier Drogba – didn't, was in his most commanding form, replacing Campbell.

The return match was much more evenly balanced and Lehmann, who had regained his place from Almunia, made an outstanding save in the second half from the prolific Real striker Raul. The goalless draw sent Arsenal through.

So to the end of March and the quarter-final confrontation at Highbury between Arsenal and Juventus, and in midfield between the precocious Cesc Fabregas and his older, larger predecessor Patrick Vieira, genially received by the crowd which had once adulated him. But he was much slower now and Fabregas would have much the best of it. Fabregas was inspired, constantly ready to surge forward in support of Thierry Henry. He scored in the first half, Henry in the second; a 2–0 win consolidated in Turin, where the Gunners drew 0–0.

The semi-final opponents were Villareal, a recently obscure Spanish club from a small city, which had risen high above its circumstances, and had a masterly playmaker in the gifted Argentine, Juan Roman Riquelme, and a dangerous striker in Diego Forlan, discarded somewhat abruptly by Manchester United.

Arsenal won by a single, elaborately worked goal at Highbury. When Henry took a corner at the Clock End the ball came back to him when it was headed clear. He ran across the field, waited until the ideal moment to find Hleb, whose cross was exploited by Kolo Toure. In Spain, Lehmann, on another of his days of grace, saved everything he had to, even a late penalty, and the goalless draw put the Gunners in the Final.

Played in Paris in mid May, the potential climax to Arsenal's so many years of European disappointment, their luck ran out. Barcelona were the multi-talented opposition, and the game was effectively decided in the 18th minute. When Lehmann brought down the powerful Cameroon striker, Samuel Eto'o, chasing a pass from the Brazilian Ronaldinho, the referee, Terje Hauge, ignored the fact that Ludovic Giuly had tapped the loose ball into the net, and expelled the German keeper. His place was taken by Almunia, by turns resilient and suspect; but it was Arsenal against the odds who took the lead. A free kick from the right by Thierry Henry – not long after Eboue himself was lucky not to be penalised – was exploited by a soaring header from Sol Campbell. This came on 37 minutes.

Thierry Henry, of all people, missed a fine second-half chance cleverly set up for him by Freddy Ljungberg. Yet it was only when the veteran Swedish attacker Henrik Larsson, a heavy scorer when with Celtic, appeared as a substitute on the hour that Barça turned the tables. In a four-minute spell, between 76 and 80 minutes, Larsson's jewelled passes enabled first Eto'o then Belletti to beat Almunia from narrow angles – should he have saved? – and the Cup was Barcelona's.

Arsenal had to make sure of fourth place in the Premier League to qualify for the following season's European Cup, which they did in somewhat torrid circumstances; twice involving the old foe, Tottenham Hotspur. At Highbury, the Gunners initially deployed a team below full strength, given the proximity of the crucial game against Villareal. Though Spurs had much the better of the first half, they failed to score until the second and then it was in controversial circumstances.

When Eboue collided with Gilberto, both lay prone. Michael Carrick of Spurs seemed at first to hesitate, then passed to Edgar Davids, on the left. He in turn served Robbie Keane, who scored with ease. A furious Wenger upbraided his equivalent, the big Dutchman Martin Jol, deploring Tottenham's failure to put the ball out of play. Jol maintained he hadn't seen what happened, Wenger called him a liar, which he surely was not. The situation was ambiguous. Had either of the fallen Arsenal men collided with an opponent there might have been a moral, rather than a legal, obligation to put the ball out of play. But since both fallen men were Arsenal's, it was a moot point. In any event, Wenger brought on Henry, who equalised ingeniously with the outside of his right foot.

There was more drama to come. Spurs were still marginally ahead of the Gunners in the fourth place which would take one or other into Europe. But when Spurs travelled to West Ham for a vital game, they ate at a hotel *en route* and players fell ill, victims of some bug which was never identified. In vain, Spurs tried to have the game postponed, but the Premier League were obdurate. They had to play, and they lost, thus guaranteeing the Gunners a European place at the following season even were they to lose, as they did, the European Cup Final.

The last hurrah at Highbury came with the final game against Wigan, preceded and followed by a vivid jamboree. The fans were dressed in alternating blocks of red and white. Two huge metal containers, ranged either side of the players' tunnel, vomited flames. In the game itself, Pires put Arsenal ahead, defensive errors gave Wigan two goals, but Henry responded with a hat trick, one goal from the penalty spot. His eighth hat trick; he would kiss the Highbury turf.

West Ham beat Spurs, Arsenal were safe, joyful celebrations followed, many an 'old glory' was interviewed on the pitch. Constable Alex Morgan, the singing policeman, evoking more melodious times gone by, sang 'Old Man River' as he used to do. Arsene Wenger counted down the last 10 seconds. Fireworks soared into the air. Farewell to Highbury.

Chapter 15

AT THE EMIRATES

At THE EMIRATES, WITH ITS TOWERING STANDS, A MARVEL OF design and engineering just as the stands at Highbury in their smaller art deco way had been, it was a whole new world. Not entirely an easy one. For a time, it almost seemed that Arsenal's natural home advantage had gone with the move, that the new stadium was no more familiar and advantageous to them than to the teams which visited it and stole points off them. No prizes were won. Manchester United, though they were beaten at The Emirates, were a full, embarrassing 21 points ahead at the close of the 2006–07 season. There were replays against two Lancastrian sides in the FA Cup. Bolton in the first of them were beaten 3–1 away after a 1–1 draw in London, after extra time despite the Gunners missing two penalties through the Brazilians Gilberto Silva and the burly newcomer, albeit on loan, Julio Baptista. Emmanuel Adebayor scored two of those goals. Blackburn drew 0–0 in London, won at home 1–0.

Previously in one of the team's finest displays of the season, Liverpool, the holders, were beaten 3–1 at Anfield with two of the goals coming from another of Wenger's shrewd transfers, the gifted Czech, Tomas Rosicky. But the fifth round proved fatal with an 87th-minute goal at Ewood Park scored by the South African, Benni McCarthy, giving Blackburn the game.

In the League Cup there was, you might say, a kind of consolation. Though fielding a reserve side, Arsenal went all the way through to the Cardiff Final, beating Tottenham's full team at White Hart Lane on the way. But in Cardiff, in a closely contested game, the Indian sign which Didier Drogba had over Philippe Senderos proved lethal again when Drogba forced his way past him to score the winner for Chelsea. And the European Cup run would end in anticlimax.

Things would surely have been different and better had Thierry Henry not been seriously injured and obliged to miss most of the second half of what would be his final season with the Gunners. Injury also kept Robin Van Persie out of many games.

Rosicky, who would, alas, succumb to a bewilderingly persisting injury the following season, defying endless medical treatment, looked initially as though, if allowed to, he could solve the Gunners' creative problems in midfield. Someone had to provide the grace notes and the opportunities furnished by the now departed Dennis Bergkamp and who, one thought, better than the Czech?

In their first European game in Hamburg, Rosicky, deployed not in central midfield but on the left, though essentially right-footed, scored the Gunners' second goal in a 2–1 success. Porto were then comfortably beaten 2–0 at The Emirates, but the next match in Moscow against CSKA saw the Gunners beaten 1–0, the goal scored by a talented Brazilian, Daniel Carvalho, whom Arsenal never mastered.

Before the return game in London, I wrote about Rosicky, who had cost a hefty £6.8 million from Borussia Dortmund. Twenty-six years old, he had played for his country 61 times, scoring 17 goals. 'Wenger', I wrote, 'seems unsure what to do with him – the player has been substituted three times, come on as a substitute twice and finished just three of the games he has started for Arsenal.' He would eventually play 22 League games, and make four appearances as a substitute. 'Used properly,' I continued, 'Rosicky could prove to be one of Wenger's most shrewd acquisitions.

'Highly versatile, he has speed of mind and foot and a fierce right-footed shot. He must be encouraged to run the show, ideally in tandem with the precocious young Spaniard, Cesc Fabregas, giving Henry and Robin Van Persie the service they need. Rosicky is a creator. As a bonus, he can also score goals. But it is futile to keep playing him out of position and still expect him to have a major influence on proceedings.' In fairness to Wenger, he may well have thought that having two essentially ball playing figures without the shield of a defender beside them could prove costly.

When it came to the return game, Arsenal, Rosicky included, would do everything but score. Arsenal at times had been accused of constantly trying to score the perfect goal and thus not scoring when they should. But this was hardly an explanation or excuse for when Fabregas, after a dazzling exchange of passes with Rosicky, went round the CSKA keeper, then stumbled when about to put the ball in the empty net. Or for Rosicky himself, when, despite an outstanding performance, he missed from point blank range.

After the game, Wenger mysteriously opined that this was Arsenal's best performance ever in the Champions League. What, without scoring, surely a fundamental object of the game? And what of those triumphant victories against Inter at San Siro, and Real Madrid at the Bernabeu? Still, Arsenal, beating Hamburg 3–1 and drawing 0–0 at Porto, did qualify for the next stage. They didn't survive. In Eindhoven, a goal by Mendez was the only one of the game. In London, the huge Brazilian centre-half Alex, on loan from Chelsea, managed to score for both sides, equalising his own goal very late in the game. Rosicky was absent, Henry arrived only as a 66th-minute substitute.

So to 5 November, which, at Upton Park, was Fireworks' Day indeed, albeit metaphorically. Eighty-nine minutes had gone in a game which Arsenal had expected to win comfortably when Marlon Harewood suddenly scored for West Ham. On the touchline, Alan Pardew, the Hammers manager, seemed to go berserk, dancing like a dervish, infuriating Arsene Wenger, who had to be restrained as he moved angrily towards him.

'You can sometimes be surprised by your bad side,' he has said. 'I have a dark side. You want to win so much that sometimes you forget that it is as well that you respect the rules. When you don't win, you have to acknowledge the respect of your opponents as well. Sometimes I can't do that. It is a dark side, because the perfect side is to say, "Well done, you played better." You never know, in fifty years, I might achieve it.'

And there would be an all too notable exit. 'Arsenal will always be in my blood and in my heart,' said Thierry Henry, before he departed for

Barcelona at the end of the season. Not only was he the most prolific of all the Gunners' goalscorers, overhauling both Cliff Bastin and Ian Wright, but he was surely one of the most gifted and spectacular attackers ever to play for the Gunners.

In drafting a replacement, Wenger showed his habitual ingenuity, signing the lithe and slender striker Eduardo from Dynamo Zagreb. Eduardo, born in Rio, was Brazilian by origin, but he had taken Croatian nationality and as such had been a thorn in the side of the England defence in their mutual World Cup qualifying group. Alas, a horrific fate awaited him in February 2008 when he suffered a dreadful foul from Birmingham's Martin Taylor which left him in agony, with a compound fracture of his left leg. Though he blessedly and comprehensively recovered, he would be out of the game for a year. And arguably, since the Gunners finished a mere four points behind Manchester United, in third place, it could have cost them the Premier League. The same might well be said of the European Cup, though the 4–0 defeat at Old Trafford in the FA Cup fifth round was – given the ebullient form of Wayne Rooney – less likely to be affected by any attacker present or absent than by the sending off of Eboue. At that point, Eduardo's disaster was imminent.

Arsenal certainly began the season in style. On a September Wednesday, they comprehensively got the better of the Spaniards Seville in the European Cup in a 3–0 win at The Emirates. Cesc Fabregas in commanding form scored one of the goals, albeit with a deflected shot. The following Saturday, again at home, he was the outstanding player in the 5–0 demolition of Derby County. 'To speed of feet and thought,' I wrote, 'to a flair for the decisive pass, to a fiercely effective right-foot shot, he adds a precocious maturity. When Wenger let his talisman Patrick Vieira go, even he could hardly have expected however much he hoped, that the smaller Fabregas would dominate in midfield. But dominate he has, and he would go on to score yet another of his spectacular right-footed goals.' Adebayor, praised as 'a fantastic player' even by the Derby manager, scored a hat trick, one goal a penalty.

In October, Arsenal would score seven without reply against Slavia of Prague. Fabregas got two of them, two more went to the teenaged Theo Walcott, expensively bought from Southampton, inexplicably taken to the 2006 World Cup without a game by Sven Goran Eriksson, but now ready to exploit his great natural talents; a born right-winger with his pace and control, though Wenger fancied him as a striker. Still sensationally to come was the 80-yard run at Anfield in the European Cup, which brought the Gunners a goal; but couldn't save them from 4–2 defeat.

Another new face was that of the tall, heavily built, Nicklas Bendtner, a 19-year-old Dane who had been on loan to Birmingham City where he had been scoring goals. He would play the whole late-November return game in Seville, where Arsenal went down 3–1. Since they had, so surprisingly, been held to a 0–0 draw by the very Slavia team which had gone down 7–0 at The Emirates, they had to be content with second place in their group, but they qualified.

It was at St Andrews on Saturday 23 February that Eduardo suffered his appalling injury, and Arsenal contentiously dropped two points, which would cost them dear in the Premier League. There may well have been no malicious intent in the horrific challenge of Birmingham City's Martin Taylor on Eduardo, though he was duly sent off, but the consequences were appalling. The defence of an Arsenal team which had seemed well on its way to victory perhaps unsurprisingly fell into disarray when a careless pass square across the penalty box put Gael Clichy in trouble, and he was judged, however controversially, to have fouled. Birmingham converted the penalty to make it 2–2. A disgusted William Gallas, the accomplished but impulsive French international defender Arsenal had bought from Chelsea, simply sat on the ground near the halfway line.

Though they deployed a number of first-choice players, Arsenal crashed out of the League Cup, beaten 5–1 in the derby match at Tottenham after a 1–1 draw in the first semi-final leg. But in the initial knock out phase of the European trophy, they had impressive success.

Milan were the distinguished opposition, and they forced a 0–0 draw in the first leg at The Emirates, the defiant 39-year-old Paolo Maldini resilient in defence. Yet even he could do nothing when, in the very last minute, Emmanuel Adebayor rose to a cross from the right by Theo Walcott. With the Milan keeper drawn to his near post, a goal seemed certain. But high as the towering Adebayor jumped, strongly though he connected – though seemingly pushed in the back – close as he was to the goal, his header bounced off the bar. Yet the performance was a substantial corrective to the 4–0 FA Cup debacle at Old Trafford, the previous weekend, one which moved Gallas, as captain, to convene a team meeting, saying his players were 'ashamed' of their performance.

But if the odds seemed on Milan in the return leg at San Siro, Arsenal would once again surpass themselves on foreign soil. Inspired by a scintillating Cesc Fabregas, who would score their first, very late, goal from 30 yards, and who quite overshadowed Milan's famed Brazilian, Kaka, the Gunners were rampant. Hleb was deployed in attack alongside Adebayor. A second still later goal arrived when Theo Walcott, brought on as a substitute, served Adebayor from the right. A display which surely ranked with Arsenal's previous 5–1 win in the same stadium, against the other Milanese club, Inter.

But one way and another, the Gunners would not survive an all-English quarter-final against Liverpool, though fortune hardly favoured them. At The Emirates, Adebayor gave Arsenal the lead midway through the first half, but Liverpool's Dirk Kuyt equalised a couple of minutes later. But should Kuyt later have given away a penalty by tugging Hleb? The offence seemed pretty plain, but the referee, a Dutchman himself, saw no evil, and Liverpool escaped, to draw 1–1.

A vibrant tie at Anfield seemed swung in Arsenal's favour when Theo Walcott's glorious, sustained solo run on the right over an 80-yard stretch brought their second goal on 84 minutes. That made it 2–2, Abu Diaby the lanky French midfielder, having put the Gunners ahead after 13 minutes, centre-back Sami Hyppia on the half hour and Fernando Torres on 69 minutes having replied. But just two minutes after Walcott, used only as a late substitute, had set up Arsenal's second goal, Liverpool benefited again from a vexed penalty decision, Steven Gerrard duly scored and an Arsenal team which then inevitably threw caution to the winds conceded a fourth goal from Ryan Babel.

Five days later, at ill-omened Old Trafford, Arsenal, though Adebayor did score, went down 2–1 to a penalty and a free kick. So, despite Arsenal's earlier 21-match unbeaten run, the League was Manchester United's again.

The Gunners made an uneasy beginning to the new 2008–09 season. They lost at home to Hull City, promoted in a Wembley play off to the top division after a century of striving, they lost at Fulham where I saw them alarmingly overplayed in central midfield – no Fabregas – by Fulham's Danny Murphy and Jimmy Bullard. Hull beat them with the help of a beautifully curled in goal by the clever little Brazilian,

Giovanni. The following March, Hull – who as we know played those two torrid semi-finals against the Gunners in 1930 – would be back again to lose an FA Cup tie in deeply contentious circumstances.

Thus Arsenal reached the semi-final of the FA Cup and made progress in the European Champions League, though the Premier League itself would be a bridge too far, with the likes of Sunderland and Fulham coming to The Emirates and forcing goalless draws.

To give the Gunners their due, they had wretched luck with injuries. Tomas Rosicky stayed out of action for months, Cesc Fabregas, the very motor of the team, was sidelined through injury for weeks in mid-season, while perhaps the supreme irony was that Theo Walcott, with his invaluable right-wing pace, dislocated a shoulder while training with the England team for their match in Berlin.

In the European tournament, progress was made. Fresh young faces had arrived: Mexico's Carlos Vela, a fluent and rapid attacker, came from Spain, where he had spent several seasons on loan. The 17-year-old Aaron Ramsey, a precocious, confident star of the 2008 FA Cup Final with Cardiff, was signed, resisting opposition from Manchester United, though, disappointingly, he was to have the scant opportunities one feared that he would have got at Old Trafford. Jack Wilshere was a rare delight, the more so as he was actually an Englishman, 16 years old on his pleasing left-wing debut, who had come through the ranks of the Arsenal youth scheme almost from childhood. And the French international winger, Samir Nasri, was a compound of balance, speed and fine technique.

February would see the long delayed debut of the hugely talented Russian attacker, Andrei Arshavin from Zenit St Petersburg. Outstanding in the previous season's UEFA Cup Final in Manchester, when he had cut the Rangers defence to ribbons, he had gone on to play two exhilarating games for Russia in the European Championship finals.

Wilshere, Ramsey and Vela all played in September in the extraordinary 6–0 rout in the League Cup at The Emirates, by a virtual reserve team, of the full Sheffield United side. Vela scored three goals, Wilshere got another.

In Arsenal's European group, they beat Twente Enschede, now managed by Steve McClaren, the unsuccessful England manager, 2–0 in Holland, 4–0 at home, and snatched a late 1–1 draw against old foes at Dynamo Kiev. William Gallas, always ready and eager to use his head in the penalty box, scored in all three games. Nine goals were scored in the next two games, a 4–0 home win against Porto, followed by one of those prodigious victories abroad; 5–2 this time in Istanbul against Fenerbahce, in which young Alex Song, much improved and a star of the last African Cup of Nations, coolly got one of the goals.

A heartening result, followed, almost mysteriously – though not altogether untypically – by a goalless draw when Fenerbahce came to The Emirates. There were strange days when Arsenal, sometimes accused of over-elaborate football, simply failed despite their dominance to score. Nor did they find scoring easy when Dynamo Kiev came to The Emirates, prevailing by the only goal. The final match away to Porto was a dead rubber. Arsenal fielded a weakened team and lost 2–0. At least Ramsey played in these last three games.

In late February, the tournament resumed on its knock out basis, and the opposition would be Roma. The first leg at The Emirates was one more example of an Arsenal dominance uncrowned by goals. There was this time again just one, and that came only from a penalty given away by the blond French centre-back Philippe Mexes, converted by Robin Van Persie. Before the game, Arsene Wenger had expressed his deep respect for the talents of Francesco Totti, the veteran Roma attacker and his incisive passing. This virtuosity would be seen in abundance in the return game despite Totti carrying an injury. But in that game he found space behind the spearhead, whereas at The Emirates, he was perplexingly played up front, where he was easily contained.

At The Olimpico, inspired by Totti, and helped by an inept piece of Arsenal defending – shades of how Chelsea had so feebly conceded three goals there in a previous group game – Roma went ahead in 10 minutes. Totti crossed low from the left (he could previously have been expelled for kicking out at Van Persie) and Arsenal's defenders stood statuesque, allowing the Brazilian defender Juan to score easily at the far post. Clichy was lucky not to concede a penalty.

There were no further goals in normal or extra time and so it came to the dramatic irrelevance of penalties. Eduardo, who had come back in fine form after his cruelly long absence, missed his penalty, but so did Mirko Vucinic, an excellent Manuel Almunia easily saving his kick and at the last Taddei missed his; so Arsenal prevailed 7–6. Their ecstatic celebrations were perhaps understandable, but somewhat excessive, given the circumstances.

Once again, deplorably, visiting supporters were subjected to brutal violence by hooligan Roma supporters. The previous season, Manchester United's fans were viciously attacked (some stabbed in the buttocks) in the city and around the stadium, inside which there was no protection by the police.

When a coach carrying Arsenal fans approached the Stadio Olimpico, it was blocked by a car and bombarded by Roma hooligans, who tried to set it alight. One of them got inside the coach and stabbed an Arsenal supporter. That nothing had been done by UEFA over the years, since, after the 1984 European Cup Final won there by Liverpool, horrific attacks were made on Liverpool fans as they left the stadium (even the Roman Press was appalled) was deplorable but perhaps, given the history of that body, predictable. Meanwhile UEFA had scheduled the ensuing European Cup Final for the Olimpico; though, since Roma blessedly would not be contesting it, perhaps optimism was justified. As for the future, it was surely intolerable that Roma be allowed to play home fixtures in Rome. Intolerable, but all too depressingly likely.

As for the FA Cup, there was a fairly easy passage through the first three rounds against teams from the so-called Championship, alias the Second Division, Plymouth, Cardiff and Burnley, all beaten at The Emirates. But when Hull City came there in March to play a delayed fifth round game, the balloon well and truly went up.

Seemingly the underdog, Hull barked menacingly as they had on their previous visit to The Emirates, when Nicky Barmby's shot from the left struck Djourou, took a baffling deflection, and curled past the reserve keeper Lukasz Fabianski high into the net. From that point, Hull defended heroically and might even have scored again, when Fabianski made a spectacular save from Giovanni's equally spectacular free kick.

As the second half wore on, so the unthinkable prospect of another Hull victory grew thinkable indeed, despite huge pressure by Arsenal. Often featuring the sublime skills of Andrei Arshavin, on the left where three days earlier he'd scored a remarkable solo goal against Blackburn, gliding past an opponent who seemed sure to stop him, before shooting high into the top far corner. And all this after having seven stitches put in his wounded foot at the Blackburn game.

At last, on 75 minutes, Arshavin it was who stroked the ball to Van Persie, whose right foot shot the equaliser. Arsenal's highly controversial winner came on 84 minutes. From Nasri's free kick, Djourou and the Hull keeper Myhill jumped together. The ball ricocheted between them, reaching Gallas alone and seemingly offside in the goalmouth, where he knocked it home. An outraged Phil Brown, the Hull City manager, called the goal a scandal. Wenger's response was that, since the ball came off the keeper, Gallas had been played onside.

But the biggest bone of contention came when Brian Horton, Hull's assistant manager, claimed that Cesc Fabregas, who had watched the game passionately from the sideline, had spat at him in the tunnel. Fabregas angrily denied it and was later exonerated by the FA. None of the officials had monitored the incident; whatever it was. The outraged Brown also accused Wenger of influencing the referee to caution Myhill for time wasting – which Myhill unquestionably had. When I asked him to elaborate on this, he replied that it had fired up the crowd, which was hard to understand. I also reminded him that Mike Riley, the referee, had been so controversially in charge of the 49th game at Old Trafford which had ended Arsenal's unbeaten run so tempestuously. To which Brown's brusque reply was that he was the manager of Hull.

And yet . . . could it be that, though Riley had unquestionably refereed the game in all honesty, deep in his unconscious, memories of that troubled time at Old Trafford might have stirred? A game after which the pizza thrower in the tunnel at Alex Ferguson was now identified as . . . Cesc Fabregas.

ADDENDUM

As THE 2008–09 SEASON WOUND TO A CLOSE, ARSENAL'S FORTUNES were decidedly mixed. The Premier League itself was clearly beyond them, but they steadily left Aston Villa behind in the contest for that fourth place which would qualify them for the so-called Champions League. In the immediate version, after the victory against Roma, on penalties, came a somewhat uneasy draw in Spain at Villareal, the equaliser superbly struck by Emmanuel Adebayor's spectacular bicycle kick. In London, Villareal were comfortably defeated, 3-0.

The ensuing FA Cup semi-final at Wembley looked a good thing for the Gunners, Chelsea, inept in defence, having conceded seven goals at home in their previous two games. As it transpired, Arsenal, on a pitch properly condemmed by Arsene Wenger for its divot-ridden condition, lost 2-1, having gone ahead through Theo Walcott. Undermined by the disastrous goalkeeping of the 24-year-old Pole, Lukasz Fabianski, deputising for the injured Almunia. Impetuous to a degree, the first goal he conceded, at his near post, mirrored the goal Bob Wilson had let through in the 1971 Cup Final against Liverpool. Though that day, Arsenal went on to win. Puzzling, however, was Wenger's failure to use the skills of Andrei Arshavin for 75 minutes.

A decision that seemed all the more impenetrable when Arshavin, a few days later, produced a remarkable display against Liverpool at Anfield, scoring four splendid goals in a 4-4 draw which so nearly became a 4-3 victory.

There is no doubt his presence would have made a substantial difference to Arsenal's drab performance at Old Trafford in the first leg of the European Cup semi-final, when they were simply overwhelmed by a Manchester United team which largely bombarded their goal, only to be thwarted time and again by an Almunia in defiantly coruscating form. The Spaniard made save after difficult and even phenomenal save, though the crossbar once saved him when he was beaten, like so many goalkeepers, by a thundering right-footed shot by Cristiano Ronaldo.

The irony being that when he was, in the first half of the second leg, beaten for the only goal of the game, it was the consequence of inept marking with the United right-back, John O'Shea, left culpably free when a left-wing cross was deflected to him. True, the Gunners badly missed the presence in central defence of the injured William Gallas, not to mention the irreplaceable Arshavin, but Wenger's choices were somewhat puzzling. To use an ineffectual midfielder in Abou Diaby on the left flank, while deploying Samir Nasri to scant effect in the middle, though he likes this role, seemed illogical.

Having crashed at home to Manchester United on the Wednesday, the Gunners promptly crashed again to Chelsea on the Sunday, in the Premier League. All well and good for Arsene Wenger, doubtless whistling to keep his spirits up, to assert that Arsenal could have been 2–0 up before they conceded the first Chelsea goal. It might well have been, since they began quickly and brightly but simply couldn't turn chances into goals. Then, alas, came, against the play, a goal powerfully headed, unopposed, by the visiting Brazilian centre-back, Alex. Fabianski, never convincing in goal, might have done better too, and the Gunners collapsed. Malouda toyed with Arsenal's right flank defence, Silvestre struggled at centre-back, the midfield was criticised for not guarding the defence. Nicolas Anelka, illustrating the old Italian 'immutable law of the ex', was given excessive licence to score with ease. There was the late embarrassment of a trickling own goal by Toure. Oh, for an Adams.

Meanwhile, the news was that Stan Kroenke was buying up more and more shares, his haul now over 28 per cent, but just short of the 29 per cent which would necessitate a bid for control, though he seemed never to come near a game. Help was offered by the Uzbek billionaire, Alisher Usmanov, nudging Kroenke as the club's largest shareholder, but Arsenal didn't want it. How far away and long ago the patrician rule of the Hill-Wood family now seemed. And what would happen next?

Rather like a bunch of spoiled children, certain shareholders turned on Wenger – shades of the somewhat remote past – at a meeting, incensed that so much time had passed without trophies. Eliciting the punchline of an old joke: 'But what have you done for me lately?'

A despondent Wenger declared, 'I'm made to feel like a murderer', yet only three days later, in the penultimate Premier League game of the season, Arsenal went to Old Trafford and quite deservedly forced a 0–0 draw. What was wrong with the defence on this occasion, in which their one bare point prompted massive jubilation by the United players and their ecstatic fans, since the Premiership had been won?

A couple of days later, there were ominous rumours that Wenger might yet be interested in responding to the siren call of Real Madrid and their re-elected President, Florentino Pérez. Never yet had Wenger broken a contract, but there was evident disagreement with his board over how much money he could spend on new players, Wenger seeming a great deal less sanguine than they. Meanwhile, who could logically replace him?

Dein's departure, when it occurred, had, in retrospect, a dimension of irony. For it might be said that he was the equivalent of what was known before the Second World War as a Premature Anti-Fascist. This because he wanted to bring into the club the American multi-millionaire, owner of various USA sports franchises, Stan Kroenke. But Danny Fiszman, now in possession of so many of the shares which Dein had sold him, and thus the major force on the board, disagreed, as did other fellow directors. So Dein was forced out, though by May 2009, when he bought some £42 million of shares from the Carr family, Kroenke with just over 28 per cent, would become, with the Uzbek, Usmanov, one of the two largest shareholders in the club. Though even then there were those who felt that, like General Douglas MacArthur to the Philippines, Dein would return. His preference for Wembley, rather than a newly built Emirates, for Arsenal's home, though frust-rated, was not thought to be the reason for his going.

Hope springs eternal and there was much of it in the last few days of the season. On the Friday evening of 23 May, in the first leg of the Final of the FA Youth Cup, the young Gunners thrashed their Liverpool equivalents 4–1 at the Emirates, with the precocious Jack Wilshere the star of the show. First, he sent through Gilles Sun to put Arsenal ahead, next he himself scored from a penalty. Liverpool hit back to score, but in the second half it was Wilshere who set up Sanchez Watt for the third Arsenal goal. Jay Emmanuel-Thomas headed the fourth.

Two days later, in the last game of the Premier League, the senior Gunners disposed of Stoke City by the same score, again at home. With Robin Van Persie, scorer of two goals, one from a penalty, in incisive form, the Gunners took ample revenge for their earlier defeat at Stoke; by an abrasive side bitterly condemned by Wenger for its bruising methods. It was thus a doubly satisfying end to the season.

On the eve of the new season, Emmanuel Adebayor was sold to Manchester City, with its infinite millions from Abu Dhabi, for a massive £25 million. 'Believe me', said Arsene Wenger, as aware as anyone else that he was taking a gamble, 'we have lost a great player'.

But a dissident and disruptive one, who had plainly tried the patience both of his manager and his teammates with his increasingly inconsistent performances, his occasional petulance on the field – despite the profusion of goals with foot and head. An average of almost 20 over the previous three seasons, though there had been such notable misses as the point-blank header against Milan's bar at The Emirates in a vital European Cup tie. It might be argued that given his super abundance of star strikers, City's manager Mark Hughes might be taking a gamble as well – a very expensive one.